To our Vincentian Sisters,
— ours, Vincent's, Catherine's —
enjoy her story!
          Sister Mary Ellen

Pioneer Spirit

Pioneer Spirit

Catherine Spalding,
Sister of Charity of Nazareth

MARY ELLEN DOYLE, SCN

THE UNIVERSITY PRESS OF KENTUCKY

Publication of this volume was made possible in part by a grant
from the National Endowment for the Humanities.

Scholarly publisher for the Commonwealth,
serving Bellarmine University, Berea College, Centre College of Kentucky,
Eastern Kentucky University, The Filson Historical Society, Georgetown
College, Kentucky Historical Society, Kentucky State University, Morehead State
University, Murray State University, Northern Kentucky University, Transylvania
University, University of Kentucky, University of Louisville, and Western
Kentucky University.

Editorial and Sales Offices: The University Press of Kentucky
663 South Limestone Street, Lexington, Kentucky 40508–4008
www.kentuckypress.com

10 09 08 07 06   5 4 3 2 1

Frontispiece: Catherine Spalding, c. 1850s. (Nazareth Archives)

Library of Congress Cataloging-in-Publication Data

Doyle, Mary Ellen, 1932-
  Pioneer spirit : Catherine Spalding, Sister of Charity of Nazareth / Mary Ellen
Doyle.
     p. cm.
  Includes bibliographical references and index.
  ISBN-13: 978-0-8131-2395-0 (hardcover : alk. paper)
  ISBN-10: 0-8131-2395-X (hardcover : alk. paper)
  1. Spalding, Catherine, 1793-1858. 2. Sisters of Charity of Nazareth (Nazareth,
Ky.)—Biography. I. Title.
  BX4456.Z8D69 2006
  271'.9102—dc22   2006002563

Manufactured in the United States of America.

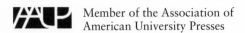

Member of the Association of
American University Presses

Dedicated to

Marie Menard, SCN

who first preserved in writing
the memory of Catherine Spalding

James Maria Spillane, SCN

who revived that memory and wrote the story
for generations of SCNs, their friends, and students

Contents

Illustrations follow page 92

Preface

Three statements made to the author in the course of researching and writing this biography of Catherine Spalding focus the book's purpose, development, and methods.

"We know what she did; we don't know what she was." Like the Sister of Charity of Nazareth who said this, almost any SCN could name the main acts and accomplishments of their first leader: she was elected at the age of nineteen and served alternate terms for the rest of her life; she developed a community of women now nearly two hundred years in service; she established the most effective and best-attended school for young women in the antebellum South, and other schools in Kentucky and Tennessee; she performed works of charity all over Louisville and established there a hospital and orphanage, the first such social agencies under religious auspices in Kentucky. Various stories have transmitted details of these actions and of Catherine's fame for charity.

"What she was" is certainly implied in "what she did." Yet for years, Sisters and others fascinated with Catherine's deeds and character have felt a strong desire to know more of what actually happened, and to know more of her personality, her spirituality, her driving motives. To learn and reveal these things, by whatever clues Catherine left to her inner world, has been the driving purpose of this book.

"Catherine will reveal herself to you." This remark by a dear friend and wise SCN elder has been a steady encouragement throughout the research. I had expected to find only limited resources from the early days; the pioneers were preoccupied with implementing the ministries rather than keeping records of them. Yet the Nazareth Archives contain resources beyond all expectation: revealing, often detailed letters of founding bishops Flaget and David; the letters of Catherine Spalding herself and of various Sisters and laity to her or about her; the Annals compiled from interviews with surviving pioneer members; the findings of several private researchers; and many and varied other materials. Some of these resources were previously gleaned from the archives in Baltimore and Emmitsburg, Maryland, and the University of Notre Dame, Indiana. The Filson Historical Society of Louisville, the archdiocesan archives and Cathedral Heritage Foundation, and the Louisville Free Public Library also yielded valuable information.

With the unforeseen lode of materials came the revelations. Pieces of puzzles fit together; events explained each other; dates coincided and created fresh connections and insights. Letters, beneath their seemingly chatty surfaces, revealed emotions and motives and ways of relating. Sister James Maria Spillane, author of *Kentucky Spring,* had indeed captured for her readers Catherine's character and spirit, though her resources were more limited and her narrative was popularized in style and could not tell the whole story.

"We want to be able to say, 'This is all we know at present about her.'" That mandate from a past president of the SCN Congregation has challenged me to keep looking for data, no matter how long or in how many volumes. Yet real limitations must be accepted. The Nazareth Archives contain more than forty volumes of assorted letters but only one thin collection of sixty-six letters by Mother Catherine herself, out of the many she must have written. Fortunately, those preserved were written to various kinds of people, revealing nuances of her thinking, feeling, and relationships. By comparison with better-known persons who were more prolific writers or who kept journals, Catherine Spalding left few verbal traces. Yet the available material still required selective use in order to be complete without swamping interest in detail, and to keep the focus on Catherine, embedded as she is in the histories of Catholic Kentucky and her religious community.

A greater challenge has been to meet various levels of interest in Catherine's story. Not everyone has a professional historian's interest in "all we know." Some want the good story, told with enough detail for a lively and meaningful portrait; it is hoped that the chapters will satisfy this desire. Others are likely to ask, "How do you know that?" or "Can we know more about it?" For the interest of these readers, the endnotes document sources and add some tangential and explanatory history. Finally, for Catherine's genealogy, a note is insufficient. To explain what can be known, two appendixes are offered.

Most challenging in a biography drawn from limited resources is interpretation. Facts are facts, supported by data; enough facts connect to create high probability of what else may have or surely must have happened. Beyond such probabilities lie justifiable inferences based on data. A circular process develops; known data reveal a personality; the personality studied long enough and well enough invites probabilities and inferences. The challenge, the demand of honesty, is to let language tell which mode is in use at any time. In this account of Catherine Spalding, an honest effort has been made to maintain such distinctions, with the realization that her private and nineteenth-century mind and feelings can never be fully known.

Note on spelling: The nineteenth century was notoriously flexible about spelling. To avoid seeming errors or multiple uses of [*sic*], spelling and capitalization have been regularized. Forms and spellings of names are especially disconcerting: Ralph/Raphael, Juliet/Julianna, Macey/Maxcy, Hazeltine/Haseltine. Catherine Spalding signed herself both "Catherine" and "Catharine," the latter quite consistently in her final years. The former, however, has been used historically and given to institutions and a street in Louisville. Both spellings will appear in direct quotations; "Catherine" will be used in the narrative.

Acknowledgments

My first and heaviest debts are to the many who preserved or tirelessly sought out and transmitted information about Mother Catherine. Chief among these are Marie Menard, SCN, without whose interviews in 1870 of the surviving pioneers, most early history would have been lost; Francis P. Clark, former director of microfilming at the University of Notre Dame, who copied and gave to Nazareth dozens of letters from archives in Baltimore, St. Louis, and Notre Dame; and Edward Barnes, SCN, who translated their French. James Maria Spillane, SCN, author of *Kentucky Spring,* revived the memory and influence of Catherine in her community and roused our desire to know her again and more fully. Sister James Maria has discussed Catherine with me for many years and throughout her own illness has urged on my study of her. Thomas Spalding, CFX, shared his own accumulated resources and his vast knowledge of Kentucky history and genealogy. He demonstrated the theory of Catherine's parentage now most widely accepted, read and evaluated the sections on her heritage and childhood, and offered to "see me through" the entire work. His sudden death deprived me of a superb historian's counsel and a friend's encouragement.

Others have done what Brother Tom could no longer do—led me to sources and read the work in progress with the needed critical eyes. The staff of the Nazareth Archives, especially Mary Collette Crone and Bridgid Clifford, SCNs, have pulled out, copied, and discussed materials with endless patience, believing against all evidence that the notes would finally become a book. Janice Poston, Reference Librarian of Spalding University, led me to medical references in the nursing archives. Helen Forge, SCL, Archivist of the Sisters of Charity of Leavenworth, contributed information and photographs for chapter 9. Rev. Steve Pohl, pastor and historian of St. Thomas, Bardstown, did the same for chapter 2. Shirley Harmon of the Filson Historical Society of Louisville dug with me in the Bullitt Family Papers for a story until then unknown to SCNs. Mary Imogene Perrin, SCN, and Trudi Maish, SCNA, gleaned archival sources and made photographs for illustrations. Anthony Garvey and the Computer Services staff at Nazareth overcame my limitations to give the manuscript secure electronic existence.

Nazareth's archivists and SCNs Lucy Freibert, Margaret Maria Coon, and Mary Ransom Burke have read the text and given both literary and community perspective. Rev. Clyde Crews, historian of the Archdiocese of Louisville, and Dr. Walker Gollar of Xavier University contributed historical information and read and discussed each chapter with an eye to accuracy and effective style. Dr. Mary Helen Washington read several drafts of the analysis of slavery at Nazareth and, with incisive thinking and truest friendship, challenged and encouraged me to grapple with the difficult topic. Finally, colleagues and friends of several backgrounds have read and tested the work's interest for a varied audience: Regina Bechtle and Judith Metz, SCs; Eugenie Coakley, SCNA; Dirk and Betty Kuyck; and Mildred Daugherty.

Beyond all others, I cite those who made the work happen in the first place: the leadership of the Sisters of Charity of Nazareth, who commissioned it and supported me through more years than they ever expected, and my Sisters across the globe who have motivated and inspired me by being so truly Catherine's daughters and by their interest and patient wait to get her story. My gratitude is immense.

Chronology of Catherine Spalding

1793–1797   Birth on December 23, 1793; early childhood in
Charles County, Maryland

1798–1812   Girlhood with Spalding, Elder, and Clark families
in Nelson County, Kentucky

1812–1822   Leader and first superior of Sisters of Charity of
Nazareth at St. Thomas Farm, Nelson County;
establishment of Nazareth Academy

1822–1823   Move of the motherhouse and academy to
Nazareth, Kentucky, near Bardstown; Mistress of
Novices

1823–1824   Opening of school at Scott County, near
Lexington, Kentucky

1824–1831   Recall to leadership as Mother at Nazareth;
building of new chapel and academy

1831–1838   Opening of Presentation Academy in Louisville,
Kentucky; nursing in cholera epidemic; opening of
St. Vincent Orphanage and Infirmary

1838–1844   Mother at Nazareth; duties in administration
of community, academy, and branch schools of
SCNs; efforts to maintain independent identity of
SCNs

1844–1850   Superior of St. Vincent Orphanage and Infirmary,
            Louisville; witness in legal test of will of Polly
            Bullitt

1850–1856   Mother at Nazareth; separation from Nazareth
            of Sisters in Nashville; building of new church
            and academy; expansion of membership in both
            school and community; expansion of missions
            beyond Nazareth; separation of St. Joseph
            Infirmary from orphanage

1856–1858   Return to orphanage in Louisville; death on
            March 20, 1858

Introduction

Daughter of the Spaldings

1658–1797

In the cold, possibly the snow, of January 21, 1813, a woman just turned nineteen crossed on horseback the empty fields at Poplar Neck near the Salt River and Bardstown, Kentucky. She had been escorted throughout the day by her cousin and cousin's husband; near day's end, they arrived at a log house on St. Thomas Farm. Nothing else was nearby but another log structure, a few outlying cabins, and stripped winter trees. The couple, her guardians, could with reason have looked at her as if to ask, "Are you sure you want to do this?"

Catherine Spalding had come to give herself to a new religious enterprise, the formation of a convent. The first bishop of Bardstown desired religious women to undertake education in that new diocese. Almost everything was new to the girl that day: the scene at St. Thomas, the two women who had preceded her, the clerics who would guide and shape the enterprise, the teaching mission she expected to undertake, and the dire poverty she would endure in this beginning. Not new to her were winter cold and hard physical work, nor the white heat of purpose with which she would give herself to this new community and its mission. Nor were the qualities requisite for group leadership new in her character; her new companions would soon recognize and affirm those traits formed in her girlhood.

Ingrained and familiar above all on that first day of her new life were commitment to an ancient faith, bedrock convictions, a spirit of pioneering, and the ability to endure hardship. For this

1

girl, who had lived at least nine of her nineteen years in families
with names other than her own, had an old Catholic family name.
She was a Spalding. More than 150 years earlier, her ancestors had
migrated from England to Maryland, partly for fortune, partly for
faith, but always ready to move, eager to build and improve, and
determined to pass on their religion.

Who was Catherine Spalding? Who were her parents? What
experiences first formed her character? Given her lineage and
name, why, in future, would her heart cling especially to children
without a name or a nurturing family? Why, above all, would she
give herself, at nineteen, to any religious enterprise?

Part of the answer to these questions lies in her ancestral heritage and in the painful summary of her early life: four homes in
two states, three fathers and four mothers, real or surrogate—all
before she was sixteen.

Despite abundant genealogies of Spaldings, there is no abso-
lute agreement on who Catherine's parents were. Yet through the
fog of data, assertions, and conjectures, some long-standing traditions and demonstrable facts emerge to reveal the key formative
experiences of the girl who came to St. Thomas Farm.

The tradition of the Sisters of Charity of Nazareth (SCN) asserts that Catherine Spalding was born December 23, 1793, in
Charles County, Maryland. She was orphaned early, and she and
her sister Ann, also to become an SCN, were reared in Kentucky
by an uncle and aunt, Thomas and Elizabeth Spalding Elder. For
the last few years before she went to St. Thomas, Catherine lived
in the home of her cousin Clementina Elder Clark. This account is
probably what Mother Catherine told of herself.

If Elizabeth Spalding Elder was Catherine's aunt, one of Elizabeth's brothers was her father. And her grandparents were Basil
and Catherine Green Spalding, the parents of seven sons and five
daughters. Since there is not a scrap of evidence for any more sons,
Catherine's father must be one of the seven named in Basil's 1791 will.
Documented locations and dates exclude all of them except Edward,
and certified facts of his life and migrations make his paternity essentially indisputable. Edward Spalding, sixth son of Basil Spalding,
was almost certainly the father of Catherine (see Appendix A).

Through her father and grandfather, Catherine inherited and would forever be influenced by the history, the faith, and the culture of the American Spaldings.[1] The first in her lineage, Thomas, born around 1640, came to Maryland from England about 1657. His trip across the ocean was financed by John Shercliffe in exchange for a period of service or indenture. If Thomas Spalding was not already a Catholic, he became one in Maryland. Eventually he received some of Shercliffe's land as his "freedom dues" and then acquired more of his own and passed it, with the faith, to his son John.[2]

John Spalding (c. 1675–1726) gained more land, moved eventually to Charles County, and kept the faith when anti-Catholic laws spread to the formerly free colony. Land was wealth. Wealth was also ownership of human beings to work the land. By the time of Catherine's birth, Maryland had one hundred thousand black people, very few of them free.[3] Faith and freedom to practice it, fortune and slavery to maintain it—these were the contradictory elements in the heritage of the Maryland Spaldings. They saw no discordance, taking their way of life for granted as a right to be maintained.

John Spalding's son Basil (c. 1720–1791), Catherine's grandfather, was a large landowner and slaveholder—also an esteemed Catholic citizen. He lived at least in his later years on "Green's Inheritance," near Pomfret in Charles County. After his death, part of this plantation, including its house, was renamed Pleasant Hill. During the time when penal laws forbade public Catholic chapels and services, Basil's house was one of the "Mass houses" where the Eucharist was celebrated, and it remained a "mission station" when religious freedom was restored.[4]

Basil died September 26, 1791, two years before the birth of his granddaughter Catherine. His will left a large tract of land to his wife and single daughters, and the rest of the land to his three youngest sons, Basil Jr., Edward, and George Hilary. It also distributed among his wife and their twelve children "negro Ann and negro Ned and negro Aaron and negro Nell" and fourteen other named "negroes," along with the "stock and household furniture."[5]

Edward Spalding had married Juliet (or Julianna) Boarman in 1789. Records of the early 1790s in Charles County show that his household included several slaves but no land. Later court records reveal that he had a son, Ralph, born in February 1792, and a daughter Rosella, almost surely Ralph's twin. In March 1792, Edward came into land, his part of his father's estate.[6]

Edward, Basil, and George Hilary had not yet divided their inheritance when Catherine was born December 23, 1793, and named, one assumes, for her grandmother, Basil's wife, Catherine Green Spalding.[7] Catherine may well have seen sunlight first from the second story of her grandfather's house. Her mother may have come to the family manor house for greater comfort and assistance at the time of a birth.[8] Even if not Catherine's official birthplace, the beautifully restored and enlarged home at Pleasant Hill stands as a reminder of her ancestral background and the service-oriented Catholic faith that she drew from her Maryland roots.

The widow Catherine Green Spalding, mistress of Pleasant Hill, was matriarch of a large extended family. Little Catherine, wherever her parents lived, had a grandmother, several single aunts and uncles still at home or in the area, and some cousins.[9] The house, then as now, had a narrow staircase and many corners, with an ample outdoors. If the children were disciplined by expected behavior, they were also served by the slaves of the household and enjoyed the amenities of food and furnishing available by that time in a well-established family. In such a soil Catherine's life was planted. She maintained in later years some contact with her cousins at Pleasant Hill, and she sought to replicate later at Nazareth the stability that comes with the sense of place, of a valued self, and of stable relationships.

Yet Catherine would be uprooted, and early. If her heritage included love of a homestead and a sense of its importance to family stability and bonds, it also included the tradition of Maryland farmers who wore out their land or lacked enough for many descendants, who heard of large tracts of fertile and available land over the mountains. Lured by hope of greater fortune, from 1785 onward, these families became the Catholic pioneers and settlers along the Salt River and its numerous forks and creeks in central Kentucky.[10]

Such a farmer was Edward Spalding. The story of Catherine Spalding's character formation is the story both of her ancestral heritage and of what her father's behaviors did to her childhood.

Kentucky Girl

1798–1812

What did three- or four-year-old Catherine understand when told in 1797 that her family was moving far away? In that year, Edward Spalding sold his inheritance of 112.5 acres to his brothers and moved his family (which by then included a fourth child, Louisa) to the enclave of Maryland Catholic migrants at Cox's Creek in Nelson County, Kentucky. Could little Catherine grasp how far Kentucky was from Maryland, how long the journey overland, across the mountains, and on the river? Did she realize at all that she could not expect to see again her grandmother or any of her extended family? What explanations or comfort were offered the child? What did she understand, anticipate, fear, or enjoy?

Catherine's mother died early in their Kentucky life, in 1798 or early 1799. No cause of Juliet's death is recorded, but the birth of her fifth child, Ann Spalding, is given as 1797 or 1798.[1] On the frontier, a mother's death at or soon after childbirth was frequent enough to render it a probable cause. Left with five young children, Edward married Sarah Housley on December 7, 1799, two weeks before Catherine's sixth birthday. We have no record of Catherine's feelings about her mother's death or her father's rapid remarriage. What is clear, however, is that the comfortable, familiar experiences and people of Maryland, and her mother, probably her best helper and comforter in adjustment to Kentucky, were all gone.

In his early years in Nelson County, 1799–1801, Edward Spalding seems to have done well. He owned several slaves and horses, bought three hundred acres on the Salt River, and was appointed constable for Nelson County. But that was the end of his good fortune. Catherine's most impressionable years were to be affected by her father's growing problems and increasingly irresponsible solutions.

Apparently Edward wanted to prosper quickly. He had five children and their stepmother to support. He may have speculated in land beyond his means or been swindled in a land deal. He may have engaged in the gambling endemic to the frontier. Whatever the reasons, in 1802 he borrowed £353 from his brother-in-law Robert Housley and mortgaged all his property, real and personal, including a slave Nancy, to be forfeit if the debt was not paid in a year. The risk of such a contract was aggravated by the fact (did he forget it?) that he had sold Nancy a month earlier to one William Edwards. Next he borrowed £120 from Hayden Edwards, probably William's brother. This time he got his sister's husband, Thomas Elder, to be his security. There were other debts, too, an accumulation sufficient to ruin him. Whether or not he intended to pay, he could not. In 1803 or 1804, Edward Spalding simply deserted his monetary obligations and his family and disappeared. His name is off the tax lists in 1803, and in 1805, the court judged he was no longer "an inhabitant of the Commonwealth."[2]

Edward's wife either decamped with him or, more probably, was also deserted by him and declined to take responsibility for his household and children. At that time, families, not courts, determined the placement of children. Edward Spalding's children became the wards of Thomas Elder, probably when their father left the state, perhaps even sooner. Thus Catherine lost her father and stepmother and experienced a second uprooting when she was ten—or younger.

As Catherine approached her teens, litigation over her father's debts began. For several years the judgments fell heavily on her relatives. Robert Housley claimed and won all the mortgaged property but had to sue William Edwards to get the slave Nancy. Hayden Edwards sued Thomas Elder, guarantor of the £120 debt.

Elder could pay that much, but not the other creditors who also sued him. In 1807, Elder spent some time in debtors' prison for his brother-in-law's debts.[3] His embarrassment, financial losses, and the ensuing hardships had to encompass his own large family and his Spalding wards.

In what surely seems a related incident, William Edwards, who ran a tavern, got possession of Catherine's sister Ann Spalding, less than ten years old. In October 1807, Thomas Elder obtained a writ of habeas corpus requiring William Edwards to bring Ann before the court. Had Edwards claimed her services when he lost the slave Nancy and while Ann's uncle was in debtors' prison, unable to protect her? Did the court return her? Were two girls, one black and one white, caught in these men's financial follies or misdeeds? And what might this experience of being claimed, shuffled about, and disputed like property have done to the emotional and social formation of Ann Spalding, destined to be a Sister of Charity in charge of slaves? The coincidence of William Edwards being legally involved with Edward Spalding's property and child twice in so short a time invites such speculation. But it seems beyond question that teenaged Catherine was painfully cognizant of her little sister's fate, her uncle's suffering, and the pain, turmoil, and hardship in the Elder home caused by her father's deeds.

In the court action of late 1807, Ann was still called "daughter" of Edward Spalding. At the start of 1809, however, when Catherine was fifteen, court records begin to note the legal disposition of Edward's "orphans." Where, when, and how Edward died may not have been known to his children any more than to history, but his death—actual or legally assumed—clearly caused further upheaval for them all. On January 9, 1809, "Ralph Spalding Orphan of Edward Spalding" was bound into an apprenticeship to learn house carpentry. On January 26, 1809, Thomas Elder, guardian of Louisa Spalding, granted permission for her to marry Leonard Pierce. She could not have been older than fourteen. Sometime after Louisa's wedding, Rosella, Catherine, and probably Ann were moved to the home of their cousin Clementina Elder, who had recently married Richard Clark. Catherine remained there until January 1813. Later that year, Rosella Spalding was married to

Ceda Wathen, with "the consent of Richard Clark her relation with whom she has lived for several years."⁴ Ann remained with the Elders or Clarks, separated again from all her siblings.

Thus, Catherine lost her father again, this time irrevocably. By her move to the Clarks' home, she was shifted again—for the third time; and in the space of one year, she lost the companionship of two siblings. By any assessment, Catherine Spalding was a girl who knew physical and emotional upheavals, losses, rejection, and instability. Not much modern psychology is needed to suppose that she must either become emotionally unstable herself or, by God's care and that of some loving adults, learn to bear losses and hardship, to find alternate sources of joy and trust, to make adjustments and move on, and to become firm in her own purposes and ethics. Over her lifetime, evidences show Catherine grappling with and maturing her own temperament, rooted surely in these early experiences. She learned to let strong feelings energize a profound care for other children orphaned by death or desertion.

In Catherine's girlhood, the primary loving adults were Thomas Elder and "his amiable wife," Elizabeth. Given Edward Spalding's history, the startling fact about the Elders is that they opened their home to his children, where they already had ten of their own. Elder had owned a farm and headed a family of eleven children for twenty-eight years in Maryland. He then sold his land and migrated to Kentucky in 1800 with his wife and all but his eldest son.⁵ Even if only for about five years (1803–1809), Catherine Spalding had in the Elder home a father figure she could respect and a mother figure she could love. Surrounded again by siblings and cousins, Catherine had, even in the years of hardest trouble, a stable, large-family life with relations she could rely on.

The three or four youngest Elders would have been the same age as the Spalding children. In her growing years, Catherine would have found playmates and coworkers at home. One may suppose that the wit and playfulness evidenced later in her personality emerged at this time despite the sorrows affecting both families. Most of the Elder children must still have been at home through the time (1807) of their father's losses and imprisonment for their uncle's debts. But nothing suggests that the family's pain was visited on the Spalding cousins or that they were made to feel they belonged any less to the family. Only when Edward Spalding was declared dead, and the growing family demanded more space, was Clementina Elder, thirteen years older than Catherine, able to persuade her father to transfer guardianship of at least some of the Spalding children to her and her husband.

Late into the nineteenth century, the Elders were remembered and cited for their love, confidence, private austerity, public mildness, and practical goodness.[6] What other virtues could their circumstances more demand—or make more difficult? Catherine must have preserved this positive memory in her community's traditions. The immediate recognition of her strength and warmth of character when she came to St. Thomas suggests that she had received from her aunt and uncle emotional support and ample love blended with expectation of the disciplined self-sacrifice required to make a large multibranched family live together in harmony and growing prosperity. They had formed the leader of a community of diverse women.

Beyond fond remembrance, what can be known or fairly inferred about Catherine's daily life with the Elders and Clarks? The Elders lived in a settlement on Cox's Creek north of Bardstown, known as Gardiner's Station or Turkey Town until it was incorporated as Fairfield in 1820. It was one of an "intricate network of faith communities, several first gathered and sustained by pious laity." Besides achieving safety in numbers, the Catholics hoped to warrant the assignment to Kentucky of one or two priests who would provide at least some of the "consolations of religion" for themselves and their children. Two priests came but left before Catherine arrived in Kentucky; two others died, and one "disappeared" between 1799 and 1804, the very years she was experiencing her father's debts and desertion.[7] The clergy as spiritual fathers were not reliable either, and she had to know it.

But one priest came and remained, and every Catholic knew him well, indeed—Stephen Theodore Badin. A French refugee, twenty-five years old, newly ordained in Baltimore, Father Badin was en route to Kentucky at the very time of Catherine's birth in

1793. His stability there, his zeal, and the force of his eccentric personality would guarantee that a primary emphasis of life for young Catherine Spalding would be on the religion that bonded the pioneers at the Catholic settlements. Badin rode the circuit of communities, nearly always alone until Belgian refugee Father Charles Nerinckx arrived in 1805.[8] Then they shared the services for the fifty families at Cox's Creek. But Badin remained the chief pastor, the one Catherine would have known in her childhood. He would have supervised her instruction for first sacraments; his sermons and principles would have been her primary church influence, and his attempts to regulate the conduct of the laity would introduce her to internal church controversy.

The regulations and the controversy were elements of a dual Catholic culture that would mark Catherine's girlhood. Some grasp of that culture is essential to understanding much of her ensuing history, especially her dealings with clerical leaders.

The Maryland Catholic migrants of her parents' era inherited a tradition of faith sustained during persecution in England and under penal laws and civil disabilities in the colony. They had been liberated by the American Revolution, with its republican ideals of liberty and equality. The first American bishop, John Carroll, translated these ideas into a mode of church governance, and the Kentucky migrants made them into the frontier spirit. These lay folk were accustomed to desiring, but not having, a priest and sacraments, adjusting to a personal, homebound prayer life fed by devotional manuals with Mass prayers, and judging for themselves what was suitable moral conduct. They had learned to be tolerant of and inoffensive to Protestant neighbors. And they had developed active lay leadership (women included) in the management of their communal religious life. On the frontier, they wanted to build churches of a size and decor they could afford. They also wanted to keep financial control of them.

When these folk of English stock did get a priest who stayed (Badin), he was French, an inheritor of a Catholic culture that was distinctly communal, clerical, and hierarchical. Upwardly mobile clergymen in France achieved social status and moral authority. In beautiful churches, they dispensed the solemn rituals of salvation to reverent and obedient laity. While rejecting Jansenist theology, many priests imbibed a good deal of its spirit, its emphasis on corrupted nature, moral weakness, and discipline of the passions by penance, devotion, and confession.[9] When the French Revolution abruptly and brutally ended both status and safety, many clergy fled to the United States, where priests were so urgently needed. The best of them left material ambition behind and brought real devotion and missionary zeal, but also their inherited spirituality, a newly formed distrust of independent spirit, and a loathing of "Republicanism." Stephen Badin was one of the most devoted and zealous—but also, by culture and temperament, sure to embroil himself in controversy with his lay folk.

Badin was indefatigable in providing the sacraments to his scattered congregations. They revered him and participated gratefully, even if they sometimes feared him. In 1801, he wrote Bishop Carroll in Baltimore that he visited Cox's Creek once a month. Thomas Elder was an acknowledged leader in that congregation, which included his family, the Spalding children, Clement and Henrietta Boone Gardiner and their three granddaughters (later Catherine's companions as SCNs), and also the family of Nicholas Miles, father of Richard Miles (the future bishop of Nashville, with whom Catherine would later have very conflicted dealings).[10]

The Mass station was the home of the Gardiners, Catholic leaders in the area. Badin's monthly arrival meant a full day of religious observances. His rule for attendance by families at a distance was ten miles if on horseback, five miles if on foot. Badin noted admiringly that some of his people did come great distances and spent the night in the church to be there for the confessions that began at dawn. Morning prayer was followed by more confessions, for each of which Badin took ample time. While he was thus engaged, catechists whom he had trained, usually women, instructed children and slaves; other adults recited the rosary. Mass, with a sermon, might not begin until past noon (the people, of course, fasting for Communion), and it might be followed by yet more confessions, instructions, baptisms, a marriage or burial, and even some other devotions and hymns. Catherine Spalding would have experienced ritual processions to the cemetery (such as those she led years later at Nazareth) and solemn processions of the Blessed Sacrament with leaders on horseback and participants with canopy and censer, banners and bells.[11]

Yet, if the distances and hours were exhausting, the services gave to the pioneers a collective identity in a faith community. They were graced members of an ecclesial body for whose sacraments they made these sacrifices. Beyond doubt, young Catherine Spalding saw herself as firmly and forever a daughter of the Catholic Church. She had a solid foundation in its sacramental and moral life and some impetus to aspire to deeper spiritual life and service when occasion and guidance would come.

Religious events were also social occasions, neighborhood gatherings of both young and old, that required a good deal of preparation. The Gardiner sisters were said to be Catherine's childhood companions. She was often with them and helped them prepare for the Masses held at their grandfather's house.[12] If the communal religious experiences helped her to have friends and playmates outside the family, one need not suppose any unusual childhood piety to account for her pleasure in preparing and participating.

Household piety, however, was the sustenance of faith throughout Catherine's girlhood. Badin's rule was "No morning prayer, no breakfast; no work, no dinner; no night prayer, no supper."[13] Many families followed the custom of blessing the children daily. Badin advocated only the basic observances, but he cooperated with Nerinckx's introduction of extra devotions and confraternities. Whatever the observances in the Elder household, Catherine certainly imbibed there a good and solid quantity of their faith and devotion.

Solid piety, however, did not prevent the clash of religious cultures, and young Catherine Spalding, ward of a leading Catholic family, certainly witnessed plenty of it. Religious disciplines affecting daily life were strict, too strict in the view of the Elders and many laity, but hardly strict enough to suit Badin and Nerinckx. There were many complaints to Bishop Carroll about both priests. Nerinckx was accused of asking for too many prayers too early in the day and too much financial sacrifice, and of opposing horse racing and women's finery. He and Badin tried hard to stop the neighborhood dances that had been customary since the early migrations. Badin, in self-defense, told the bishop he had tolerated dancing by day but not late at night, when it brought in "most profligate characters . . . uninvited" and became "an infallible occasion of sin for most of the actors or spectators."[14]

The English Dominicans, who had arrived in 1805, did not share the French priests' moral strictures. Samuel Wilson, OP, soon advised Bishop Carroll that Kentucky needed a diocese and "a prudent bishop" to limit the powers and "too great zeal" that went so far as to refuse women absolution for their husbands' permitting a decent dance in their house, and to deny young people admission to the sacraments without a "solemn promise of not dancing on any occasion whatever, which few will promise."[15] Whether teenaged Catherine Spalding ever danced or was required to submit to regulations about dancing cannot be verified, but the Elder family surely hosted social events and was notably engaged in the struggle with Badin about his inflexible severity. She certainly grew up knowing that one could disagree with a cleric and even appeal over his head to his bishop.

However important religion was in young Catherine's life, it could hardly have absorbed the bulk of her thought, energy, or time. That must have gone into the essentials of survival on the frontier. Her girlhood would have followed the patterns of the families on Cox's Creek: plentiful work, limited recreation, and homespun education. What is known of the general lifestyle can fairly be inferred of hers.

When the Spaldings and Elders came to Kentucky, life was advancing beyond the primitive stage of log cabins with dirt or puncheon floors, clothing of buckskin or homespun, wooden dishes, beds on the floor, and wild game, hominy, and corn bread for food. Yet, in 1807, when Catherine was thirteen, Father Nerinckx could still describe to his family "all the nays of this country": no wine, beer, oil, coal, turf, bells, or sparrows; no stoves, spices, fine herbs, peaches, or fruit trees except wild apple and pear; few vegetables or singing birds, little fresh meat.[16] The settlers did have corn, pumpkins, molasses from pumpkin juice, turnips, melons, and wild cane. Cows gave milk for cheese, butter, and curds; trees gave nuts and maple sugar; turkey and game were in the woods, fish plentiful in the streams. Catherine would grow up on plain food but probably a sufficiency of it. She would know, however, that hardships, crop failures, and illness often left others hungry, and that both neighborliness and Christian charity called for a generous response.

Catherine was equally prepared for hard work of many sorts. Her primary education was that of any girl in a frontier settlement—chiefly domestic. Participation in "women's work" of cooking, cleaning, and production of clothing for the large household would be expected, as well as care and medication of the sick. Probably she learned to prepare flax for spinning by "pulling, threshing, spreading, drying, breaking, swinging"; to pick cockles and burrs out of wool; to weave wool and linen together into the staple fabric, linsey-woolsey; and to make dye from nuts and tree bark, lye from ashes, and soap from lye.[17] Tanning leather and then making shoes was a family affair or even a neighborhood enterprise that lasted a year or even two, a fact that explains why Catherine and the first Sisters saved their shoes by carrying them to church. She was prepared to continue all these domestic tasks when she came to St. Thomas; the first mission of the Sisters was to weave cloth and make clothing for the seminarians and themselves.

Gardening, if not field labor, was certainly part of Catherine's girlhood training. If Thomas Elder had slaves (as he very likely had, at least before his fortunes were shattered), they probably did the heaviest work. But in new and rugged settlements, white family members often worked along with their servants. When Catherine came to St. Thomas, she was clearly accustomed to outdoor work, to raising her own food and preserving it. She could not have been surprised to see both slaves and seminarians raising the vegetables and erecting the buildings.

From the Elders, influenced by what the local clergy demanded, she would learn the accepted policies toward "servants," as Kentucky Catholics nearly always called their slaves. Badin owned slaves himself and defended the need of the institution. But with Bishop Carroll's backing, he opposed cruelty to slaves and insisted they be instructed and allowed to practice their religion, not kept at home to care for young children or work while the family was at Mass. They were to receive the sacraments, and their marriages were to be respected. The "servants" were enslaved persons, and no euphemism or policy can soften or justify the fact. The rules did at least modify the inhumanity that was expected and all too often practiced by Catholics as well as Protestants, in both Maryland and Kentucky.[18]

How much formal education Catherine had before coming to St. Thomas is unknown. Many early readers, spellers, grammars, arithmetics, and quaint geographies were published in Kentucky after Lexington got a printer in 1787. Salem Academy, founded in Bardstown in 1788, may have had some Catholic students. But that school was not near Turkey Town/Fairfield, and the pupils were doubtless boys. Flaget wrote of "our Kentucky girls, who scarcely know how to read or write."[19]

Yet Catherine does not seem to have come to the community illiterate. The Elders, long residents of a more developed state, very likely had basic education sufficient to pass on to their children and wards. Certainly they had enough pupils in their care to constitute a substantial little home school. A colony of Catholic families, visited with some regularity by Badin—himself educated, intellectual in taste, and a writer—may have set up some system of basic schooling for groups of neighboring children. In any case, Catherine was undoubtedly as naturally bright then as she later proved herself to be. What she did not know by 1812, she learned rapidly.

Badin strongly encouraged Catholic reading. He lent out his own books and sought to obtain copies of books that were popular and available in the East: Francis de Sales, *Introduction to the Devout Life;* Thomas à Kempis, *The Following of Christ;* Lorenzo Scupoli, *Unseen Warfare: The Spiritual Combat and Path to Paradise;* Alban Butler, *Lives of the Saints,* and others. In late 1799, the time of Catherine's sixth birthday, when she may have been learning to read, Badin had some catechisms printed. In August 1805, when she was eleven, he wrote and published in Bardstown *The Real Principles of Roman Catholics in Reference to God and*

Country. Finally, when she was about fifteen, eighty-seven Kentuckians, including Catholics of Cox's Creek, subscribed for a reprinting of an unknown author's *Reflections on the Spirit of Religious Controversy.* Some of these books very likely found their way into Thomas Elder's home. If Catherine did not read them, she would have heard discussion of their contents by her uncle and aunt and other leading Catholics, including such women of the congregation as Grace Newton Simpson, an esteemed local intellectual and speaker.[20]

Any scarcity of books during Catherine's girlhood was offset by a form of oral education. In a large family with children much older than herself, with plenty of neighbors not too far away, and all gathering for Mass at least monthly, much could be heard and learned by an attentive young listener. In 1805, Father Badin reported to Rome, "We have nine or ten printers of gazettes, of lampoons, of hymns and of political or heretical brochures." Before 1812, there were twenty-nine newspapers in Kentucky and papers from New York, Baltimore, and Philadelphia, which came via Lexington to subscribers in Bardstown. People would gather to hear them read aloud.[21] A young lady was unlikely to be in that crowd, but Catherine had plenty of menfolk to hear the news and repeat it at home.

Catherine could have heard discussions of local and national elections and political propaganda, of the Louisiana Purchase, of foreign relations and the approach of war with England, of virulent anti-Catholic sentiments and statements, of controversy over slavery among the Presbyterians, Methodists, and Baptists, including the "Emancipating Baptists" in Nelson County. The fact that the same groups opposed both Catholicism and slavery was shaping the Catholic defense of both institutions. Catherine could also hear at home or among the neighbors Catholic opinion of the "Great Awakening" among Protestants, and diverse opinions about Protestant-Catholic relations and the value of controversial speeches and pamphlets. She surely knew about Badin's defense of Catholicism as compatible with loyal and free citizenship.[22] In general, Catherine would have grown up aware of the political and religious activities and issues around her.

She came to St. Thomas young but not naive or unprepared for her coming role in society.

By 1807, the biggest, most discussed issue for Catholics was the need and probability of a diocese. The possibility that Badin would be made the bishop was enough to set off what historian Thomas Spalding called the "Tempest in Turkey Town." It was "a story of turmoil that could not but have affected Catherine's attitude toward family and church," since "the Elders were in the forefront of a concerted effort" to prevent Badin's selection.[23] Although that motive was never stated, letters filled with charges and counter-charges began to go to Bishop Carroll. The list of Badin's offenses included opposition to dancing, denial of the sacraments even to the sick, excommunications, grotesque and cruel penances assigned in confession, and forbidding confession to the Dominicans. The letters created an uproar that involved many people of different families, did not end until 1809, and was certainly observed by the teenaged Catherine.

Among the Elders involved was Thomas Elder himself. He apparently helped persuade his sister's son, John Lilly, a state legislator and a skeptic (thus personally unaffected and supposedly objective), to write Bishop Carroll a description, with "certificates" from local witnesses, of Badin's egregious severity. Elizabeth and Nancy Elder, Thomas's wife and daughter, were among those cited in John Lilly's letter as having reported Badin's reprehensible statements and actions. Another set of letters involved Nancy and Thomas's son Basil in Baltimore (thus close to the bishop). The dancing issue became personal, as it occurred and was condemned at the wedding (which Catherine probably attended) of Polly Elder, a relative.

In June 1808, Badin told Bishop Carroll that "numerous friends have endeavored to atone for the ingratitude of a few, viz. the Elder family, to whom I have been partial."[24] But the Elders were divided among themselves. When Badin's friends, seventy-seven of them from the Bardstown and Turkey Town congregations, sent a statement to Carroll denying the calumnies against their pastor, the signers included a younger Thomas Elder, nephew of Thomas

Sr.; Robert Housley, brother-in-law of Edward Spalding; and Richard Clark, almost certainly the one who married Thomas's daughter Clementina. Thomas Elder Jr., his wife, Susanna, and a Matilda Elder also sent a certificate saying that Grace Newton Simpson had voiced threats of leaving the church and of John Lilly's injuring it in the Assembly if the bishop did not give satisfaction. Badin himself sent Carroll a certificate from one John Blandford, saying that Thomas Elder, John Lilly, and Joseph Gardiner had tried to get him drunk enough to sign the certificate against Badin; he had signed but repented. In August 1808, Badin received from Carroll the list of charges and penned a forty-page rebuttal. He noted that Nancy Elder and Grace Simpson "cease not to circulate their stories. . . . Oh! what a glorious spectacle for Infidels, to see two pious Amazons leading a coalition, to divide in a Protestant country the Catholic Pastor from his Flock, and the clergy between themselves."[25]

Somewhere in all these countercharges among the people of Catherine's foster family and other people of good, even high, repute was the truth about Badin's excessive demands, rigidity, and imposition of some truly bizarre penances, but also the truth about some of the wild dances and drinking that he deplored, and the exaggerations, misrepresentations, and even falsehoods of those who feared the extension of his authority. And somewhere in the midst of the wrangling, feverishly commenting people was the observant teenaged ward of Thomas and Elizabeth Elder, listening, surely, and learning.

In November 1808, word reached Kentucky that Benedict Joseph Flaget, a French priest of the Society of St. Sulpice, teaching in the seminary in Baltimore but familiar with the frontier from a previous mission in Vincennes, Indiana, had been appointed bishop (with Badin's own urgent recommendation).[26] The tempest subsided. In January 1809, Badin told Carroll that the Elder family and others had acknowledged their errors and were willing to make satisfaction. By September of that year, he reported that the "Turkey Townists . . . become more tame," and in May 1810, that Mr. Thomas Elder Sr. had made his peace with him at Easter and that he still respected the Elder family.[27]

What could Catherine Spalding have learned from being a close witness to this unseemly commotion and slow healing of divisions in the local church? She never mentions the episode in her later extant letters, but those she wrote to Bishops Flaget and Martin John Spalding defending the independence and the fervor of her own SCN community suggest that she had learned a good deal about modes of relationship with clerical authority. Her mode would include freedom and forthrightness in expressing and holding a position, even counter to her superiors, and even as a woman. But she also was aware of the damage done by religious quarrels and congregational divisions, and the eminent necessity of truth, justice, and mutual respect. It is noteworthy that in the independence crisis of 1841, the most serious she was ever to face, she sought and obtained Badin's advocacy for her position.

Flaget's arrival in Kentucky was delayed well over two years, first by his own frantic efforts to avoid the bishopric, and then by winter weather and lack of money.[28] Finally, on May 13, 1811, like the Spaldings, Elders, and other Maryland migrants before him, he left the relative comforts of the settled state to plant something new on the frontier. He was accompanied by John Baptist David, a fellow Sulpician and teacher, his closest friend and strong, voluntary support. This priest was soon to become the single most powerful influence on the life and mission of Catherine Spalding.[29]

The niece of Thomas Elder may well have been on the edge of the group of "notable Catholics" who came out to greet the bishop in Bardstown on June 8, 1811. Flaget described an arrival without exchange of public "compliments," everything occurring "with true American composure." His own composure hid his "broken heart" at the sight of his "episcopal palace" provided by Badin at his own residence, St. Stephen's on Pottinger's Creek. Still worse, the "cathedral" had "no chairs, not even an altar." David's description of it as a "chapel of logs poorly joined together, unplastered, having a sorry altar made of some pieces of board—all in a pitiable condition" may be unfair to Badin's efforts.[30] It does illuminate one priority of these French clerics, which David later gave to Catherine when he told her to build first a house suitable for her God, who would then help her build one for the Sisters.

Flaget nevertheless took possession of his see and church with solemn ceremonies and was soon bringing the new diocese to active life. To meet diocesan needs, he established three priorities: seminary, cathedral, and convent. The first and third were initiated by his collaborator, Father David. With all their respect for Badin, the two soon noted that to reach the people and to form a new sort of clergy, a new location was needed. This they found on the farm near Bardstown willed by Thomas Howard in 1810 to Badin and Nerinckx, and "the then Roman Catholic Bishop of Kentucky."[31] This land and will would quickly create conflict over title between Badin and Flaget; it would eventually create Catherine's first great crisis. For the immediate need, however, it provided the necessary independent location for the seminary begun in November 1811 by David and three seminarians who had accompanied him from Maryland.

As early as the previous July, David had written his Sulpician friend Bruté in Maryland of the desire to form "a society of virtuous girls for the education of young people of their own sex." The original plan was a motherhouse at St. Thomas from which Sisters would go in twos to the rural congregations and be recalled for retreats and other occasions. He soon began to speak about this at the mission stations, and by early September 1812, he expressed hopes to begin that autumn. In November, Teresa Carrico presented herself, followed shortly thereafter by Elizabeth Wells.[32]

The First Annals cite "two young women of the country, poor and illiterate but of good repute." Flaget later described them as "two poor girls, one of whom had a complete set of cooking utensils and some furniture." Betsey Wells, in fact, was neither young nor entirely uneducated. The poverty, however, is not in doubt. David hesitated to begin in winter, without money. But the "poor girls" argued for a start. Though David was uneasy and experienced moments of "grief and anguish" at the responsibility, he acceded to their urging.[33] The two arrived at St. Thomas on December 1, 1812. That date has ever since been honored as Foundation Day of the Sisters of Charity of Nazareth.

Much uncertainty has persisted about where the Sisters first lived at St. Thomas. Bits of data from Flaget and David, other

Nazareth traditions, and the known sequence of events in 1812 combine to make virtually certain that the "cradle" for the new community was the sturdy two-story log and poplar-sided house still standing at St. Thomas. Originally the Howard house and then the seminary, it had become Flaget's episcopal residence in August 1812. In December, he was in Baltimore and could not return over the mountains until spring. The seminarians were in a newly built dormitory. The second story of Flaget's house was vacant if needed. And needed it was. The "house that the priest had destined for them . . . was occupied by a renter, whom it was very difficult to dislodge." Nazareth's tradition says that "of his own scanty lodging—a log cabin, the saintly bishop spared two rooms for the first Sisters." More likely, David appropriated the rooms in his absence for the Sisters' present necessity. It seems likely that the occupation lasted until close to the bishop's return in May.[34]

Catherine joined Teresa and Betsey on January 21, 1813. The Clark family tradition recalls that Richard Clark "took some young woman on horseback across the fields to enter Nazareth. I think this must have been Mother Catherine." According to another Clark descendant, both Richard Clark and his wife, Clementina Elder, "took her on a horse. . . . both went with her."[35] Both would have been thirty-two years old when they gave consent for their nineteen-year-old cousin and ward to choose a radically experimental future in a sure-to-be-arduous environment. Perhaps they themselves had the pioneers' daring and faith-filled spirit; they must have recognized it in her, seen her impelled by a desire to serve and by personal determination. So it became their honor and their moment in history to escort Catherine Spalding to the enterprise of her life.

That enterprise was to be central to the life of the new diocese planted in the seedbeds of the local churches and St. Thomas Seminary. Community and church, Catherine and clergy, would influence each other to permanent effect. Together they would collaborate on religious and social missions that would influence Kentucky for generations and spread far beyond it. But that much could hardly have been within the vision of the girl who dismounted at the door of the log house at St. Thomas.

Two

Pioneer at St. Thomas

1812–1822

To stand today before the log house at St. Thomas on a frigid winter afternoon, to observe the woods behind and beside it, to erase from imagination all contemporary buildings and replace them with only the log seminary and a few slave cabins—all that evokes wonder at the power of faith and motivation that emboldened young Catherine Spalding to pass the doorway, intending permanence and commitment.

The house certainly represented a break with the homes of her aunt and cousin. By 1813, both the Elders and the Clarks, if not highly prosperous, were at least able to provide ample warmth, comfortable furnishings of the time, and more than sufficient food. Catherine, entering this new home and looking around, could see what she was sacrificing.

Though the house is described as "well built" and "of the better class," those phrases relate to its size and construction, not to amenities for daily living. Home of the Howards, it had been refurnished for a group of young male students and two clerics with a high regard for asceticism, all laboring in the necessities of a new and poor diocese. Father David and the seminarians had moved furniture into their new dormitory and study building, leaving little more than a table and benches for the parish Mass in the large downstairs room. Upstairs were two twelve-by-fifteen-foot rooms, one that David had occupied and another recently vacated by the seminarians for the bishop. One of these rooms and the adjacent "small study"—equipped with cots or only pallets and perhaps some benches or chairs—were probably the "two rooms" of the Sisters.[1] Only the narrow chapel off the main room below would have signaled an effort to achieve beauty. Catherine looked, confronted her reality, then moved on in. She would hold to her intent.

The most important unknowns to Catherine Spalding at her entry to St. Thomas were the four people who would most influence her immediate future: Teresa Carrico and Elizabeth (Betsey) Wells, Bishop Flaget and Father David. Records provide variant amounts of information about these pioneers of the new venture.

Teresa Carrico, the first volunteer and ever after honored as the first Sister of Charity of Nazareth, came from a Maryland family settled in Washington County. She was almost four years older than Catherine. The distance between pioneer counties probably meant that they had never met. Community tradition indicates that Teresa had little or no education; she never did become a teacher. Yet that tradition also is very strong that Teresa Carrico, though not a leader, appreciated character and possessed a warmth and fidelity in friendship, together with robust health, practical domestic skills, a capacity and willingness for heavy manual labor, and an ever-deepening spirituality. These combined attributes made her Catherine's lifelong support and the heart of community life and ministry at Nazareth.

Elizabeth Wells, sister of two military men and a convert instructed by Father Badin, had been housekeeper for Father Michael Fournier, one of Badin's short-lived helpers. Now, at nearly thirty-seven, she was the oldest and the highest in social status of the three women, surely somewhat educated, and probably the one who brought "some furniture." Later memory described her as "a good but very peculiar person." Her welcome to Catherine was doubtless sincere, yet their subsequent relationship proved strained and relatively short.[2]

While little is known of the women, much more survives of the two men who were to be such immense influences on Catherine's personal development and on her exercise of leadership in her community. Whether Catherine had previously met Flaget cannot be known. He had spent much of his first year in Kentucky on horseback visiting mission stations. When Catherine entered, he was in Baltimore with Badin. Father David must have interviewed Catherine before he accepted her, but she could hardly have known well this cleric who was now to become her superior and mentor. She simply took the risk of placing herself under his authority. She would soon know both men well.

Both priests, refugees of the French Revolution, resembled yet differed from Badin as pastors. They brought to Kentucky the same objection to "false liberalism" and the same French Catholic culture, with its respect for tradition, religious ritual, and strong clerical authority. They expected lay cooperation but accepted only minimal lay leadership. Both habitually referred to those subject to their authority as their children, beloved indeed, but expected to obey without resistance.[3] When challenged in his role, the gentle Flaget could be severe, even threatening. His letters echo a sort of refrain: I did not want to be a bishop, I am unworthy to be a bishop, I begged not to be made a bishop; but having obeyed and accepted the burden, I am the bishop!

Still, if Flaget and David were clerical monarchs or parents, they exercised authority far more gently than Badin. David expressed satisfaction that the people treated them "with all the respect and attention due the Bishop and his clergy" but lamented a "certain aloofness caused by respect or fear" in those previously directed "with an iron rod" rather than by love.[4] Both men brought to their dealings with Catherine and the other Sisters this concept of authority as benevolent and unquestionable. She would not contravene their due authority, but in her time of leadership, the girl raised by the Elders would offer serious questions about some of their wishes and pending decisions, and even offer successful resistance.

In another respect, Flaget and David were both like and unlike Badin. Less tinged with Jansenism, they had still inherited what has been called a "subtractive spirituality," a flesh-denying, will-denying approach to earthly life.[5] Discipline to control the untamed flesh, rule and regularity of observance, conviction of one's nothingness and sinfulness, with consequent humility and penitence—these were powerful norms they strove to inculcate in their priests and women religious. David wrote that Sisters should confess every month, maybe every two weeks or even more often, yet "monthly communion is sufficient." A "premature ardor" to communicate more often showed "they do not perceive sufficiently the enormity of sin."[6] Such views and counsel would influence Catherine's community for a long time, yet her personal spirituality, as seen in her letters, reflects no such scruples or Jansenistic fears.

As Sulpicians, however, Flaget and David were sons of Jean-Jacques Olier, priestly disciple of Vincent de Paul. Through him they inherited Vincent's gentler approach to God, his Christ-centered, tender love, his charism of charity, his zeal for the church, and his pastoral service of the poor. For these motives they rejected clerical ambition, materialism, and worldliness, gave earnest and faithful service at any cost to self, and exercised the urgent concern for the poor and slaves that so often appears in their letters. Their Vincentian connection also predisposed them to choose the charism and the Rule of the Daughters of Charity for the community they wished to establish.

The two clerical friends were, however, quite distinct personalities. Flaget combined great physical strength and zeal for the long missionary journeys with acute sensitivity to unpleasant or unseemly physical conditions (such as a tavern where all the women had "the itch" yet handled the food, or a house where guests and family, women included, slept in one room). His feelings were easily hurt (a fact that Catherine was evidently considering in her later letters to him), yet he was not inclined to harbor resentment; and sensitivity to the feelings of others enabled him to bend to customs that were not sinful and to reconcile people long estranged from each other or from the church. He was essentially personable, humorous, and very outgoing; he loved especially to have recreation with the seminarians and reproached himself with "not being sufficiently grave in their company."[7]

John Baptist David, in his letters, reproaches himself for various failings, but lack of gravity is not one of them. A precocious intellect and spirituality—tutored in childhood, encouraged in seminary years, and exercised as a professor of philosophy—had shaped his naturally introverted personality to a seriousness that still retained great warmth of feeling. His gifts precisely fit the Sulpician charism to conduct seminaries and elevate the character of the priesthood. For that goal he had offered himself spontaneously to his friend Flaget. The force of their friendship never diminished. Flaget protested vehemently his Baltimore superior's intent to recall David, "'the pole bolt of my coach'—of the entire establishment . . . as necessary for me as my two eyes, and also my counselor and the friend of my heart and affection . . . the only one on whose knowledge and wisdom I can count with certainty."[8] With allowance for differences in roles and degrees of mutuality, the same words could express the coming relationship of David and Catherine Spalding, as together they established a religious community.

Catherine and all David's "daughters" would benefit from his deep and genuine affection for them and from his theoretical and intensely practiced knowledge of the interior life. One of the Sisters left an anonymous sketch of him: "Not naturally eloquent, solid tender piety, modest, learned, excellent advice in all times, especially Church matters. Director of souls here. Wit sometimes, not talker."[9] They would also know the force of his regard for rules, rituals, and self-discipline. On occasion, they would experience what he himself lamented as "my brusque and sometimes harsh disposition." Yet he felt sure that his charges understood him and knew his love for them; "they love me more than they fear me." At a conference in 1823, he publicly apologized to the young clergy for past expressions of impatience. He sought to model what he urged on students and Sisters: perfection through humility, obedience, industry, order, punctuality, and regularity in work and prayer.[10]

Young Catherine Spalding in January 1813 could have known little of all this except rumors. And surely she did not know David's recent history of authority over women. Between Father David and Elizabeth Ann Seton, the clash of religious cultures had occurred immediately and played out painfully. When he was ap-

pointed ecclesiastical superior[11] and spiritual director at Emmitsburg, Maryland, Mother Seton had already founded the Sisters of
Charity and their school and had exercised her mature judgment
and experience in leading them. He expected, by virtue of his role,
to direct everything: the spiritual and community life of the Sisters,
the school program, and the management of temporalities. The
requirements stated in his letters to Mother Seton and the torment
reflected in hers to Bishop Carroll remind one of the Kentuckians'
trouble with Badin, but the grounds of her conflict with David are
much more certain.[12]

Against that background, David received Catherine Spalding
and the first volunteers for the Kentucky convent. And against it,
one must read several episodes of their early and subsequent history. Catherine apparently had no conflicts with David compa-
rable to those of Elizabeth Seton. This fact may be due to her
much younger age, the pliability of her temperament, or her sense
of obedience—perhaps also to a more canny and intuitive knowledge, seasoned by observation of Badin, of how to deal with a man
like David. To give David his due, experience may have taught him
some caution and the wisdom of consulting and affirming a woman of intelligence and natural leadership recognized and honored
by her peers. He would need to relearn that lesson in the 1830s, in
an episode that would afflict both of them deeply and nearly split
the community. But that could not be foreseen by either the girl
Catherine or the priest who welcomed her.

David's bent for order and regulation Catherine must have mentally noted at once. She might have expected a respite from her
day's journey on horseback, some hours or days to get to know
her companions and the ways of living together in the house. If so,
she had to be startled—or perhaps amused or even pleased—when
David presented, within hours of her arrival, a "provisional rule."
It unfolded "the nature, objects, and duties of the new society."
According to the early Annals, he "also read and fully explained
to those present an 'order of the day' which he had written out for
the regulation of the exercises." These included mental and vocal
prayer, study, work, and recreation. This new life "was still further

organized by the temporary appointment of the oldest member [Betsey Wells] as superior, until the society should be sufficiently numerous to proceed to a regular election, according to the provisions of the rule."[13] Religious vows were yet to be determined.

If the prompt beginning of regulation dazed the weary newcomer, at least it assured her that she really was beginning a life with sacred purpose and character, however small and bare the setting. Bare it was—dangerously so. The spiritually regulated life still requires other life-sustaining priorities: basic housing, food, and steady, serviceable, supportive work. The first two needs were in decidedly short supply.

Housing in the bishop's residence did not last longer than it took David to persuade the tenant to move. David described the house to which the new religious moved as "half a mile from the Seminary . . . a house 18 feet square . . . adding a small log-house which serves as a kitchen and as a loom-room." In the early 1870s, the remaining pioneers who had lived there described what they remembered: a "dilapidated log cabin" with one room below for community and dining room and a half-story attic for sleeping. The prior occupants had left the house in such bad condition that the floor boards and supporting planks ("sleepers") underneath were burned away around the fireplace; to eat their meals, the Sisters sat on projecting ends of these boards with their feet hanging down before the fire. Their "full set of utensils" consisted of one frying pan, one spoon, and two knives, with which to prepare in succession, and then eat, corn bread, middling (a dish made from coarse grain), and sage tea.[14] This apparently unvarying and impoverished menu resulted partly from the extremely limited financial resources of both the Sisters and the sponsoring clergy, and still more from the choice to begin their new life in the middle of a frontier winter. The Sisters ate what they had and awaited a new planting season.

Reference to the women's prior experience of frontier life cannot soften the severity of their lodging and board. Few, if any of them, had been accustomed to a lifestyle so stark. Later praises of the heroic and unvarying cheerfulness of all the Sisters carry an aura of hagiography. No letters home reveal Catherine's feelings directly, but Richard Clark's stories to his grandchildren included the memory of "how very homesick she was."[15] She was young and accustomed to the planning and work of provision for the Elder and Clark households, as well as their camaraderie. The true source of her perseverance, surely, was her spiritual purpose, well laced with warm sympathy, native humor, and determination, and also with practical wisdom to see needs and the skills to provide for them. All are traits cited later, which she must have developed in her girlhood homes and which must have influenced the other Sisters to establish her leadership officially.

That bare house was named Nazareth and gave to the community its permanent full name. David is said to have reminded the Sisters that in the residence of the Holy Family, "seeking to be unknown, the Son of God gave us the example of perfect purity of life—of the obedience, humility and poverty that ought to be the riches of religious houses."[16] This quotation, oddly, does not mention charity—the virtue that suffused the house of Nazareth in Galilee and is the key element in both community name and charism. The desire and will for charity-driven service had attracted the pioneers and enabled them to endure hunger, meager lodgings, and winter cold.

Catherine had come to give service, and she very quickly had the opportunity. The Sisters' ministry consisted of teaching and "works of mercy . . . especially those that can contribute to aid the work of the mission." They had not yet means or skills to teach, but with a view to that end, David included in the daily order two hours of study, and he himself gave weekly lessons in grammar and writing. The "work of the mission," however, was assigned in short order: "manufacturing all the clothing worn by the seminarians." Catherine put to use all the skills she had learned at the Elders'. She and the other Sisters were daily busy with spinning, weaving, and sewing for the seminarians, for themselves, and for the slaves whom Flaget had inherited from the Howards. Flaget sent one or two slaves to help clear the land and cut wood, but the Sisters themselves did field labor, along with cooking and washing clothes. They slightly alleviated their poverty by making clothes for neighbors who could pay for them.[17]

The first works of mercy were not to children but to the elderly, some poor men and women who lived and worked on the property in three or four former slave cabins. Two of these people have retained names in community history: Mr. Morgan, age seventy-four, was a skilled weaver; Mr. Wesley is described as a feeble saint, a man of constant prayer. The men worked in cabins that had been converted to a laundry and loom room, and Mr. Wesley was one day found dead standing at the loom with both hands on it.[18] This first death created consternation. For Catherine, it was a call to reactivate emotional energies she had developed and expended in comforting her siblings and the Elders.

Loss by death was balanced by a gain in community life. April and May 1813 brought Catherine three more companions, Mary (Polly) Beaven, Harriet Gardiner, and Sarah (Sally) Sims. In the memories of later years, Polly is described as "calm and edifying," strictly exemplary, kind, and devoted, a quiet woman who talked little, had much virtue but no special talents and no education. Harriet Gardiner, two to three years younger than Catherine, is characterized by "zeal for religious observance," which made her seem "too severe to many, who feared her and loved her less on account of that strictness of character." Yet she was "ever kind and compassionate in the occasion."[19] Nothing is known of Sarah Sims; she would be gone by late October.

These six members constituted the number required by Father David for the holding of an election to choose their superior. David gave the small community a seven-day retreat, and on June 2, 1813, six months after the foundation, the six walked the half mile to the episcopal house for this event. A biographer would give much to know what was in Catherine's mind on that walk. Having lived with the other five and observed their character traits and limitations, she might well have intuited her own candidacy and felt some painful ambivalence.

Whatever Catherine thought or felt, in community tradition, Teresa Carrico is credited with causing a revelation in the minds of the others. According to the story, the Sisters customarily walked barefoot to church to save their valuable shoes, stopping nearby to put them on. While doing so on election day, Teresa remarked,

"Well, I know who will be our Mother; it will be Sister Catherine."
"Yes, yes, Sister Catherine!" was echoed by all—except Sisters
Catherine and Betsey Wells. Sensitivity must have generated embarrassment and painful sympathy in the younger woman; the remark
was, in effect, a public rejection of the older. Teresa, in her later
years, would tell younger Sisters that "we elected Mother Catherine
while we were tying our shoes."[20] She may never have realized the
emotional implications of her spontaneous enthusiastic outburst.

The formal election took place in the little chapel on the first
floor of the surviving house. Bishop Flaget first said Mass; the Sisters communicated and made a quarter hour of thanksgiving. Then
they went one by one into the next room and gave to the bishop
and Father David their votes for Mother, Assistant, and Procuratrix. Catherine Spalding, nineteen years old, heard herself declared
the first Mother of her community. She must now, by her intuitive wisdom and kindness, lead and guide her Sisters in developing
their common life and mission. Harriet Gardiner, even younger
than Catherine, would assist her, and Betsey Wells, as Procuratrix, would administer whatever goods they could acquire. "They
elected no treasurer, for they had no money to keep." Whatever
Catherine's own emotion, her sensitivity surely made her aware of
Betsey's feelings, which in the next year would take their toll on
both of them. Nor could this American pioneer girl have felt much
at ease in the old-world ceremony of having her hand kissed by her
new-made "subjects." Flaget gave the group "counsel which was
evidently dictated by the Holy Spirit," and they withdrew.[21] The
short ceremony would shape the rest of Catherine's life.

Flaget's response to the Spirit also took effect in material ways.
Summer alleviated extreme cold, but the serious limitations on
food continued until the garden could produce. Catherine and Sisters of the era held in grateful memory that Flaget gave five dollars
after he noticed Catherine's distress. The gift was then a notable
generosity.[22] Catherine Spalding's acceptance of dire poverty and
her balancing labors to alleviate it are equally recalled.

The cramp of the lodging, at least, did not last much more than
a year. In September 1813, the seminarians prepared logs for an
addition to the tenant's house. They duplicated the original house

of one room with a half-story attic dormitory, made a twelve-foot passage between the two lower rooms, and extended the attic over it to make a dormitory for students. The new lower room was the schoolroom, and the passageway was closed in to form a reception room. Then a "small log house was also added for a kitchen over which was a loft in which the Sisters slept." This added structure provided Catherine's special joy; it allowed their attic dormitory in the old tenant's house to become a chapel "arranged as their scanty means could best allow."[23]

In the summer of 1814, Father David carried the Blessed Sacrament to this little loft chapel and installed it with the ceremony of Benediction. To Catherine, a frontier girl accustomed to Mass once a month and no reservation of the Sacrament in the church, this event was of immense spiritual significance. She referred to it often in later years as a source of great joy. The presence of Christ in the Sacrament of Love within their house, she said, lightened all trials and increased all joys and the sense of belonging to him.[24] Her letters suggest that this memory was not exaggerated; they refer to other hours spent in a chapel before the Sacrament and the relief or courage or counsel she there attained.

On August 8, Catherine and the Sisters attended the first Mass in the little chapel. Thereafter, they had a weekly Mass, followed by an instruction from Father David. For Sunday and at least some weekday Masses, the Sisters walked the half mile to St. Thomas. In the "subtractive spirituality" of that century, Communion was a Sunday-only privilege. Despite that limitation, Eucharistic devotion became a key element in Catherine's spirituality.

Whatever relief and pleasure the practical Catherine was taking in physical improvements, she could not but be suffering from the tension in the community to which David alludes in a late 1813 letter. Of "my six Philotheas," he says, "only one gives me any trouble . . . a changed person, a spirit out of gear, singular, etc. I am afraid I shall be obliged to send her away." The silence with which Betsey Wells had greeted the eager endorsement of Catherine during the shoe tying had evidently become a persistent alienation from community. The early account says "she seemed dejected from that day."[25]

Betsey's moods may be understandable. Catherine now led prayers and discussions of community business, made final decisions, and assigned tasks. Betsey, old enough to be her mother, was to participate gladly and obey. If her troubled and troubling spirit distressed David, it surely stressed her young superior, her "supplanter" in authority, as they tried to form a religious community life in their close quarters. Perhaps Catherine was not always a model of tact and patience. Letters show that she had her sensitivities and a native capacity for forthright speech. But whatever the two women and their companions suffered, they did not lightly break the bond. Unless the community register is in error by a year, Betsey Wells remained fifteen months after the time of David's letter. She left Nazareth on December 1, 1814, exactly two years from her arrival as a founding member. She and Catherine may never have met again.[26]

Two of the first six Sisters, then, Betsey Wells and Sarah Sims, had left before the community was firmly established or any of them had professed vows. Remaining with Catherine were Teresa Carrico, Polly Beaven, and Harriet Gardiner, who had joyfully elected her, and five others who had entered after the election and before Betsey's departure. The two departures, however appropriate, would have introduced Catherine to the self-questioning, the sense of possible failure, that are endemic to leadership.

The exact status of her leadership, moreover, was not yet firmly decided, as she must have quickly realized. As early as 1811, David had been exploring a possible connection of a Kentucky community with that in Emmitsburg and had requested the Rule of St. Vincent as modified and used in Maryland. When he had some candidates, he asked for two or three Emmitsburg Sisters (of his choosing) to train them. The Emmitsburg Council refused. The newly elected Catherine probably knew of these requests, which would have been presented with all their real advantages. Her feelings may have been ambivalent, the possible confusion of authority weighing against the pleasure of fresh contact with her Maryland origins and with other religious women, who would bring the Rule of Charity and the systematic education the Kentuckians needed. But in the culture of the time, she probably was not consulted in any discussion of her status vis-à-vis those who would come to train her and the others still presumably under her authority. She certainly did not have the decisive word about it.

Nor would Catherine have been included in the discussion going on about full union of the Nazareth community with Emmitsburg. Flaget and David wanted it, but only if the novitiate was in Kentucky and the bishop could modify the Rule and appoint the ecclesiastical superior. The Emmitsburg superiors opposed this confusion of authority and any responsibility for Kentucky's finances and personnel. In late 1814, Archbishop Carroll resolved the question by advising that "a clear distinction should be made between the two institutions." In 1815, Emmitsburg sent a copy of the Rule, and with it David accepted the separate identity of his foundation and his responsibility for it. But Catherine did not know all this. Many years later, when Flaget again sought the union, Catherine would oppose it and say that the early Sisters "never dreamed that a change would be required of us; otherwise our zeal and energy would have been paralyzed."[27]

Before the dispute was resolved, the Sisters were granted their wish for a distinctive religious habit: a black dress, cape, and apron and a black cap like that worn in Emmitsburg. This they donned on April 7, 1814, "after they had made their paschal communion, it being Maundy Thursday."[28] In 1825, Flaget quaintly described the habit as differing little "from that of sedate persons . . . who are not following the styles of the world," the dress being "only a little fuller in the body and sleeves" and the cap "also that of the unworldly woman." His description indicates that Catherine and the community had then the idea of dress upheld by later members—great simplicity but no radical difference from the women around them. The cap by 1825 was white, a sign of the distinction from Emmitsburg. Catherine would again have to defend both the color and the independence it signified, on which the mission itself depended.

Catherine's desire for the mission of education and also her powers of persuasion are revealed by David's notation that the Mother and her Assistant, Harriet Gardiner, had begun to teach as early as September 1813: "Already four boarders, seven or eight day-

scholars." By April 1814, he counted "seven good Sisters at Nazareth" who had in the winter "made the small beginning of a school
in their little house" (the tenant's house before the addition). After
Christmas, however, they had interrupted the school until the addition to the house was finished.[29] Perhaps Catherine, both zealous
and practical, had learned that some limits on shared quarters and
food were necessary. The Sisters needed to live their religious life,
and the children had a right to be children.

Catherine also learned that, if teaching was to be done well,
the teachers must first be taught. Only she and Harriet Gardiner
seem to have been found "quite gifted, and already able to assist
in the classroom."[30] They all needed better preparation than David was able to give. He was limited in time and in knowledge of
American language, culture, and elementary pedagogy. His own
awareness of the need had provoked his anger at the refusal of
Sisters from Emmitsburg. But Providence was about to supply another who would become one of Catherine's chief collaborators,
a one-woman normal school, and the mainstay of the educational
mission for the next twenty years.

"There is a Miss Connell [sic], a school mistress, . . . who
wished to come dwell in one of the convents that I have established," Flaget wrote to a prospective seminarian in Baltimore.
"This young lady will be essential for our schools. She would be
worth a missionary to me."[31] Flaget hoped the man would encourage and escort the lady to Kentucky.

Ellen O'Connell actually needed permission rather than persuasion to undertake the mission planned for her. She was the
daughter of a professor of languages and rhetoric, an early widow-
er who had devoted himself to cultivating her fine mind and taste
for learning and the arts. With her father she had closely studied
the Scripture. In 1813, she was already an experienced teacher.
David had been her spiritual director, and after his departure from
Maryland, they had maintained a correspondence. To him Ellen
proposed entering the new Kentucky congregation. He told her
frankly the contrast she could expect to her Baltimore lifestyle.
When she was undeterred, David welcomed her as the agent of
Providence to begin and develop a school.[32]

An assessment of Ellen O'Connell as instrument of Providence for David's relief and assistance applies equally and incisively to Catherine Spalding's needs and feelings. Ellen validated Catherine's faith that Sisters really could develop a teaching mission in rural Kentucky, that the eighteen months of hardship and constant manual labor would finally bear fruit. Catherine, it is said, had "intuitively the gift of choosing suitable persons for every work, and trusting them to pursue it untrammeled in every detail."[33] She entrusted to Ellen O'Connell leadership both in establishing a school and in training its teachers. She doubtless profited by that training herself as much as she could.

On a more personal level, when Ellen arrived in June 1814, she brought to Catherine a new companionship. The six Sisters then with her included Betsey Wells, with her problematic moods; Harriet Gardiner, intelligent, zealous, and helpful, a good conversationalist, but also serious, perfectionistic, and rather scrupulous; and four others who were certainly companionable and unselfish workers but seem not to have had the talents of mind or the lively interests, personality, and wit that were Catherine's. Ellen had all those traits in abundance, plus maturity from experience to share with her young superior, to stimulate and release the like traits in her, to enliven and enlighten the community recreation.[34]

Community recreation was vital sustenance for these women. Days were long, work exhausting, food plain, if not also scarce— all a strain on the psyche as well as the body. But every evening an hour was set aside for no purpose except to relax and enjoy companionship, to amuse and encourage each other by conversation, storytelling, jokes, laughter, mutual interest, and sympathy. With no appliances for entertainment, not even books, the Sisters and their twenty-year-old superior relied on what all frontier people have employed—their own wits, memories, and tongues. From their own appreciation of small events, ironies, foibles, and discrepancies, a good tale and a good laugh might be made for common pleasure. Hands might be doing needlework, but the goal of the hour was production of sisterly love, renewal of spirits and energies, and that bond of "belonging" created in every culture by shared talk in front of fireplaces and doorways. Since Catherine let

David hear her humor, even lightly targeted him with it, she surely let it flow spontaneously and freely within the community circle. As for Ellen O'Connell, she would be remembered many years later as the center of glee at community recreation.[35]

Through the summer of 1814, Ellen helped prepare for the reopening of the school on August 23. Cecily O'Brien arrived as a "day scholar," followed in a week by Ann Lancaster as a boarder. The teachers were Ellen O'Connell and Harriet Gardiner, assisted by Catherine. In the next year, there were thirty-seven girls, thirteen of them not Catholics. The distance between farms made boarding the norm for most students; that and the high proportion of non-Catholics would set the pattern for the school for decades. By 1816 there were so many boarders that the Sisters gave up their beds and began to sleep on straw mattresses in the kitchen loft and smaller outbuildings. Catherine would struggle a long time both to take an equal share in that discomfort and to end it for everyone.[36]

While the school was beginning, Catherine and the Sisters were also learning the spirit of St. Vincent de Paul, the driving energy for the charism and mission of the Sisters of Charity. In 1815, Father Bruté had hand copied and sent from Emmitsburg to Kentucky the "Common Rules of the Daughters of Charity, Servants of the Sick Poor." The spirit of this Rule gave Catherine Spalding a way to express the urges of her heart formed in her girlhood by both her own severe familial losses and the gratuitous and loving care of her other relatives. She would refer to the Rule many times in later letters, urging faithful observance and the "true spirit of religion," calling it "the only way to secure the blessings of God on our labors."[37]

Catherine, like many other first readers of this Rule, may well have been caught by the beauty of its opening chapter, "Of the Purpose and Fundamental Virtues of Their Institute." Certainly, to follow Catherine Spalding's life is to see the evidence of her commitment to the core values there expressed: honoring and serving Christ in the poor, uniting interior spiritual life with exterior service, and acquiring "the Christian virtues," especially those characteristic of the Vincentian spirit: humility, simplicity, and charity; trust in Providence; and readiness for any sort of service, anywhere, any time. Echoes in her later letters suggest years of meditative absorption of the spirit of this one chapter, which is the life of all else in the Rule.[38]

Catherine also would have noted at once that the core values are hedged about and supported by abundant details for observance of the religious vows and communal charity, and by spiritual practices and daily schedule. She may have felt the doubtful application to the Kentucky frontier of rules developed during the notoriously licentious and luxurious era of Louis XIV. Yet, if the Sisters were puzzled by the elaborate code of behavior to safeguard the vow of chastity, they had Badin's rules to remember and David's concerns about frontier liberty to explain his insistence on what may have seemed, even then, an excessive reserve and propriety. Observing the details of poverty could hardly have been a problem. They had barely enough to sustain life and no wealthy ladies to provide their favorites with extra food, better clothing, or expensive medicines, let alone with birds or little lap dogs. In their log house, it was a given that all resources were held in common and that each would be "dressed, coifed, shod, housed, nourished or furnished no better than the others" unless by way of exception for health. A code of obedience extending from the bishop to the bell "as the voice of Our Lord who is calling them" was not much more than they had already experienced. And if a system of permissions, specified times of silence and recreation, acknowledgment of faults, apologies, and pardons would help them to maintain the "charity and union which they ought to have among themselves," even in their tight quarters and constant presence to one another, so much the better.

Some of the Rule was adapted to the situation of Kentucky, but the "subtractive spirituality" practiced under the French clergy could not be entirely erased. It does seem to have been contained during Catherine's leadership. While her letters often urge such observances as community prayer, neither her own words nor others' memories of her reflect a negative or overly cautious spirit. She may, in fact, have suffered from seeing such asceticism imposed on her Sisters. But charity and the English Catholic spirit of freedom seem to have formed a shield around her spirit.

Catherine herself absorbed the spirit and practice of the Rule with remarkable success—so much so that sometime before the end of 1815 or early in 1816, David turned over to her the direction and formation of the novices, himself continuing only the weekly instruction. At one level, this decision was prompted by his need to give more time to the increasing numbers of seminarians. He also faced the looming threat of recall to the Baltimore seminary or, even worse, elevation to a bishopric. Throughout 1815, both Flaget and David were sending desperate letters to their superiors, to Bruté, and to Archbishop Carroll, urging David's health problems and especially the needs of the seminary.[39] Perhaps they did not think their correspondents would be as impressed by the need of David's presence to the newly formed Sisters of Charity, but surely he was conscious of it. And it is more than probable that Catherine, ever alert to what was going on around her, had a notion of what was threatening her little community. A clerical superior was required. If David departed or died, there was no one to replace him—except perhaps Badin or Nerinckx. If she knew the situation, she must have prayed desperately and led the community in doing so.

Despite the exigencies of the situation, David would hardly have appointed Catherine Mistress of Novices had he not been convinced she was ready to take the responsibility. Historian Sister Columba Fox says that he "watched with satisfaction Mother Catherine's remarkable gifts of mind and soul beautifully unfold as the years advanced," that he noted in her a generous response to grace, a humility willing to be servant of all, and a zeal that would embrace the world. "The firmness and maternal kindness with which she ruled and the respect of the Sisters for her authority assured him a solid foundation of the Sisterhood was being laid." This description is corroborated by an earlier one from the memories of Sisters who knew Catherine well: she was "intelligent, kind and considerate, as well as firm and zealous in securing the observance of the Rule, therefore she was much esteemed and beloved."[40]

Even so, David was doing the unusual in appointing Catherine to her new office. Strictly speaking, in 1815 she herself was a novice; none of the nine or ten members had yet made profession of religious vows. From a contemporary perspective, the sequence of events is amusing: Catherine was elected Mother Superior first, then appointed Mistress of Novices, then admitted to her own vows. Such were the exigencies of a new frontier community. But no objections or questions seem to have been raised by the other Sisters. Catherine would hold this office, of prime importance to all their futures, until 1823.

Her own vows, however, were soon to come. On a feast day of Mary, Mother of Christ, February 2, 1816, Catherine, together with her earliest companions, Teresa Carrico, Harriet Gardiner, and Polly Beaven, made first profession of religious vows in the large first-floor room of the log house where they had entered. Bishop Flaget presided, gave an exhortation, and received the vows in the presence of clergy and parishioners. An old formula of vows was found many years later; it reads:

O Almighty and Eternal God, I Sister N., though unworthy of appearing before thee, yet confiding in thy infinite goodness and mercy and moved with the desire of serving thee: in the presence of the ever Blessed Virgin Mary, my Mother and protectress, and St. Joseph, my tutelar Father, of St. Vincent of Paul, the Father of the poor, and of all the Heavenly Court, devote my whole being and faculties to thy service and that of the poor members of Jesus Christ, binding myself by simple and yearly vows to EVANGELICAL POVERTY, CHASTITY AND OBEDIENCE and PERSEVERANCE, in the Society of Nazareth, according to the meaning and extent attached to the same Vows, humbly beseeching thy infinite Goodness, through the blood of Jesus Christ to receive this my Consecration to thee; and as thou hast enabled me to conceive the desire of it, so mayst thou give me the Grace faithfully to accomplish it. Amen.[41]

This vow formula is enough like that of later years to suggest Catherine may have used it. The surprise in it is the fourth vow, Perseverance. To women making annual vows, it would represent a strengthening pledge to face all challenges to commitment; the heart's intent would be fulfilled by their renewals. What her commitment meant to Catherine is indicated by the community memory that she always celebrated the anniversary of her vows with special joy.

More vow ceremonies throughout 1816 added to Catherine's happiness: on March 25, Nancy Lynch, Mary Gwynn, Ellen O'Connell, and Martha Gough; on August 15, Mary Watson and Agnes Higdon; and on December 31, Elizabeth Suttle. Eleven professed Sisters as the New Year began, only four years after the foundation.[42]

In addition, another election on August 30 confirmed Catherine as Mother for three more years, with Harriet Gardiner, Assistant; Agnes Higdon, Procuratrix, and Ellen O'Connell, treasurer. Catherine must have felt a vindication of her hopes for the community and its mission. Still few and poor they might be, but they stood now together on solid ground.

What Catherine could not know, though she surely understood the health hazards inherent in their poverty, was that five of the women at whose vows she had rejoiced would be buried in the next ten years, and one (Mary Watson) would leave the community.

Deaths and departures were to be her continuing affliction, but life also kept blossoming. Four new members arrived in 1816. Three stayed and would live long for those times. One of the four was Catherine's own sister Ann. That doubling of the bond of sisterhood would give Catherine special delight. Her youngest sister, with whom she had shared childhood, would now share her religious life. As Mistress of Novices, Catherine would even have the privilege to teach and guide Ann in her new life.

While the community was growing and stabilizing in 1816, so was its educational ministry. When the school had thirty-one students, more than the Sisters could house, Catherine, a twenty-two-year-old leader with an eye for needs, began to plan improvements and make them as fast as the communal resources allowed: small outbuildings "fitted for domestic use," a stone spring house for a dairy, and in the summer, a small frame chapel in the woods behind their house. Once again, Catherine led Sisters and students in procession while Father David transferred the Blessed Sacrament. In October, Bishop Flaget wrote that the Sisters at St. Thomas were giving an education that attracted and served "more particularly the wealthy class of the district"; the term probably meant the more prosperous farmers and Bardstown business and professional people, who could afford tuition. Their payment, from the very beginning, allowed some orphans to be included in the student body.[43]

The prosperity of the Bardstown area had also overflowed on St. Thomas by the completion in 1816 of the brick church that still serves that parish. The proximity of all the buildings at St. Thomas meant that the Sisters were necessarily included in liturgical celebrations, seasonal processions, and other events and were aware of the many persons who came there as the diocese developed. It appears that they were also, on occasion, asked to help prepare a dinner. Flaget requested one "purely and simply à la Kentuckienne," with "a dozen or two little biscuits and a lot of Johnny cakes."[44] In November 1816, twelve Europeans, including three Vincentian priests, arrived at St. Thomas en route to assignment in St. Louis. They spent about a year living in the area, learning English from David and practicing the life of a missionary. Catherine certainly knew some of the individuals fairly well, especially Vincentian Joseph Rosati.

By March 1817, Rosati had mastered English well enough to preach to the Sisters, and he and other Vincentians served them as chaplains. Thus, the Sisters of Charity had their first opportunity to learn the spirit of St. Vincent de Paul directly from members of his congregation. Catherine's first preserved letter is addressed to Father Rosati in St. Louis, as "a true son of St. Vincent," her "Rev. & Dear friend, and may I presume to say it Brother." She appeals to him to send information about a former student and convert who might be in his area and undergoing family opposition to her religion, and to give the girl spiritual and material assistance.[45]

For Catherine and her Sisters, the years 1818–1821 might well be proclaimed "a time to live, and a time to die, a time to build, a time to weep, and a time to laugh, a time to lose" (Eccl. 3:2–4, 6). Prosperity and a sense of Providence guiding the mission influenced a major decision, the ramifications of which Catherine could not have imagined. In 1818, prosperity, defined by expansion of the student body, signaled the need to build again.

This time, Catherine and her councillors, with the essential approbation of David, who surely consulted Flaget, decided to act with a view to permanency. No more frame buildings exposed to the deterioration of time and weather; this building would be in brick, and the income from the school would pay for it. By the end of summer, a structure to accommodate thirty to fifty boarders was up. It was considered large, well built, and sufficient for a long time. The furnishings were few, but the Sisters were content to remain on their straw pallets.[46] The zealous and practical young leader must have felt blessed and pleased, expectant of the harvest of this summer labor.

The test of her faith in God and of her own wisdom came quickly. In December of the same year, 1818, David wrote to a priest who was proposing to send some young women to Nazareth as postulants:

> I must tell you everything. The school of Nazareth, so much in favor and so filled during a certain time that they were obliged to refuse students . . . is at this time reduced to two or three boarders. The Mother does not lose courage; her confidence in Divine Providence is great, and she believes that after Christmas, pupils will apply. They could receive a large number of poor girls who offer to work in return for their schooling; they have taken five or six of this description, but their work brings in so little that it is not nearly equivalent to their expenses.[47]

David added that Catherine "cannot make up her mind to refuse" two or three more postulants despite his insistence on their poverty: "She smiles and asks me whether we should refuse the way to heaven to these souls for fear of going bankrupt. I do not dare to contradict such Christian views." But he does insist that his clerical friend "explain all this to your young ladies, as well as the hard life that they will have to lead." And since the bishop can pay for the trip to Kentucky of only one, "it will be necessary to find some good souls" to pay for the other. The Sisters "are in debt and would not be able to assume this expense." David wrote this revealing letter on SCN Foundation Day, after six years of deprivation and hard labor that had seemed to be finally ending in a harvest of membership and mission.

Why the enrollment of the school so suddenly declined just after completion of the building is unknown, but the fact had to concern deeply the two superiors, David seemingly more than Catherine.[48] It did not deter her progressive outlook but certainly did test her ability to live by the Vincentian rule of "entire trust" in the Providence that would "assist them with everything needed . . . even when they think that all will be lost."[49]

But if the "time to build" had required Catherine's faith and trust, it paled in comparison with the "time to die" that began the same summer the brick school was finished. In August, Mary Gwynn, pioneer Sister with whom Catherine had made her vows, died of consumption. Very little is recorded of Mary or her labors in those early years, only that she was kind, very charitable, scrupulously observant of Rule, and intensely fearful of sin and of offending God. Catherine, who by all evidence was practical, not at all scrupulous, and very largehearted, may have tried all along to relieve Mary's anxieties and intensified the effort at her deathbed. Nearly at the end, Mary's fear changed to an intense desire to be united with God; in the early morning of August 12, 1818, she died. All seven priests present at St. Thomas for Robert Abell's ordination said Mass for her that same day; Catherine and the Sisters took that as a sign that Mary's desire was fulfilled.[50]

But Catherine's personal grief could not have been rapidly assuaged, especially if she had any intuition that the demon consumption, bred in the damps of the rivers and valley around Bardstown and encouraged by the Sisters' cramped quarters, straw pallets, poor nutrition, and hard labor, would become a regular invader of their homes.[51] It would respect neither status nor age. Among the boarders in 1818 was Elizabeth Swan from Scott County. She often asked to sit in the room where the Sisters were weaving and spinning, and Mother Catherine let her. She said she wanted to become a Catholic and was receiving instruction. She received her First Communion just before her death on November 4—three months after the burial of Mary Gwynn.[52]

A year and three months after Mary Gwynn, the community lost Martha Gough, the oldest member. She was the sister of Mrs. Thomas Howard, donor of their first home, and was fifty-one when she arrived in June 1814. The enthusiasm with which she announced herself, "Mother, I have come, a soul to save, and a God to serve!" had amused the Sisters. She endeared herself by the fidelity and zeal with which she observed the rules, obeyed "a superior young enough to have been her granddaughter," and shared in the privations and domestic labor. Sickness tried her patience severely before she, too, died in February 1820.[53] Consumption would claim many more Sisters, but no more during the years at St. Thomas.

The qualities of Catherine's leadership may be inferred partly by the kind of women she attracted to and retained in the community, as well as by the circumstances they encountered together. In 1818, Charlotte and Elizabeth Gardiner came to join their sister Harriet and Catherine, the woman they had known as a girl. As Sister Clare and Sister Frances, they would initiate or participate in key community enterprises. Though Frances was so small, young, and meek that she was nicknamed "little Moses," she would become Mother, eventually alternating terms of office with Catherine and serving as one of her principal collaborators. Just as vital to the expansion of mission and thus equally close to Catherine's concerned and grateful heart were the women who would pioneer the earliest missions. Some would face not only the hardships but also the failure of those missions; others would make the mission survive though they did not. Nothing important that Catherine Spalding did or caused to be done was a solo enterprise. The extensions of the mission that began about 1818 especially indicate that her leadership was collaborative.[54]

In the first place, Catherine had to cooperate with the changes occurring in the diocesan scheme of things. Construction of the cathedral in Bardstown was well under way. Flaget now wanted a coadjutor bishop and asked for David. Both his friend and Rome agreed to the appointment. Flaget then planned to move himself, his coadjutor, and his seminarians in theology to Bardstown near the cathedral. Only the preparatory seminary and parish, along with the Sisters and school, would be left at St. Thomas.[55] David would still be the community's ecclesiastical superior and would attend most business meetings, and Catherine's decision making was still subject to ecclesiastical authority in major matters. But David as her consultant and guide would now be much less available. In most matters, Catherine and her Council could and would have to act without readily accessible advice or approval. Her leadership would be both enhanced and tried.

That Catherine was ready to collaborate was made evident when Bishop Flaget asked that the Sisters serve the cathedral parish in a day school and by "the care of the linen, etc. of the cathedral."[56] The school would be a fine feature of the cathedral complex, no doubt; for the Nazareth community, a first branch house would indicate and stimulate growth. Yet it was a risk. The school at St. Thomas could again lose boarders, some of whom had come from families of Bardstown. Nevertheless, Catherine and her Council, doubtless urged on by David, agreed, and plans for this school were under way when the historic month of August 1819 began.

Early August saw the move of the bishops to Bardstown. Whatever regret Catherine and the others felt that day may have been assuaged by witnessing the consecration of St. Joseph Cathedral on August 8 and, a week later, on August 15, David's consecration as bishop. David had invited as many of his Sisters as possible to be present. As she watched and prayed, Catherine had more than her affection for Father David and her pleasure in the music or preaching to rouse her grateful devotion. Whatever her mix of feelings, the girl who grew up in Turkey Town, with a sacramental life fed once a month by one or two circuit riding priests, could not have failed to note the implications of both these elaborate ceremonies—evident Catholic growth, acceptance by local Protestants, and a stability to promote more growth.

With these blessings of growth, Catherine, her Sisters, and school were allied. Twenty-one Sisters had entered the community during her six years as Mother. Only two of these had left before vows; none had yet failed to renew their annual vows. The community, too, was living and growing. And now, after six years of leadership, with the expiration of her term, she could turn her demanding office over to another.

About that intention, however, both Sisters and bishops had other thoughts. Flaget and David insisted that the young community needed consistent leadership, that Catherine should do as both Louise de Marillac, foundress of the Daughters of Charity in France, and Elizabeth Seton in Maryland had done—remain in office for life. In response, qualities in Catherine that would reappear later emerged. Motivated by both principle and humility, and doubtless encouraged by her girlhood observation of the Badin crisis, this twenty-five-year-old woman made bold to disagree. The Annals say she refused despite "the deep maternal love that swayed her broad generous heart and made her feel towards the community she had cradled, perhaps as none other could feel."[57] She argued that the greater age and varied experience of the two foundresses justified their being kept in leadership, but that it would be better for the Kentucky community and for her own soul to put the Constitutions into effect from the start. She pleaded well enough to touch the bishops (both of whom had tried to evade office); they stopped insisting. On August 27, 1819, Agnes Higdon was elected to replace Catherine Spalding.

Catherine was retained as Mistress of Novices, apparently without protest on her part. The novices were the human future, the expansion on which she could now focus her heart and her attention. She began this period with five novices and two postulants; they included Clare and Frances Gardiner, Agatha Cooper, and Angela Spink, all of whom made six months to a year of novitiate under Catherine's tutelage; Angela and Frances would later succeed her as Mother. Cecily O'Brien, the first student in 1814, was now to receive her entire spiritual formation from Catherine.

But the community Register more than hints at what Catherine experienced as candidates presented themselves. The office of Mistress of Novices requires one to discern with the candidate her suitability for religious life and her ability to endure its hardships. It follows that one must say many good-byes, sometimes with peaceful conviction, often enough with reluctance, disappointment, even frustration. During the remaining years at St. Thomas, seventeen more women entered; ten left. Before 1821, only five members had left the community, none of them professed. In April 1821, two sisters whose health had collapsed had to be sent home; before the end of 1821, three more left the novitiate. Five candidates gone in a year, four of them within four months, and they constituted most of the novitiate at the time. Any illusion that Catherine was able to form and lead a consistently expanding, enthusiastic, strong, and even heroic community of pioneers, or that she could find consistent joy in observing its expansion, collapses before the statistics.[58] She was both practical and sensitive; all the preserved testimonies of the early Sisters and her own letters reveal this fact. She must have felt painfully those early losses of potential members.

Yet there were causes for joy. Though such a number of novices left in the first half of 1821, it then became the big year for entries—twelve, of whom eleven received the habit. They came in "classes" of two, three, five, and two. Only one of that crowd did not persevere to vows, which were again made mostly in groups, in 1822 and 1823. Catherine may well have felt consoled for the losses by persevering new members and new relationships.

Besides Catherine's primary work with the novitiate, Mother Agnes almost certainly consulted her on important matters as mission outreach began. In September 1819, the house and school in Bardstown opened with Harriet Gardiner as superior and headmistress, and Polly Beaven and Nancy Lynch, all Catherine's pioneer companions.[59] At the newly established College of St. Joseph near the cathedral, Betsy Bowling took charge of a linen room and sewed for seminarians and boarding students.

Catherine, no longer on the Council, may not have been consulted and definitely did not have a vote on the next two ventures. Bardstown is only a few miles from St. Thomas, not too risky or painful a parting. But Long Lick in Breckinridge County, where Flaget and David were persuaded to open a school, was sixty miles away. Flaget stopped there in 1821 and reported that three Sisters had "a school that is quite flourishing."[60] When Catherine learned of the actual poverty, insufficient housing, and sickness endured by Barbara Spalding, Elizabeth Suttle, and Susan Hagan, she was surely relieved by the decision to close the school a year later.

Before the closing of Long Lick, another mission was begun yet 120 miles farther away.[61] The story of the establishment of St. Vincent's in Union County, western Kentucky, may well have astounded, edified, amused, and deeply worried the former Mother when she heard it. Angela Spink, Frances Gardiner, and Cecily O'Brien, accompanied by a priest, made the journey of several days on horseback in December 1820. Their baggage was in their aprons, sewed up like sacks. En route they sought and received lodging from kindly Protestants; one morning they woke to find a decidedly live hog under their bed. On another day, diminutive Frances Gardiner was literally frozen stiff; her clothes were solid, and she had to be lifted from her horse and carried to the house to thaw out.

The Sisters then relived the experience of the 1812 foundation. The house intended for them had not been vacated. With no vacant "episcopal residence" to fall back on, they cleaned and occupied a henhouse. At that distance, there was no turning back. In the newly settled area, they bought land, built a log house, and worked the fields. Angela, only four months in vows, was superior of the Sisters, overseer, builder, and laborer in the fields. Her legendary physical strength and her intense labor probably saved them all.

Again one wonders what Catherine thought of this story as she heard it, whether she had been consulted about sending the Sisters on such a venture, whether she knew the extremity of their hardship before it was alleviated. Courageous as she had been in the harsh winter of 1813, and hard as she had worked to provide for the Sisters and students in the early years, she might well have hesitated to ask a repetition of such sacrifices. Yet she could not but deeply admire as she sympathized with those who repeated the pioneers' endurance.

By 1821, however, Nazareth on St. Thomas Farm, with its

school, surely seemed to Catherine firmly established, the ripe fruit of the years of hardship, saving, planning, and building. Because the school was again flourishing, it seemed to Mother Agnes and to Catherine, her consultant, that the time had come to enlarge the building. Assured of the need and confident of the bishops' support, they began planning. They could not have foreseen the crisis about to break over them.

Leader to New Frontiers

1822–1824

When Mothers Catherine and Agnes enthusiastically proposed to the bishops their plan for enlarging the brick school, they found that its strongest promoters had apparently lost their interest or their nerve. Columba Fox begins the story rather dramatically: "A postponement of all discussion was advised. What could it mean? Was it the shadow of a coming cross? Soon the revelation came, and what a shock! The ground on which they had built was not their own, and never could be theirs."[1]

This quotation implies a revelation in two phases, each with its shock and questions. First, the refusal to build or to discuss it. Why not build? Why not even talk about it? What was being concealed? That first phase, at the very least, jarred Catherine's sense of mutuality in trust, on which she had built her steady collaboration with both bishops. And they in turn must have sensed some negative difference and realized they had to reveal more, to defer no longer a decision based on what they knew.

Sister Columba also refers tersely to "whatever explanation was offered" and a "situation over which prudence once saw fit to throw the cloak of silence." The explanation offered to Catherine and Agnes was obviously incomplete and left them with agonizing questions. It was probably the account that for decades was passed down in the community: that the will of Thomas Howard precluded alienation of the land to any agent other than the diocese, and that the two bishops, not having previously understood the terms, had expected in time to transfer ownership to the Sisters. This is undoubtedly a true portion of "the situation." The will, made in 1810 before the expected arrival of Flaget, gives Howard's land to Fathers Badin and Nerinckx "and the then Roman Catholic Bishop of Kentucky," and to the "lawful heirs of the last survivor forever."[2] It is entirely possible that the Sisters of Charity of Nazareth could not be given a legal status as those heirs.

But that was only part of "the situation" and possibly not the definitive part. The land under the school not only was not the community's; it perhaps did not even belong to the bishop. Flaget's diary for early 1812 had recorded one after another "extremely painful conversation with Mr. B——n." Flaget was insisting that Badin transfer to him all titles to church lands, and Badin was refusing. Perhaps he was clinging to his long authority over the Kentucky missions, but mainly he hesitated to entrust to Flaget the numerous debts on these properties for which he was personally responsible. The Howard farm became the focus of the intense dispute, mediated by Archbishop Carroll during the two men's 1812–1813 trip to Baltimore. Flaget agreed to end the fight if Badin transferred the title to the entire Howard plantation. The Howard will, however, gave the land in two parcels. Not until 1815 did Flaget hear and then verify that Badin had ceded to him only one parcel, and not the one on which stood the bishop's house, the seminary, and the Sisters' home and school.[3]

Flaget was furious. Letters of accusation, threats to refuse absolution to Badin, "a *sharper* of my ignorance," countered by Badin's long explanation and defense—all in highly inflated and inflammatory language—were speeded to Archbishop Carroll. Badin vehemently accused David of influencing Flaget from "behind the screen"; "the mildness of the one, the assuming and overbearing temper of the other are too well known . . . to need proofs of this assertion." In 1819, Badin left for an indefinite stay in France, and it is said "the problem solved itself in his absence."[4]

What did Catherine know of this affair? Both the embattled bishops living at St. Thomas were in constant contact with her. Astute observer that she was, she surely had some notion of the uproar in 1815. And if Flaget thought he had a settled claim after 1819, Catherine must have so assumed. So their grievous "situation" in 1821 had to raise some burning questions in her: What did the bishops really know before the brick school was built in 1818? If the issue of landownership was not yet settled, why were the Sisters allowed to build then? If it was settled between Badin's departure in 1819 and their request to build again in 1821, why was that request delayed and then refused?[5] Catherine may never have received answers to these questions; no historian since has offered any.

The Sisters could never own the land on which they had built. Whatever the causes, that was the consequence. The extreme sacrifices of ten years, the resources that had been earned, saved, and spent so as to build in brick, the hopes and securities for the future—all were gone. To survive as a community, to expand in mission, they would have to find a new location on land they could own. Columba Fox, despite her admiration of Bishop David, records truthfully that the Sisters had to draw from the strength of Christ who had "borne wrongs and injustices," had to try to "keep unshattered their love and confidence in their leaders," and to pass those sentiments on.[6] A volume of pain, disappointment, and struggle is implied in her brief phrases.

For Catherine, the entire episode must have revived memories of the behaviors of her father and his creditors that had destroyed her family. The dispute also resembled that between the Elder family and Badin. The disruptions, the moods, the virulent language on both sides are distinctly similar. Now she had again to pick up her own life and support others in doing the same. The community Annals record tersely that "the blow fell upon her as the most dire calamity she had ever known."[7]

How many months Catherine had to grapple interiorly with the loss of St. Thomas cannot be stated. She had to wrestle with the Providence that had allowed her to lead the 1818 building project, had not warned her to ask her superiors the crucial questions that might have prevented such a waste of community resources and efforts. It would be some time before she would recognize the loss and the suffering as a "special blessing of Providence." But the strength to go on deepened with the challenge, and it is said that the community felt "no time was to be lost in repining."[8]

By early 1822, Catherine knew that the resources for new land and new life were at hand. Providence was enfleshed in two unlikely persons: a Presbyterian minister and an SCN novice. In his 1825 "Report," Flaget says merely that the Sisters felt the need of more space on land they could own and that "a very convenient place [was] then up for sale." This place was 237 acres north of Bardstown (the site of the present Nazareth) offered through an agent in Bardstown by Rev. Joseph Lapsley. The offer seemed perfectly timed for the relief of Catherine Spalding's distress. "The terms were moderate and the location seemed in all respects desirable."[9] But how were the terms to be met by the now impoverished community?

As Ellen O'Connell had brought education at a crucial time, so now another cultivated Baltimore woman arrived with at least the promise of funds. Mrs. Ann O'Connor, a convert rejected by her own wealthy family, was now the young, childless widow of a successful doctor. Like Ellen, she had been directed by Father David. She entered the novitiate in July 1821 and became Sister Scholastica. Dr. O'Connor had bequeathed his land in Baltimore jointly to his wife and his sister, Mrs. Sabina Tyson. In the normal course of church procedures, Scholastica's land would not be sold before she sealed her membership by vows. But in the distress of the landless time, she urged her superiors to move on the sale and use the proceeds to purchase the Lapsley estate. Mrs. Tyson also donated her share of the inheritance.[10] Catherine, Mistress of Novices, had to affirm to the Council her confidence in Sister Scholastica's perseverance. Her gratitude to the novice for such generosity must have firmly bonded their sisterly love and appreciation.

The superiors negotiated and got possession of the Lapsley land even before money from the O'Connor land was available to close the sale and give them the deed. Catherine may or may not have been consulted about so rapid and risky a move. Whether or not she thought it advisable, it could not be her decision. That lay with the bishops, presumably in consultation with Mother Agnes and the Council; their decision was Catherine's to accept. In early spring, 1822, a few Sisters, two orphans, and the two slaves owned by the community went ahead to prepare the Lapsley house for student residents and to plant a garden. On June 11, 1822, Catherine left all the associations of memory and emotion at St. Thomas. With Agnes, she led the entire community of Sisters and boarders, more than thirty in all, in procession to the new Nazareth.[11]

There Catherine discovered at once that to leave St. Thomas in 1822 was to return to the St. Thomas of 1813, to its hardships and labor. No brick building awaited her. The "Preacher's House" was a frame dwelling of four rooms, two below and two above. They would have to serve as the classrooms and dormitories for twelve boarders. The two Mothers, nine other Sisters in vows, ten novices and one postulant, and the slaves would sleep and work as best they could in the other "buildings," actually cold, cramped cabins intended as kitchen or work areas. Food and clothing would have to be produced on the property. The two slaves, brought by early members, were Abe, a young man, and Teresa or Terry, "scarcely grown."[12] Though subservient, these two must have been treated with a measure of dignity. Several miles out on the edge of town, their mistresses had to depend on their loyalty and cooperative sharing in the cooking, washing, sewing, and labor in the garden and fields. These tasks would be the Sisters', too, along with their teaching, for a long time to come. Whatever share she could manage along with her other duties, Catherine would take.

With all her well-known optimism, Catherine could not expect the school to prosper very soon. How many boarders could they expect to attract into such a space? Expansion was a desperate need, but the diocese could not provide funds. And as David wrote Bruté, the Sisters' "own slender means had been already exhausted in the improvements made on their first establishment."[13] Still worse, and surely a cause of grave anxiety to the prudent Catherine, they did not yet have clear title to the new land.

David's letter of September 1822 had made the purchase sound like an easily done deed: "Our Sisters have just bought a plantation. One of their novices from Baltimore made them this gift."

Five months later, however, he writes that the Sisters are "finding great difficulties" paying for Nazareth, as "the properties of Sister O'Connor, on which they were counting, . . . have lost their value because of the yellow fever" in the area. In August, he reports that they cannot build because they still have no deed to the property.[14] In March 1824, Ann O'Connor legally relinquished to David money for which she had drawn an order from Luke Tiernan, her lawyer in Baltimore. But not until February 1825 could David write to Bruté that he had "at last obtained a deed from Mr. Hynes," the real estate agent in Bardstown. He complains that Hynes was hard to deal with. In fact, double interest may have been paid on Nazareth's debt, by both David and Tiernan.[15]

For three full years, then, Catherine Spalding (along with Agnes Higdon and others who knew) had to worry and wait, to wonder whether this whole exchange of land was merely a repetition of the errors of 1818. Well might Catherine have wondered whether she could trust the judgment and actions of the clerical and civic gentlemen on whom her hopes and mission depended. But could she trust her own judgment either? It is impossible to suppose that Catherine went through those three years with entirely placid spirit. Experience had matured her own judgment. She knew a lot about human nature that she had not known at nineteen. But she still had to trust and obey, and it cannot have been easy.

Catherine had, however, her one constant support in trial and hope. Lapsley's study, separate from the house, had become the chapel, and her steady reliance on the Eucharist could be exercised there, though not without the hardship of heat or cold. Mass was said daily by a priest from St. Joseph's College in Bardstown. The celebrant's arrival time was uncertain, so the Sisters often went to the fields after meditation until the bell for Mass was rung. David came each Wednesday for confessions and instructions and remained for Mass on Thursday. He often enough made Thursdays into communion days, a concession Catherine would greatly value.[16]

As confessor, spiritual director, and instructor, David inevitably had a high degree of influence on Catherine's and the Sisters' developing spirituality. In confession and direction, he was liberal with his time, knew individuals well, and was said to be "ever ready to encourage, to console, or to chide with justice and gentleness." His weekly instruction was made simple and practical: "Duty was plain, once he had unfolded its import." The content was generally drawn from the "riches of his own heart" or from some chapters of the Fathers of the Church and the Desert, with whose asceticism he had a strong affinity, and whose heroism he wished to encourage in the Sisters. Yet he urged, for Nazareth as previously for Emmitsburg, prudent care of health. Sisters should not complain but declare their state of health in "sincerity, candor, and simplicity," since the "true spirit of religion is a spirit of infancy, which knows no disguise." He insisted on the daily spiritual exercises: mental prayer made in dispositions of recollection and "disengagement," examination of conscience, and spiritual reading in common and in private.[17]

This mixture of common sense with asceticism and regulation, of loving concern for his honored friends with paternalistic authority over "daughters" or "children"—this paradoxical combination seems ever to have marked David's relations with the Sisters. Catherine's later letters suggest that she, daughter first of the English/Kentucky Catholic culture, had reflected on David's spiritual teachings, had prayed and sought her own balance. She will, for instance, urge "full observance of the rules & fulfillment of all duties" and recognize that Sisters "must daily carry a portion of their Savior's cross & often deny themselves." She will also send to Nazareth "soft gloves for your poor chapped hands" and the "Rosin soap [that] some of the Sisters used to want," also a coffee pot "of good quality," with the promise to "try to send you better coffee" next time.[18] Her influence on David is noted in some of his letters, indicating that she brought her spiritual balance to community life and religious practice.

To the extent that such spiritual equilibrium became characteristic of Catherine's community, it must be traced to these years when she was training the novices. The best clues to her instructions are the letters she was later to write to young Sisters on their missions. In them, she combined deep affection and sympathy for their difficulties with encouragement to bear trials for the sake of

Christ and his poor; she urged them to work faithfully at their assigned tasks, to support each other by prayer and loving communication, and to avoid any form of divisive personal ambition. Her
best instruction was her own example, for which she had plenty of
occasion in this first year at Nazareth.

Whether or not Catherine fully admired the stoicism of the
French priests, circumstances assured ample opportunities to practice whatever detachment of spirit she needed. The log chapel and
the small community room had no benches or chairs; for Mass and
instructions the Sisters sat on the bare floor. They slept on straw
pallets; novices who brought beds gave them up to share the general poverty. Beds were for students who could not bring their own
but could pay a modest charge for one and thus help the school.
There were only two beds for Sisters, one reserved for the sick, the
other assigned over her protest to Catherine. She wanted nothing
unavailable to the others, but at St. Thomas, Teresa Carrico had
got Father David to order Catherine to "accept that little mark of
deference." She had to turn the unwanted comfort into an instance
of obedience and even let it become a sort of community joke that
would soon follow her on mission. As for food, the staples were
still corn bread, middling, greens or other vegetables, sage tea, and
rye coffee without sugar, often without milk. Day work went on
in fields, kitchen, and wash house as well as the school. Evening
recreation was taken with sewing or knitting. Small wonder that
Bishop David exhorted from his heart that they cheerfully endure
poverty in hope and fidelity, and pray that "when you have gone
hence . . . those whom Providence shall call to continue the good
work you have begun may be animated by the same spirit."[19]

Catherine's training of novices in a spirit of mission and devotion to duty supplemented Ellen O'Connell's intelligent curriculum
planning and training of teachers. Both these women and David, a
fine musician, had to be delighted when one or more pianos were
somehow acquired. Sister Scholastica introduced music instruction, taught several Sisters, and thus developed a music depart-
ment. By June 1823, only a year after the arrival at Nazareth, the
boarders numbered fifty, "not counting 10 girls who work half
the time to be taught the other half." Though Catherine was still

awaiting the deed to the land and relief from debt, and though it was still true that the expense of poor girls could exceed the value of their work, their reception was a satisfaction to her heart.[20]

Before that first anniversary, Catherine had been called to move on yet again. In February 1823, David writes not only of the problems paying for Nazareth but also of preparation "we" are making to send four Sisters to Scott County "about 60 miles away." His "we" seems not to have included Catherine as a consultant. She was "said to have been surprised" when chosen to lead the project. Well she might be. She had been less than a year at the new Nazareth, and in addition to any work she was doing in the school, she had her major task as Mistress of Novices. Ten novices and a postulant had come from St. Thomas to Nazareth. She had seen eight of those make vows and nine more women enter. On the day following David's letter, February 5, 1823, she saw six of these postulants receive the habit and become novices.[21] The community might be poor in lands and funds, but it was being enriched by substantial clusters of willing women. Catherine was the heart of their intensive spiritual formation, and her heart was in her work.

Nevertheless, she was asked to leave that work and go to Scott County. About three months after the February ceremony for the new novices, Catherine witnessed two other novices make vows; on the same day, April 30, 1823, she and one of the two (Sister Bibiana Tiriac) said good-bye to the other newly professed Sister and to the novices and left for the new mission. Those who have experienced or witnessed the bond formed between novices and a loving woman who is guiding their formative years know what pain such a parting can cause.

Bishop Flaget was quite aware that Scott County promised grief of another sort. To Guy Ignatius Chabrat, pastor there, he wrote: "Sisters Catherine, Josephine, Bibiana & Mildred leave this morning for Scott Cty, and I assure you it is for them a great sacrifice to obey; for these poor children know that scarcely anybody in that country sees them come with pleasure. The road from Nazareth to St. Pius Church will be for them a real Via Crucis; and this is what makes me hope that God will bless them." He begs Chabrat to be urged by his "kind heart and the love of religion" to support them with his "instructions" and to "do all in your power to utilize their services." He hopes the school will "take well" and promises to do all in his power to make it "solid and flourishing."[22]

One may well ask, What was the problem at St. Pius? Was a school really wanted, or was it merely a hope that Chabrat could start one or make some other use of Sisters? If the Sisters were so unwelcome, why were they sent? Why was Catherine at their head?

In fact, Catherine was leading a mission to a parish variously labeled "the shame and reproach of the diocese," "that almost ungovernable congregation," "that perennial seat of trouble," "decidedly the least subject to pastoral authority," where "something was always boiling."[23] The parish at White Sulphur in Scott County was a cauldron that had boiled with controversy at least since 1793, when Badin began there his ministry in Kentucky. Through a succession of pastors, all the familiar problems had continued: trusteeship and land titles; monetary support; opposition to dancing, foxhunting, and horse racing; and the crossfire of the French diocesan clergy and the English Dominicans. The Dominican superior notified Flaget to send *his* choice of priest. Flaget's less-than-wise appointment was the humorless Chabrat, controversial by temperament, who made matters worse by taking sides vocally. It was apparently Chabrat's idea that the presence of Sisters would help to cool and calm the waters. Flaget and David agreed to his request, and Catherine was chosen to lead as the most likely to succeed (or at least survive). Again she had to trust her superiors' judgment (or the Providence that would shape a better and as yet unforeseeable future). She may or may not have been reassured by David's putting the school under the protection of her patroness, St. Catherine of Siena.

David himself escorted the four Sisters on the journey. The slave Abe drove the wagon with Catherine's unwanted bed, sleeping mats, and what other household goods they could bring. Their destination was the hundred acres deeded by Ignatius Gough to Flaget for the benefit of the SCNs in exchange for a small annuity for his lifetime (which turned out to be quite long). The gift meant, of course, that the Sisters would have to not only build a log school but also manage a farm for their own and their pupils' sustenance. Abe was probably kept with them to share this labor. Catherine had to make a third start on a frontier, again in the poverty of St. Thomas and the new Nazareth.[24]

Circumstances would dictate that Catherine spend only eighteen months at St. Catherine's—time enough to test her "ready spirit and desire to do the Master's will." Chabrat promptly told the Sisters tales of the dissension, "and this did not reassure them." The good brick parish church a mile from their land, however, may have given hope of support for a school. For four months, with Abe's help, they cut trees, plowed and planted, and prepared to begin a school.[25]

The day it opened, five pupils enrolled. Catherine never saw more than forty. The local population was scattered, and parents placed limited value on education. Many students stayed only long enough to learn to read and "cipher." Nonpaying students were also received, so that altogether funds were never enough to match expenses. Because the hilly land was hard to till and insufficiently productive, Catherine and the Sisters were again eating chiefly corn-hoe cakes and clabber. Finally, in an area predominantly Protestant and not without prejudice, a sectarian paper tried to rouse opposition to the new Catholic school.[26] Catherine had to face, in Scott County, a failure of sorts, the consequence of others' poor judgments and the hostility or indifference of those she had come to serve.

Nevertheless, the Sisters did win a general respect, and Catherine was particularly revered. When, in the early 1830s, a Sister "fractured her limbs," Catherine accompanied Sister Claudia Elliott to Scott County to replace her. Along the way she was recognized, and "to her great confusion and mortification," people knelt to ask her blessing. She protested she could not give blessings but spoke kindly and promised prayers.[27]

No amount of respect, however, could make the school flourish at the original site. Ultimately, the combination of problems there and remoteness from Nazareth undid hope for the school's success.

In 1833, the pastor advised moving the enterprise to Lexington. By that time, Catherine had been long gone from the area.

Her recall to Nazareth was sudden and grievous in its cause. After a very short illness, Mother Agnes Higdon had died on September 24, 1824. The cause of her death is nowhere named, and little is reported of her personality except that she was modest and personally loved. She did not wish to be called "Reverend Mother" but desired to retain "Mother" as "a name of pure and tender love."[28] She had been Catherine's friend and collaborator in important decisions and suffered with her in crises and losses. She could not but be intensely missed.

In her final year of office, Agnes had been deeply engaged in building the much needed new school. For both community leadership and supervision of the construction, Catherine was judged to be the best, if not only, possible replacement. On September 30, she was elected to complete Mother Agnes's term of office. The early Annalist comments that she would need for the task "all the energy of her clear sighted mind," since the "new trials that awaited her were simply appalling."[29]

The first trial was appalling grief as Catherine had to visit not only one grave but three. Around Agnes lay two other especially dear companions, Scholastica O'Connor and Polly Beaven. A fourth grave she could not reach. Agatha Cooper had died and been buried at St. Vincent's in distant Union County. Their dates read like a drumroll of death: March 29, June 3, and August 8, 1824. All had been leveled by the consumption that would continue to be the community's worst enemy.

Each death represented a particular wound to Catherine's heart. Scholastica had sacrificed the elegance, comfort, and culture of Baltimore to enter the community, had given her financial all for the purchase of Nazareth, and had brought music and art to the curriculum and culture of the school. Yet she had lived less than three full years in the community and was the first to die on the land she had given. Agatha Cooper had been one of Catherine's first novices, was already consumptive when sent to St. Vincent Academy, and had died after only a few months on the mission.

A uniquely painful loss, Polly Beaven had been one of the six pioneers, had joined in electing Catherine, and had taken the habit and made vows with her. Kind, obliging, and gentle, she had pioneered the school in Bardstown, then given domestic service at St. Joseph's College until her final months of painful yet patient endurance.[30] Although word of these deaths must have reached Scott County and caused deep mourning, Catherine's return to view the empty places and the filled graves had to be an excruciating suffering.

Nor was the bereavement of 1824 yet complete. Catherine found on her deathbed Sister Columba Tarlton, former student at St. Thomas, one of her novices, only eight months in vows. Community traditions have made this sister virtually a legend for her sanctity. One may well question the wisdom of those who directed her from girlhood and, in an area rampant with consumption and requiring so much hard labor, allowed austerities that had weakened her health even before she entered the community at nineteen. In two years of community life, she had acquired a reputation for observance of duties as a religious and music teacher, and also for enormous interest and charity for anyone in need of attention, comfort, or encouragement. Now she was dying of consumption.

Mother Catherine gave permission for Margaret Carroll, Columba's most devoted student, to visit her mentor in the cabin that served as infirmary. Columba asked that her name be given to Margaret, soon to enter the community. Catherine insisted that Columba have a night watcher. Columba insisted that the Sister lie on a pallet by her bed and, when the exhausted watcher fell asleep, stayed still so as not to disturb her. The morning of her death, she insisted the watcher go on to Mass. A few minutes after the Mass, the community gathered at Columba's bed. Catherine led them in prayers and witnessed the sudden joy in Columba's face and her death in "rapture."[31]

Five deaths in seven months, out of a community numbering about fifty—what grief must its young leader have felt, what fears for its future? In fact, Catherine would never again experience so many deaths in one year, and only one more Sister would die before 1830. But Catherine could not have known that as she mourned.

Yet all her experiences on the return from Scott County were not about death. In her absence, no one had left the community, and thirteen new members had entered. Ten had made vows, all but one of them her former novices. Among the ten was Martha Drury, the first postulant at the new Nazareth and destined to out-live all there at that time. Martha had brought and given up the bed that David required Catherine to use, the bed that followed her to Scott County and became a community joke.[32]

Martha was also the center (and later reporter) of a joke that had occurred in Catherine's absence, one that revealed some of the difference in her style of authority from Mother Agnes's. Com-munal poverty required special care of dishes. Breakage was to be acknowledged and a mild penance performed. The custom origi-nated with Father David; Catherine had implemented it gently. Mother Agnes, however, is described as "more rigid and severe." To halt the breakage, she required Martha, among others, to wear a shard of crockery on a string like a necklace. Sisters Ellen and Scholastica thought this excessive, and when Martha "polished" her shard into a "medal," Ellen mischievously wrote "Diligence" on it.[33] The story was in circulation when Catherine returned.

Catherine was well able to appreciate ironies and good hu-mor; that fact is well attested. She could appreciate even more the generosity of spirit, the sacrifices that had caused the new growth she now saw all around her. The most obvious development was a foundation and low shell of brick walls. It could not have been long before Catherine learned that the building in progress was also cause for yet another appalling trial that she, as the Mother, would have to face.

Four

Educator and Mother

1824–1831

When Catherine resumed her leadership at Nazareth in 1824, she could hardly have supposed the full symbolic meaning of the walls she saw rising there. What could never have grown in the space at St. Thomas would spread and flourish at this new Nazareth. The next seven years would effect a transformation in her, her mission, and her community. When her term ended, she would no longer be a very young woman pioneering education in small rural schools but the recognized leader of one of the very few fine schools for young women in the South. She and her Sisters would no longer be a small band of willing volunteers needing every sort of physical and spiritual assistance, but a firmly rooted community of religious women, ready to spread beyond Nazareth in a variety of missions. And she herself would have matured by the exercise of collaborative leadership, in times of affirmation and joy, in times of opposition and loss.

The immediate and most visible task before Catherine was completion of the new chapel and academy, buildings rising on land still not deeded to the community. Until the deed was in hand, she knew well that every added brick represented a fresh risk of expenditure and debt that could end in loss. What else that shell of bricks would cost she was soon to learn.

Five months after Mother Agnes's death, David wrote to Bruté, "I will miss her for a long time. She has, however, left more debts than I thought. We are somewhat burdened and reduced to expedients." Flaget stated more bluntly that the "good Sisters of Charity, through the bad administration of an imprudent mother, leave me almost [$4,000] to liquidate for them."[1] Both prelates were plain in their opinion that the debts were insurmountable unless Providence stepped in; the Sisters were invoking that with confidence. If the bishops were nearly desperate, what was the shock to Catherine Spalding, who really inherited the debts and found herself, at thirty, with the responsibility of saving the community and its mission from bankruptcy?

Such a weight of debt had accumulated because of the urgent need for more room. In 1824, twenty-eight Sisters, about thirty boarders, three elderly women, eight orphans, and three slaves resided at Nazareth. That summer, four boarders came from the South and paid tuition in advance. Bardstown merchants offered to provide groceries on credit for the year. It had seemed feasible to begin a new academy. Such a venture, however, required a prudent pace and careful monitoring. Because Mother Agnes had, according to Flaget, "enjoyed a great reputation as administrator of temporal affairs," the two busy bishops had evidently authorized the construction and left the management to her. The debts piled up and became Agnes's unfortunate legacy to her successor.[2]

Authentic debts were not the worst problems Catherine inherited. Mother Agnes may have had a head for planning and remembering temporal affairs, but she apparently could not read or write well enough to record them. Her treasurer, French Sister Eulalia Flaget (the bishop's niece), had a similar handicap with English. This dual linguistic deficiency was a deep crack through which injustice could seep. No written plans or contracts had been kept, no accounts, no statements of liability or receipts for payments.[3] Conditions were set for a windfall to the creditors, financial disaster for the community, and trauma for Mother Catherine.

Merchants and builders rapidly discovered their opportunity. Bills arrived; Sisters assured Catherine some had already been paid; she could do nothing but pay them again. In this crisis, no Scholastica O'Connor appeared. Providence took form only in the courage of the Sisters to endure further deprivations and in the spiritual strength and practical wisdom of Catherine Spalding. No doubt she kept charity in her memory, judgments, and speech as best she could—with whatever struggle she could not escape. She kept the accounts and paid the bills as she could. The community supported her and each other in the common struggle to survive. The Sisters involved later recalled Catherine's saying often that she did not know how they had struggled through the time and that it was a special act of Providence that they did so. Small wonder that David should write to Sister Rose White at Emmitsburg that "the dear Catherine . . . enjoys but a weak health."[4]

Whether or not the two bishops felt any responsibility for failing to forestall the crisis, they did now exert themselves to alleviate its misery and end it. David begged from Scholastica O'Connor's lawyer in Baltimore, adding that he wished especially to render the school "useful to the poor class" of whom eight or nine orphans were already being educated without charge. Flaget went to the largest source he could tap, the Grand Almoner of France, appealing to the "inexhaustible charity of our virtuous compatriots" for a liberal contribution to the Sisters' "pious project."[5] However much or little these appeals reduced the debts, the bishops and Catherine were soon obliged to face up to the urgent need to continue the building project.

David obtained the Sisters' agreement to build first a chapel, trusting that "Our Lord after being decently lodged, will procure his Spouses the means of lodging themselves conveniently." He solemnly performed the blessing of the chapel on his feast day, June 24, 1825, with Flaget, priests and seminarians, Sisters, forty-eight boarders, day students, and some visitors all there. The chapel was dedicated to St. Vincent de Paul "at the request of Mgr. [Flaget] and of the Mother."[6]

Recorded debates about the interior decor invite speculation on Catherine's part in the decisions. Flaget and his "holy daughters" wanted a large picture over the altar of Vincent de Paul with some of the Daughters of Charity. David, however, wanted a picture of the Holy Family and on either side paintings of St. Vincent and his patron St. John the Baptist. He asked a bishop for the "grand tableau" and that of the Baptist, promising a donation to the Dominican Sisters of a painting of St. Catherine of Siena—Catherine's patron.[7] No evidence indicates who won this small skirmish.

Regardless of decor, Catherine Spalding would find deep satisfaction in this second chapel built during her leadership. For her, it was not only another dwelling place for Christ among her "family," where she could find strength, solace, and guidance; it would also be a pledge that Providence would see the community through its crisis, see her through her efforts to complete the new brick academy.

The dates and duration of Catherine's struggle with buildings and debts can only be pieced together. Eliza Crozier Wilkinson, reminiscing as an elderly woman on her student days in 1825–1826, says that as the youngest student and the first from a southern climate, she slept in Mother's room adjoining the chapel. Throughout 1826 and 1827, David tells Bruté of the progress. Not until August 1827 does he describe a complete building: dormitories, refectories, the "gym of the Sisters, that is, their recreation hall," classrooms, music rooms, wardrobe, entry passage, Mother's room, treasurer's room, and exterior galleries. The promised "convenient lodging" for some Sisters refers to the dormitories the boarders had before, presumably in the Lapsley house. Finally, in June 1828, a student describes to her mother the improvements made outside the building: a yard and garden and a new lane.[8]

Catherine Spalding's main labor and source of concern, therefore, from 1825 to at least 1828, was constructing and paying for buildings intended to be large enough for future needs. This labor required numerous decisions about purchasing, paying, and oversight. She had to collaborate with Flaget and David (who were certainly supervising more closely than before), with merchants whose goodwill she had to keep whether or not she now trusted them, and with workmen. Some of the latter probably were slaves under an overseer; their treatment would be at least partially hers to supervise. With the buildings, one hundred acres of timberland were added, and David assured Bruté that "Providence has furnished us with the means to pay for it." By 1828, Catherine had expended $20,000.[9]

With the success of the project, Catherine also experienced

criticism for the size and quality of the buildings, comments sufficiently harsh and widespread to have been heard and remembered
by young Eliza Crozier. Catherine was viewed as an extravagant
visionary, the buildings as signs of lost religious simplicity. She had
no option but to wait out the storm and let wisdom be known in
her deeds. The "large and commodious edifice" was designed to
receive "upwards of one hundred" boarders. Catherine said room
would be needed in time for three hundred.[10] She was right, and
the burden of more construction (and more criticism) would in
time fall on her again.

Wise manager and builder at age thirty-five, Catherine was not,
however, insensitive to the judgments made on her. In May 1829,
writing to Flaget on a very different topic, she abruptly interjects:

> Moreover, dear father, we are not unmindful that if there
> are now splendid buildings, comfortable lodgings etc., it
> is not precisely for us who "have borne the heat & the
> burden of the day," but for those who will perhaps never
> appreciate what has been undergone, the privations that
> have been endured to procure the comforts & advantages
> that they will enjoy, but vain and foolish would I be, if
> I expected my reward in the acknowledgements of mor-
> tals. No, I do not. I ask for nothing, I desire nothing but
> the grace & mercy of my God. You may think perhaps,
> dear father, that my feelings are too deeply wounded to be
> healed, but believe me I am not.[11]

Given the subject matter of the rest of the letter (misunderstanding
about a change in the color of the collar), this passionate digres-
sion about the buildings surely reveals the depth of Catherine's
pain. Her feelings may not have been beyond healing, but they ran
deep and were sore indeed. The letter creates the impression of
anger, struggle, and prayer behind that plea for grace and mercy, as
if Catherine wishes to desire nothing else, while her human nature
asserts its claim. She seems to have realized how frankly she had
revealed herself; rather than pen the whole letter again, she adds a
sort of apology for having "expressed my sentiments . . . probably

in too awkward a manner" and assures the bishop she will "now endeavor to be tranquil."[12]

By the end of this first great construction project, Catherine had become a shrewd and careful businesswoman. No more monetary dealings would escape written form and signatures. A promissory note for $100 specifies details of payment, in "small sums," "without interest," into "the hands of said Ann Bamber for her mother." In 1828, elderly Mrs. Elizabeth Wescott wished to retire "from the noise and bustle of the world" and to be taken care of for life in the "Nazareth Monastery." Catherine became "the one part" of a legal, witnessed agreement: Mrs. Wescott would have a private room, board, clothing, and care "as a member of the family"; Nazareth would educate her niece as a boarder until she was sixteen and provide a total $500 to her dependent relatives. For these benefits, Mrs. Wescott would convey to Bishop Flaget "a certain tract of land [136.5 acres] and some negroes for the benefit of the Monastery." The widow Wescott may have made the best of the bargain, and Catherine agreed to a charity.[13] She did not fail, however, to have the agreement in writing and the terms specified. What Catherine had not learned about business from observation of her own relatives, she was learning fast by experience of her office and its difficulties.

The "splendid buildings," Catherine said, were not for the comfort of one generation but for accommodation of many future students. Such a large building, however, presented questions that had not arisen in the limited space at St. Thomas: who those students should be, how enrollment and curriculum would express the school's purpose, and how that purpose would express the mission goals of the Sisters of Charity. In this period, both David and Catherine had to look at these questions. Both expressed opinions and desires and made decisions showing concern for the way the developing school would follow the fundamental Rule and tradition of St. Vincent de Paul.

The original Rule states the principal purpose of the Sisters of Charity: to serve Christ "in the person of the poor,"[14] and in others whose needs are discovered. When the tradition of Charity came to Maryland, the need first discovered was education. Archbishop Carroll believed that the church would be rooted in American soil and culture only by the education of women who would transmit faith and learning. Girls, rich or poor, were to have intellectual opportunity. Schools must enroll both groups; the rich would enable the poor. Such was the authentic response to the essential Vincentian questions, "What is the need? What must be done?"

In Kentucky, the first need was the same: children must be taught. At St. Thomas, nearly all the children were rural poor, but with the move, the economic issue confronted Catherine. In 1825, fifty young men from Louisiana transferred to St. Joseph College in Bardstown. Their sisters soon followed them to Nazareth, and its reputation spread. Soon more and more "young girls of well-to-do families" arrived at the only academy in the South offering "a highly finished education."[15] David and Catherine clearly saw this as a true call in mission. These girls, Catholic or not, could become educated women, influences for moral good, not mere "ornaments of society."

Yet neither Catherine nor David viewed a school for the rich or prosperous as a sufficient response to the purpose of Sisters of Charity. In 1827, when the new building was housing only thirty-six, ten orphans or poor girls were also receiving upkeep and education. David proposed to increase that number as the debt was paid: "I wish to bring our Sisters, little by little, to their first vocation, that is, the care of the poor." As for Catherine, her Sisters' memories recorded that each mark of growing prosperity increased her hope that "ere long the day might dawn, when its members would be enabled to devote themselves more to the service of the poor."[16]

Catherine received girls of some means, but the school thrived on the Sisters' poverty. They made their habits, stockings, and shoes. They lived by the farm and all manner of labor besides their teaching. Even the first paying students shared in the general poverty. Eliza Crozier Wilkinson remembered the attraction of the orchard to children not fully sated by an "abundant breakfast of bread and coffee (with meat on Sunday, and occasionally butter)," dinner at one, a lunch of dry bread at five, and more bread and tea at seven. The Sisters' fare was no better. They were sustained largely by motivation and hope.[17]

Whatever the food, the curriculum had to be of high quality. This was the accomplishment of Ellen O'Connell, both teacher and instructor of teachers, abetted by the constant collaboration and encouragement of the headmistress, Catherine Spalding. They prepared good teachers from young women who came to the community with "a mind bare of knowledge, knowing hardly how to read."[18] By 1826, the curriculum included all the subjects usual in the eastern female academies: reading, writing, arithmetic, English grammar and composition, geography with use of globes, survey of history, French, pianoforte, drawing, and needlework.

David was final arbiter of curriculum, but Catherine was the prime influence on his decisions, and she did not hesitate to debate them. He expressed to Bruté a scruple about citing the Sister faculty in the prospectus as "ladies," fearing the name would create vanity in their weak "female minds" and "not believing it to be according to the spirit of St. Vincent de Paul, who wanted to make only Servants of the Poor." The Sisters "practically laughed at my delicacy, and our little Mother, who has much humor, has given me many arguments in which there is a little sarcasm which she does not mean."[19] Various later publications refer to the faculty as "ladies" of Nazareth. Catherine was certainly not much exercised about such trivia, yet one may readily understand her sarcasm and suppose she *did* mean it—good-humoredly.

On a much more important matter, Catherine had a strong opinion and prevailed. David explains to Bruté that Catherine "let" the president of St. Joseph's College revise Nazareth's curriculum, and he had placed in it "many articles which I do not approve of very much. But since our excellent Mother thinks them very useful, I let them pass it." Later that month, he wrote again, "I did not approve the introduction of the four branches that you have marked, but our little Mother insisted very strongly . . . and her reasons were convincing." The branches were "Botany, Natural Philosophy, Optics, and Chemistry." Catherine's cited reasons were that "the parents of the young ladies desired that we teach sciences. That gives a certain prestige to the school and procures a great number of boarders and consequently greater profits." He hastens to add that the profits will be applied to the education of orphans and other poor girls.[20] That, assuredly, was also one of Catherine's reasons.

What really bothered the clerics, it seems, was the necessity of sending the young students at Nazareth to the men's college to witness experiments in the laboratory. But the arrangement, David concedes, is not so inconvenient. Only "3 or 4 times a year two prefects (Sisters) bring over 4 or 5 physics students" to the laboratory in Bardstown, where "in their presence, we perform some experiments . . . with the necessary explanations."[21] "Our little Mother" was obviously less concerned than her clerical mentor about the dangers of science and performance of experiments, and less defensive about male contacts for her students.

Another issue of prestige Catherine had to deal with was annual public examinations, the norm in most nineteenth-century academic institutions. Flaget and David insisted that open examinations would inform and assure the public of the school's quality, and so attract a higher enrollment according to the intention of Providence. For a long time the success of the practice seemed to validate their confidence. Local people and relatives from a distance came to watch the professors of St. Joseph College or visiting dignitaries pose questions to the well-prepared students. The famous Kentucky statesman Henry Clay presided at examinations and commencement in 1825.[22]

Catherine, headmistress of the academy, accepted these examinations as a public relations necessity, but she was not wholly in favor of their duration or methods. By 1830, they lasted two full days, and the crowds attending and requiring some form of hospitality had grown in proportion. Catherine was heard to say she "looked forward to the day when all of this would be changed" and the Sisters and girls would be spared the fatigue and trial of the examinations. Such a change would be "more consonant with the spirit of Catholic female education."[23] Her remarks much impressed Eliza Crozier's mother with their good sense and sensitivity.

Eliza also says in her memoir that her mother, then a Protestant, had met Catherine at Old Nazareth (St. Thomas). "She was only nineteen years of age, when the impression made by her manner, her intelligence, and her beautiful modesty . . . caused my mother to say, stranger though she was, that she recognized one to whose care she would, with confidence, entrust her daughter. In those days there were few Catholics, and she was my Mother's first Catholic friend."[24] A similar impression on other parents produced a similar result. By the mid-1820s, most of the students at Nazareth were not Catholic, and a policy in their regard was necessary.

Zealous for Catholicism as Catherine and the bishops were, they had the integrity to honor conscience and the rights of parents. They were also pragmatic enough to know that "solicitation" would soon leave them "without students except 2 or 3 Catholics." They knew by experience that conversions opposed by parents might not survive the students' return home. The regulation, therefore, was that a student wishing to convert to Catholicism was refused unless her parents consented. Some parents did consent, and Catherine and other Sisters served as sponsors at student baptisms.[25]

The policy was firmly applied, but not without occasional divergence between Catherine and the prelates. A Catholic man from Alabama begged admission for his young, wholly uneducated, Protestant wife—who would bring their infant daughter with her. The clergymen, fearing scandal, refused absolutely to have a baby in the arms of Sisters "crying near the parlor where strangers are received." Mother and baby came nevertheless, and Catherine's word was certainly decisive in the admission. No one else had her authority to intervene or her influence with the bishops. In four months, the young mother learned to read and keep house, then chose to study her husband's religion and accepted it. Flaget and David were duly impressed by the work of Providence.[26]

The great hope of Catherine and the bishops was that instruction, good experience of religious observances, and the example and loving personal attention of the Sisters would reduce anti-Catholic bias, first in the students, then in their societies. The tone of the school at first reflected such bias. Young Eliza Crozier heard "many unkind and contemptuous remarks" about Catholics and "the old nuns." Her descriptions of the Sisters, however, seem to account not only for some conversions but also for the respect won from the majority who never became Catholic.[27]

Catherine as headmistress set the pattern for the personal interaction of the Sisters and students. Even as a youngster, Eliza was struck by the Sisters' individuality as well as their common spiritual quality: "women of such decided characteristics that their impression is stamped indelibly. Each with her own special gifts and graces, all devoted to God." Catherine herself was reputed to be "kind and tender, especially to the erring or turbulent young creatures who drew courage and strength from her words." Indeed, her reputation declared that the worst girls were her "pets."[28] But no taint of bias seems to have touched the loving respect for her that Eliza reports.

One of Catherine's lessons Eliza could not forget. Catherine had allowed her and other students to be present at the reinterment at Nazareth of the Sisters who had died at St. Thomas. The next evening, Eliza and her French class went to recite to Catherine:

> I had, I suppose, arranged my curls and band comb with special care. As I took my seat, Mother Catherine, looking at me quietly said, "Were you at the cemetery last evening, Eliza?" "Yes, Mother." "Did you see the remains?" "Yes, Mother." "Was the hair arranged in that way?" Recalling the smooth skulls I had so shuddered at, I fully recognized my own vanity.[29]

Catherine can be criticized for allowing a child of eleven years to attend such a ceremony and then censuring her girlish curls by the contrast. Eliza, however, seems not to have felt that stricture; she calls the episode her "first lesson upon the nothingness of this world." Her summary words on Catherine are: "I think that even had I not known her in after years, I could never have forgotten the tones of her voice, so soft, so gentle, but so deep and earnest, or the expression of her dark blue eyes, which seemed to me to read your inmost heart. Her words were few and concise with an enunciation so distinct that they were sure to be remembered."[30]

Eliza's reference to Catherine's voice and eyes is one of the rare notations of her physical traits. Another sketch says she was of "medium height" and "heavily built," with eyes so deeply blue as to seem black. "Her countenance was beautiful; it bore a very benevolent, motherly expression, but one read in it firmness and strong determination as well." Frightened new students remembered her face for its warmth and encouragement.[31]

Intent as Catherine was on the mission of Nazareth Academy, she was also waiting and trusting in Divine Providence for the extension of the community's good works. By 1829, Catherine knew the time was right for a major step necessary to that advancement. As the leader of her Council, she knew that the community's property was held in the name of the bishop; "the Sisters [were not] able to personally attend to the various contracts and other temporal concerns."[32] They could never achieve that deeply desired mission to the poorest children and the sick without a corporate and legal identity. Contracts, large purchases, collection of debts, or defense against unjust claims—all necessitated incorporation by the State of Kentucky. In December, a bill for incorporation was presented to the legislature.

As a woman, Catherine could not have been present for the debate, strong as were her concern and interest. But she would hear of it from the two clergymen who were there for any needed explanations. The common objection—that the bishop would be moderator of the Board of Trustees, and that through him the pope, "this foreign Potentate," would have control of property in the state—was presented and explained away. The defender of the bill, however, was not a bishop but Ben Hardin, Protestant father of two Nazareth students. He based his arguments on the quality of the school, the excellence of the curriculum, the "character and virtue of these good Nuns," and the expansion of the buildings. He exhorted the legislators on the propriety and the practical need to give "legislative aid to the efforts of these helpless females, who have already done a great deal for virtue . . . for piety . . . for charity . . . for literature!"[33] Hardin and other supporters prevailed; incorporation of Nazareth Literary and Benevolent Institution (NLBI) occurred on December 29, 1829. Catherine and the other "helpless females" doubtless read and enjoyed the newspaper's full account of the debate.

Flaget was moderator of the new NLBI Board. No woman, however astute, would be given that role at that time. Catherine and Angela Spink, the builder of St. Vincent Academy in Union County, nonetheless joined Bishop David, Father Francis Kenrick, and lawyer Ben Chapeze as members. They met on May 3, 1830. Catherine remained a member until the last years of her life. Board minutes indicate her regular attendance, her rapid learning of legalities, and her participation in the processes.

Catherine's influence in decisions is evident from the start. The second meeting included the appointment of the bishops and Catherine to choose a seal, and the decision that no obligations should bind without signatures of "the Mother and her Assistant." At the third meeting, Catherine herself moved that the "state of the Institution's resources should be presented to the inspection of the Board" yearly in May.[34] Over the years, Catherine was given increasing authority to find and purchase land and buildings, especially for the expanding mission in Louisville.

Although Nazareth Academy was the chief beneficiary of the incorporation, legal identity opened the road to the other ministries and foundations. Catherine, while fully devoted to the service of the school, was simultaneously straining at the financial leash that held her from works of direct charity to the poor. She applied to herself and tried to obey Vincent de Paul's counsel not to anticipate Providence. While she awaited the signal and release to move ahead in mission, she led at Nazareth such informal charities as the limited resources of the community permitted.

In a sort of divine irony, the first call, as formerly at St. Thomas, was not to unsheltered or helpless children but to the elderly. Catherine sheltered in the midst of the community a group of old women, otherwise homeless: Mrs. Tyson, Sister Scholastica's sister-in-law; Aunt Polly Blandford, godmother of Sister Frances Gardiner; Granny Speak, a destitute widow; Mrs. O'Brien, mother of a mentally ill priest who had left the diocese; and Mrs. Wescott of the previously mentioned contract. Their presence offered edifying, constant prayer and service by sewing, combined with such eccentricities as sneaking off with the firewood, shouting news at the deaf, and wandering in a confused search for the lost son. Catherine wanted to provide a separate place, better for the needs of these women, but could do it only "in part." Despite the "quite burdensome charge," the community maintained them until their deaths.[35]

Care of the sick in these years consisted of home visits to neighbors, carrying what medicines and skills were available. Sister Rose White in Emmitsburg had sent rules for hospitals along with the life of St. Vincent. With desire stimulated by both documents, Catherine began, in 1828, to gather more information about the management of hospitals and asylums.[36] Resources still eluded her, but she burned to be about these services. Her time would soon come, and she would lead the new directions herself.

Meanwhile, she was still "Mother Catherine," the superior responsible for leading the daily life and business of a growing community. It was her role to assign duties, visit the sick and oversee their care, receive new members, and relate to all by admonitions and affirmations, by encouragement and instruction, sympathy and rejoicing. In her position, she required a skillful balance with the authority of the indefatigable Bishop David, who spent two days a week at Nazareth, giving himself to "directions, consultations, affairs, etc."[37] He was both ecclesiastical superior and chaplain. As the superior, he could make decisions independently, though he seems not often to have done so without consulting Catherine. She could not make significant changes, as in daily schedule and spiritual practice or even school procedures, without his approbation—however she might have been tempted to do so.

Catherine had to exercise tact also in balancing her spiritual guidance of the Sisters with David's role as chaplain. He gave three weekly instructions to the Sisters, presided at liturgy, heard confessions, gave spiritual direction, and preached the annual eight-day retreats. A hint of the extent of David's control is apparent in his appreciation sent to Bruté for "interesting news" that he had shared with "our good Sisters of Nazareth . . . at least that part which serves to edify them." Nor was he willing, even when nearly exhausted, to surrender his position at Nazareth "for lack of a man according to my heart to whom I could confide the care of the dear sisters and their pupils." He could give the students to a good Jesuit, "perhaps even after a certain time, the sisters themselves."[38] Even granting the submission to clerical authority accepted at that time, a woman as capable as Catherine had her diplomatic challenges.

In this term as Mother, Catherine experienced several special events sure to rouse either great joy or great sorrow. Every entry of a woman to the community, every profession of vows, caused a jubilee, a celebration of life for Catherine. The entrance of Margaret Carroll in August 1825 and her profession in 1827 were uniquely joyous. Daughter of Irish immigrants in Louisville who had died of typhoid contracted from nursing a priest, Margaret was sent by her guardian to Nazareth. There she became the protégé of Sisters Ellen O'Connell and Columba Tarlton, and the academy's first graduate. As Sister Columba Carroll, she would become a mainstay of the faculty and eventually Sister Ellen's replacement. Her devotion to Catherine is evidenced in her later letters. Catherine felt a special kinship with this thoughtful, prudent, lovable—and orphaned—young woman and must have been able to see her potential for future community leadership.[39]

September 1826 brought to Bardstown a literal Jubilee, the delayed celebration by the Catholic world of the Holy Year of 1825. For forty Sisters of Charity, the Jubilee occasioned their retreat, a daily schedule of Mass, sermons, and private prayer. Some from Nazareth, perhaps including Catherine, stayed with the Bardstown Sisters.[40] Rather more solemn than jubilant, the event was, nevertheless, an occasion for Catherine and her Sisters to affirm and rejoice in their faith and vocation, as well as to gather with those they did not often see.

One month after the Jubilee, Catherine would need all the strength of spirit the event had given her to bear another especially grievous death. In March 1824, presumably at Bishop Flaget's request, Mother Agnes had sent four Sisters to open a school in the frontier outpost of Vincennes, Indiana. Catherine almost surely heard about "the fevers of that region" and the extreme spiritual privations. The sole priest for the large territory was traveling for months at a time. In 1826, he had been gone for two months when all four Sisters became ill and were crawling out of bed to care for each other. Three survived, but Harriet Gardiner died. Adding to Catherine's personal grief at the death of her childhood friend, her companion and first assistant at St. Thomas, she learned that Harriet had grieved "enough to melt a heart of stone" at her impending death without benefit of the sacraments. Catherine had also to try to console Harriet's sisters, Frances and Clare Gardiner. And neither she nor they could attend the funeral at Vincennes or bring their sister's remains to Nazareth.[41]

Grievous as it was, Harriet Gardiner's death was the only one Catherine had to deal with from her return in 1824 until her final seven months of office. Then, however, she had to bury three Sisters, all from consumption, all young, one a novice. The last two deaths were only ten days apart. More consistently painful in those years were the departures not only of novices but also, each year except 1830, of one to three professed Sisters who did not renew their annual vows.[42] There may have been excellent reasons: insight on personal vocation, health, or family needs. But for a woman as committed and affectionate as Catherine, these good-byes had to be painful.

No loss could have been more traumatic to Catherine than one in 1827. This episode was dropped from published history, doubtless to spare family members and descendants. But it was so important at the time, so drained Catherine's emotional and spiritual resources, that it requires attention. She had known well both the people involved, so that her sensitivities had to be deeply wounded.[43]

The first person was Father Charles Coomes, who had come to St. Thomas in his early teens. Catherine had known him there as a seminarian and then as pastoral minister. There is no reason to doubt she had given him her respect and friendship. The other person was Sister Perpetua (Frances) Alvey from Union County. Catherine had been her Mistress of Novices at Nazareth and her superior for eight months at Scott County. Whatever her assessment of this young Sister, Catherine had to feel for her a sense of responsibility and a mother's hope.

Coomes and Sister Perpetua met when he was assigned to Scott County, where he created "inquietude" by "private interviews with some sisters at undue hours and against the rules." Flaget told Bishop Rosati of St. Louis that Coomes had committed no grave faults against morals. It seems clear, however, that this very young priest was wrestling with his promise of celibacy and endangering the similar promise of equally young Sisters. The local superior sounded a warning, and Catherine went to Scott County to deal directly with the issue. She escorted Perpetua and another Sister back to Nazareth, where, said David, "we thought we had brought them to their senses by the most charitable, paternal and maternal treatment by the Mother and myself."[44]

But Catherine's suffering had only begun. It peaked on a Sunday afternoon when Coomes came to Nazareth to persuade the two young Sisters to return to their homes under his escort. According to Flaget, "In vain the mother [Catherine] offered him some thoughts full of wisdom to arrest his imprudent step. Each statement he opposed and made bitter reproaches to the superior."[45]

Catherine knew her need for practical and emotional support. Though it was Sunday and she knew Flaget's occupations, she and her officers sent for him. They gathered with the priest and two Sisters, and Flaget tried to persuade the young women of the "indecency" of the proposed journey, promised to send them home at his own expense with a proper escort, and begged them to trust his age and experience of the world. One Sister heeded him, but Frances Alvey went with Coomes, probably that very afternoon. One can only imagine how Catherine's emotions were wrung out by the day's end, how much she needed consolation and whatever sleep she got that night. Flaget says "her heart was profoundly wounded."[46] It is worth remembering that the Mother who had to summon all the wisdom she had in this crisis of young emotions was herself thirty-three years old.

That Sunday, however, was not the end of Catherine's trauma. Instead of taking Frances Alvey to her parents, Coomes took her to Missouri and placed her as a guest in a convent of the Sisters of Loretto, while he vacillated about returning to the Bardstown

diocese or transferring to that of St. Louis. Flaget now refused
Coomes because he had "conceived a kind of hatred" for the Sisters of Charity and had written a "violent and insulting" letter
to Catherine.[47] Flaget wrote this account on Good Friday, 1827.
Catherine, too, had her share of the day's sorrows in Coomes's reproaches and especially in her concern for her young Sister adrift
at the whim of an unstable young man already unfaithful to his
own vows of ordination.

Throughout the summer of 1827, new episodes prolonged the
story, all surely known to Catherine through the bishops. In the
autumn, Frances Alvey finally went to her home. Coomes followed
her, and they were married in the Alvey parlor by a Methodist
minister. Church law required public excommunication of the unfaithful priest. This was performed in the Bardstown Cathedral on
All Saints' Day, 1827, with a huge crowd there to witness Flaget's
stern but intense grief. No record tells whether Catherine was
present. She might have stayed away to minimize the pain to all
concerned, or attended to take her community's share in the shame
and grief. Her own grief for one she had trained, affirmed for the
habit, and welcomed to Scott County had to be met in private.

Even that climactic event may not have been the last pain in-
flicted on Catherine. David, who was often at Nazareth and in
conversation with her, had been deeply wounded and angered by
the betrayal of Flaget's and his own trust and affection. Over the
next nine weeks, in letters to Bruté, he vented both the facts and
his feelings about both Coomes and Alvey in diatribes of intem-
perate language. Catherine's extant letters never refer to this sad
affair, nor do they ever use splenetic language. One hopes that
David was sensitive to her feelings and did not release his pain and
resentment in her presence. For surely she had her own reflections
on the incident, her self-questions, her own long-lasting sorrow for
a separated daughter and the sullied name of the community.[48]

In early 1828, Catherine experienced a comforting and truly
pleasant event, one more important and enduring in the long view
of community history. At David's request, the Sisters at Emmitsburg had copied for the Sisters of Nazareth the conferences of St.
Vincent de Paul to the Daughters of Charity. These conferences are

actually dialogues transcribed by St. Louise de Marillac. Vincent would initiate a topic, then solicit the views and experiences of the Daughters of Charity. Thus they gave Catherine not only the principles of the Rule but also an example of the relational style of leadership she valued and practiced. Well might she appreciate the generous labor in the gift; well might she find consolation for recent sorrow, and renewal of her joy, courage, and motivation, in this reminder and assistance to develop the charism of Charity. On receipt of the final volume, David asked Bruté to thank the Emmitsburg Sisters and assure them that "our Sisters will never forget that kind deed. I am taking it today to our dear Mother to whom this great proof of charity of the Sisters . . . will be a great joy. I desire the greatest union of prayers and good deeds between the two communities." A few months later, David reiterated to Mother Augustine, SC, his and Catherine's desire for correspondence with her, for the spiritual union of the two communities "in our Lord," and the "mutual help of their prayers."[49] No letters of Catherine to Emmitsburg are extant, nor did she ever visit there. Surely she did cherish the sense of prayerful union and of the deep common root from which her spirit flowered.

Catherine's sisterly spirit included women of the other two local religious congregations. In June 1826, she extended herself to the neighboring Sisters of Loretto. Established by Father Nerinckx in 1812 in St. Charles Parish, this community had endured the pioneer hardships Catherine knew so well, increased by their founder's austere rule of life, which they fully accepted. That Rule had created a serious conflict of Nerinckx and the Lorettines with Chabrat and Flaget. The disagreement led to the departure of Nerinckx and the enforced move of the Sisters to St. Stephen's.[50] They built there a new church and convent; to its blessing Chabrat invited the other religious orders. Catherine and another SCN attended; David, preacher for the event, described it.[51] He gives no hint of the painful background. Yet Catherine surely knew something of the coercion behind this celebration and, however she felt about the Loretto Rule, shared her sisterly affection and sympathy with the Sisters who had been commanded rather than consulted in changing it. Her own future actions about changes in Nazareth's way of life suggest she was still, as in her girlhood, observing, learning, and being prepared for her dealings with ecclesiastical superiors.

In 1829, Catherine had one more such test of her strength of spirit and her wisdom in dealing with the bishops. Compared with what else she had been through, the new matter was annoyingly trivial, certainly unworthy of the attention she was forced to give it. As recounted in her letter to Flaget, she had either initiated or approved the idea of wearing a white collar and had proposed it to David, who was willing to consider it and said so in the presence of Sisters. On her second proposal, he sanctioned introducing it; Catherine then permitted some Sisters to make and try possible designs.

How the sensible Flaget became exercised about this remains a mystery. Community historian McGill thinks the controversy was whether the change signaled vanity and that Catherine's "great spirit, so free from all pettiness," would have summarily ended it.[52] Catherine's letter to Flaget notes the issue of vanity and also suggests that other voices had interjected an issue of authority causing some change in David's attitude. She begins with a plea "on my knees and for the love of God" that the two prelates "will say to me decidedly what you wish me to do and what you wish me not to do." She continues:

> Ah! Would that you could both see my heart just as it is known to my God. . . . I think that same God of mercy knows that I never wished to act in anything independently of any Superior, but Oh! If I only could always know *immediately* from my *superior* what is disapproved in me & what he wishes me to correct . . . , how much lighter my burden! . . . If my Superiors could only always know things as they are with all their circumstances! . . . I know and repeat that I am very capable of erring . . . but it seems to me if I know my own heart, that my Superiors have only to say I *will* this or I *will it not* & I have no other desire than to do what *they will*, tho' I sometimes try to represent things as I conceive them to be. . . . perhaps it would be much better and more perfect in me, always to let everyone

think and believe according to the first impressions or representations that have been made. . . . I sometimes on those occasions yield too much to the feeling of nature. As to the collars I shall certainly await your joint answer before you will see another worn in the community.[53]

One can read in this long and impassioned letter an appeal to her own motives, to her knowledge (better than theirs) of the real story, and a virtual demand that they listen to the truth she tells (rather than to community gossip) and then respond directly, unambiguously, and without delay. She is bold and blunt, restraining anger, at points almost sarcastic ("I have erred but I hope that it is not unpardonable"), as well as submissive. She seems to sense that she may have gone too far and begs pardon for anything "improper" in her speech. But she cannot resist some self-justification, even self-pity: "I feel that my life has been spent & my peace sacrificed to the good of the community, my better days are gone [she was thirty-five], and it would now . . . be foolish in me to wish to introduce what would only serve for the vanity and enjoyment of those who come after me." Here she interjects the comments on the "splendid buildings" and her desire for "nothing but the grace and mercy of my God." She tells Flaget he is "entirely welcome" to show the letter to David; "I have no secret in it for him." Apparently the two men decided to back out of their awkward position. All pictures of Catherine show her wearing the white collar worn by SCNs until the late 1960s.

In the final years of Catherine's second six-year term of office, she could see around her the results of her labors for the school and also some lingering sorrows in community and her lasting causes for joy.

By 1830, the school was flourishing enough in numbers and reputation that it drew notice in the Catholic newspaper for its part in celebrating the consecration on June 6 of Francis Kenrick as bishop for Philadelphia: "Forty of the Community of Sisters of Charity and fifty young ladies from the female Academy of Nazareth occupied seats immediately in front of the sanctuary." Among the clergy was a stellar guest—John England, bishop of Charleston, famous for his oratory. Nazareth was on the list of diocesan establishments he had visited prior to the great event.[54]

On his arrival at Nazareth the evening of June 2, Bishop England delivered to the Sisters and students assembled in the church "a most appropriate, pathetic and eloquent discourse." Visiting prelates spent the night at Nazareth. The next morning, Catherine and her Assistant, as hostesses, conducted them to an "elegantly decorated" room, "there to suffer the daughters of Nazareth to offer the humble tributes of their high esteem and veneration for Dr. England." Before he left, Catherine escorted England through "the principal buildings and apartments of the institution."[55] One wonders if the niece of the frontier Elders actually enjoyed all this honorific ritual and ceremony. They surely did not hurt her simplicity, and she had reason to be grateful for joyous occasions and the success and stability of the mission.

As for community life, Catherine had a less happy note on which to end her term. The immediate shock of the Coomes-Alvey scandal was probable cause that no postulants had entered in the seven months after it. Then six women entered, eight more in 1829, and six in 1830. Five of the twenty left, however, as well as ten professed; so the numbers of Sisters barely increased. During the last fifteen months of Catherine's term, no new members arrived at Nazareth. No one received the habit in 1831; she received only two Sisters' vows that year.[56] Catherine Spalding's famed trust in Divine Providence was not gained without much practice.

Nevertheless, David's and Flaget's letters near the end of the 1820s indicate their satisfaction with the general well-being in both school and convent. Catherine had earned her share in this praise and seems to have had at least her final year of this term without a crisis. Begun in the depth of debts, the term ended debt-free with the election of Angela Spink on August 5, 1831.

On January, 22, 1832, F. Hertsog of Natchitoches, Louisiana, obviously unaware that Catherine had already left Nazareth, wrote to "Madam Spalding/Honored Sister" expressing his pleasure at the achievements of his daughters "with your honorable kindness." They had assured him they were "enjoying your friendship," and he is assured that she will "be a second mother" to them; this gives him a great "feeling of security."[57] When Mr. Hertsog wrote, Catherine was on the verge of the mission she had so long and deeply desired. The mother of the sick and orphaned was about to appear on the streets of Louisville.

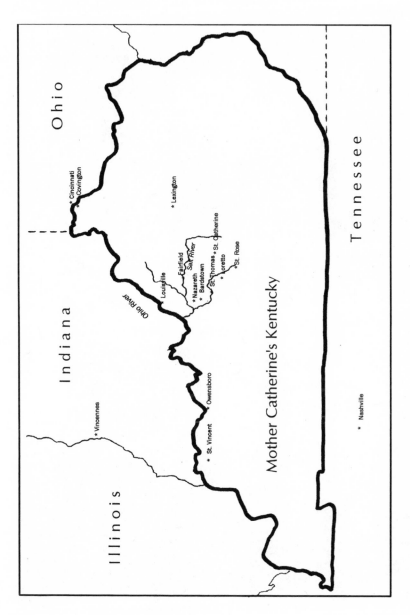

Mother Catherine's Kentucky. (Courtesy of Trudi Maish)

Howard/Flaget log house at St. Thomas, residence of first Sisters of Charity of Nazareth, c. 1890. (Courtesy of Trudi Maish)

Howard/Flaget house during the process of restoration, 2005. (Courtesy of Trudi Maish)

Pleasant Hill, home of Basil Spalding, Catherine's grandfather. (Courtesy of Shaun and Kathryn Donnelly)

Father Stephen Badin. (Nazareth Archives)

Bishop Benedict Joseph Flaget.
(Nazareth Archives)

Bishop John Baptist David.
(Nazareth Archives)

(Above) Sisters of Charity of Nazareth on their way to Union County, Kentucky. John Watson Davis, 1944. Illustration from the Society for the Propagation of the Faith calendar, 1945. In its compositional format, this painting bears a resemblance to George Caleb Bingham's *Daniel Boone Escorting Settlers through the Cumberland Gap* (1851–1852). *(Below)* Graves dated 1824 in Nazareth cemetery. (Courtesy of Trudi Maish)

Nazareth Academy, c. 1825–26. Lapsley house on left, new academy on right. (Nazareth Archives)

Father Joseph Haseltine. This portrait hangs in Heritage Hall, Nazareth. (Courtesy of Trudi Maish)

Mother Catherine's desk. Heritage Hall, Nazareth. (Courtesy of Trudi Maish)

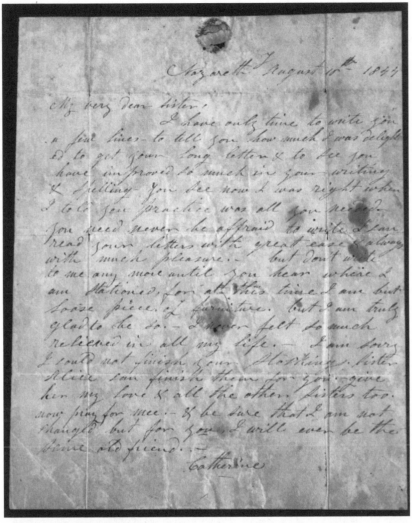

Letter of Mother Catherine Spalding to Sister Claudia Elliott, 1844.
(Nazareth Archives)

(Above) St. Joseph Infirmary, Louisville, after 1852. (Nazareth Archives)
(Below) St. Vincent Church, Nazareth, 1854, with academy of 1825 to left.
(Nazareth Archives)

(Above) Nazareth Academy, 1855. Drawing for advertisement. (Nazareth Archives) *(Below)* Mother Xavier Ross. (Courtesy of archive of Sisters of Charity of Leavenworth, Kansas)

Sister Columba Carroll.
(Nazareth Archives)

Bishop Martin John
Spalding. (Nazareth
Archives)

Catherine Spalding, tintype. (Nazareth Archives)

Statue of Mother Catherine Spalding in front of present motherhouse, Nazareth. (Courtesy of Trudi Maish)

Statue of Bishop David in front of present motherhouse, Nazareth. (Courtesy of Trudi Maish)

Mother Catherine's grave site. (Courtesy of Trudi Maish)

Five

Pioneer in Louisville

1831–1838

No person has an adequate idea of the business and bustle of Louisville until he has arrived at the town." So wrote one visitor of the 1830s.[1] The comment can surely be applied to Catherine Spalding's experience when she arrived in October 1831. The contrast to all her previous surroundings and lifestyles could hardly have been greater. Catherine was now thirty-seven. She had been raised on the rural outskirts of a very small village and, so far in her adult years, limited to life in rural convent schools and visits in Bardstown. But Nazareth and Bardstown were, by this time, fairly comfortable and genteel settings where a woman might easily settle into a long, useful life.

Louisville, by contrast, was a rough river city at the Falls of the Ohio. Father Nerinckx had described it in 1807 as a place "where there is much trade and wickedness . . . few confessions heard, but plenty of curses uttered." By 1830, it was a depot where barrels, bags, and bales of goods were unloaded for sale or sent through the new Portland Canal around the Falls to eventual connection with the Mississippi River. Entrepreneurs believed the city had a destiny "by Nature and Providence" to become a great center of expanding commerce, the "chief city of the West." Wharves and streets were busy and noisy, sometimes dangerous, with all the various characters and activities that such a locale and goal invited. Catherine may have visited the city previously on business, or she may have only passed through en route to Nelson County at the age of four. At that early time, the city's population was less than six hundred. By 1830, it exceeded ten thousand, a number that would double by 1835.[2] Urban "business and bustle" matched the numbers. The woman from the country may have been stunned, even a bit frightened; or she may have been excited and eager. Clearly she was not deterred from her new venture.

Catherine's carriage or wagon approached Louisville through lovely wooded outskirts. Her destination was in the center of the city, St. Louis Church, recently erected on Fifth Street near Walnut. The city limits, as incorporated in 1828 and mapped in 1832, extended only about eight blocks south from the river to Prather Street (now Broadway) and approximately from Twelfth Street eastward to Wenzel. Two-story residences were intermingled with stores and factories, potteries and foundries, mills and breweries, a hotel, bank, and theater, on lots along Main, Market, Jefferson, and Green (now Liberty), and their cross streets.[3]

Catherine may have shared visitors' mixed views of these streets. Were they straight, wide, and handsome, or were they unlit, deserted, and dirty, "never cleaned except by rain"? Were there large and splendid buildings or only a few nice houses? Catherine would judge by years of walking those streets, even beyond the city limits. But very soon she had to share the general awareness of filth and the opinion of one citizen that "it would contribute much to the health and comfort of our citizens if our streets, backyards, and cellars were kept clean."[4]

St. Louis Church was in a "Range of Five Acre Lots" below the busiest area but within city limits; below the southern boundary, lots of ten and twenty acres awaited development. On one such lot was the Poor and Work House, where the sick poor were said to be "attended most honorably by the Medical faculty, gratuitously," and others were confined to labor to pay court fines. There also was the Marine Hospital, established by the legislature for relief of riverboat men who "become sick and languish at the town of Louisville." Many continued to languish. In 1836 the local newspaper lamented that many were unable to find care at that hospital and "have suffered in our streets or have received temporary relief from individual benevolence." Catherine would soon know well the need of benevolent relief for sailors and passengers, transients and residents, in a city once labeled the "Graveyard of the West" for its vulnerability to consumption, pleurisy, typhus, dysentery, and various lethal fevers.[5] To provide relief would become her goal. Unforeseeably soon, she would begin to realize it.

Catherine's immediate mission was educational. Prosperous citizens, dwelling in the city or already moving into its outskirts, were aspiring to learning and gentility. So far education had been only for those who could afford private arrangements. In 1830 a "spacious and airy" public school was built on the southwest corner of Fifth Street and Walnut, thus in close proximity to St. Louis Church. The middle story was for girls, who received elementary to "higher studies."[6] Whatever the curriculum, a public school in the nineteenth century had some religious overtone, and in Louisville, that meant Protestant.

Father Robert Abell, pastor of St. Louis, wanted Catholic education for his parishioners and asked for the Sisters he had known as a seminarian at St. Thomas. Very soon after Catherine left office, in September 1831, Mother Angela and her Council at Nazareth convened to deliberate on sending Sisters to White River, Indiana, and Louisville. White River was postponed, but the Council resolved to send to Louisville Sister Barbara Spalding (no relation to Catherine) as superior, with two other Sisters. They also determined "that Sister Catherine Spalding should go to assist in the commencement."[7]

Some dynamic of personal judgment and preference entered at this point. On October 3, the Council assembled at the request of Bishop Flaget to "make a change in the last agreement, and after much talk without coming to any determination, at the request of one of the Officers, the Council adjourned with a grant of two days for further examination and deliberation." On October 5, 1831, the Council reconvened "to decide finally": Bishop David, Mother Angela Spink, Sister Francis Gardiner, Assistant, and Sisters Joanna Lewis and Anastasia Luckett. They deemed it "better for the good of the Company that Sister Catherine Spalding should go as Sister Superior if she is willing, with Sister Clare Gardiner and Sister Serena Carney and Sister Apollonia McGill."[8] A new, more seasoned cast had been chosen for Louisville; the drama of White River, with some of the same participants, was yet to come.

It is noteworthy that "much talk," discernment, and reconsideration of decisions occurred even in early days so regulated by obedience. How much Catherine was informed during the process, what she thought, felt, hoped, or even advised, must be conjectured. Her wish, however, was considered in the appointment, and she, with characteristic readiness, took on a challenging new mission when asked.

The *Louisville City Directory of 1832* noted that St. Louis Church had "schoolrooms in the basement story" and that the "building in the rear of the lot upon which the Church is built, is occupied by the Ladies of the Order denominated 'Sisters of Charity,' a Society justly celebrated . . . for their success in the education of young ladies." According to an archaeologist, the "building" was a small, two-story frame house that must originally have been some sort of adjunct to the church.[9] Catherine, just arrived in 1831 from the newly constructed residence at Nazareth, may have remembered her early years and other beginnings.

The perceived need for a specifically Catholic school indicates another dimension to the culture shock Catherine would have had in transferring to Louisville from Bardstown/Nazareth. All her former environments had been heavily Catholic, if not in numbers, at least in tone and culture. Louisville was not only heavily Protestant in numbers but also, in the 1830s, a tonal mix of friendly cooperation, occasional hostility, and general indifference to Catholicism. The laying of the cornerstone of St. Louis Church in 1830 had been formally celebrated in the nearby Presbyterian church, with preaching from the Protestant Bible. But in 1834, the Sisters of Charity would be called mercenaries in their care of the sick. And in 1836, the *Louisville Public Advertiser* supported the war for Texas's independence from Mexico under the headline "Liberty Triumphing over Tyranny and Priestcraft." More characteristically, the official opening of Presentation Academy, November 21, 1831, did not even make the papers.[10] Catherine, through many years of ministry to the poor, would learn to draw on Protestant fairness and goodwill and to challenge increasing religious hostility.

Public bias notwithstanding, the school attracted within a year fifty to sixty students and grew rapidly. Presentation was not only affordable for Catholic families; it also attracted affluent Protestants. The curriculum, in basics and higher branches, developed as far as possible in conformity with that of Nazareth.[11] Catherine was once again building a school from almost nothing except the zeal and determination of her own heart and of her band of Sisters.

Resolute as Catherine was to establish firmly a source of high-quality private education for young women who might become socially influential, she always intended more. Tuition from the professional and business classes was stretched to provide education for poor children, including the so-called "levee rats" who resided near the wharf. Catherine and her Sisters evidently visited that area soon after their arrival. Very early in 1832, she wrote to Nazareth about a severe flood that had carried away houses and left more than five hundred families homeless. No record remains of her immediate response to that crisis, but it must have roused her will to extend the mission in a new direction. And she must have made her desire known at Nazareth. A month later, the Council met there "to deliberate some plan or regulations for the Orphan Asylum." Bishop David offered to copy the regulations used by Emmitsburg.[12]

That same year, the city *Directory* noted of Presentation: "When their means will be sufficient, they will receive, clothe, educate, and support a number of orphan children—to which purpose the profits of this admirable institution are devoted."[13] The statement implies a publicly declared long-range plan, even a savings account of some sort, in fact or in hope. Action, however, would come, as it often did in Catherine's life, by immediate response to an unforeseen, urgent need. That first response is one of the best-known stories in Catherine's life. It set off a chain of actions that would lead to a long-lasting community ministry.

According to the oldest Annals, in late June 1832, a Protestant family from Pennsylvania stopped at Louisville. The mother took sick and died of an unknown disease, leaving five boys, two girls aged sixteen and five, and an infant girl. Just before the mother's death, a Catholic gentleman heard of the family's distress and appealed to Mother Catherine. She and Sister Apollonia McGill went and found the mother dead, the father helpless from grief and liquor. They comforted the terrified children and, with the help of neighbors, saw to a funeral. Catherine then begged the eldest girl, already frail with a heart condition, to go home with her. She tearfully refused and expressed her determination to keep the family together. But in two weeks, the little girls became ill, and the older girl died.

The rest of the story is told with details and fervor that suggest the author was either one of the remaining "Penn babies" or a Sister who had cared for them:

Again were the "Angels of Mercy" called in, and over the grave of his daughter, the afflicted father . . . gave up the babe to Mother Catherine until he could find some one to take care of all his children, but he would not yet part with his last girl. When Mother Catherine received the infant, she said with tender solemnity, "Mister ——, I will look upon this child and raise it as it were my own. . . ." But the little babe would not be separated from the little sister . . . and after two or three days trial, Mother sent for its father and entreated him to consider again his children's welfare. The end of the matter was that both of the little girls were given up to the sisters and never removed from their care. . . . The little babe always stayed in mother's room, and Mother's little "Penn. Baby" wept bitterly when she learned at seven years of age that "Mumsie" was not her own mother.[14]

The "Penn babies" were only the first of a succession of orphans Catherine received at Presentation. According to another story, she heard of two orphans whose parents had died en route from New Orleans and who were landed at the Louisville wharf "friendless and without means of support." Catherine went for them and brought them home.[15] As Catherine's trips to the wharves or to homes stricken with illness or poverty grew more frequent, the stories grew into a sort of legend. Reportedly, she made "long journeys" from one place to another, on horseback, wagon, or carriage, over "well-nigh impassable roads" through "snow and sleet and pouring rains" to gather up orphans.[16] The rhetoric actually understates the reality. In fact, she mostly had to *walk*. But there can be no doubt of more and more "instances of orphaned children" in the expanding city or of Catherine Spalding's consuming desire to meet their need.

The real and constant inconvenience that Catherine and the Sisters endured for the sake of orphans was not distance but crowding. In the frame convent, "that small building with four rooms, besides the basement kitchen and dining room," lived six Sisters and six children who slept with them in the small dormitory. And more were sure to come. Obviously, they required more space and more support for the basics of food, clothing, and daily care. Catherine's skills for organization, collaboration, and construction met a new challenge, perhaps equal to any so far. In meeting it, her chief helpers would be Louisville women, mostly former students from Nazareth.[17]

In 1884, the diocesan paper included a historical column "copied from Mother Catherine's memorandum-book, in her own hand writing": "A meeting was held for the founding of an Orphan Asylum in the vestry room of the Church of Saint Louis, August 10, 1832. After a short address from the Pastor, the Rev. Robert Abell, it was resolved that a fair should be gotten up to procure the means. The sisters agreed to receive into their small dwelling near the church, where they carried on a day-school, as many orphans as could be accommodated. The lady managers of the Fair were: [twelve names listed]. The Fair was held in Dec. 1832."[18]

Various Annals tell that "Mother Catherine Spalding with three other Sisters . . . joined their exertions with the ladies to effect the good work, and also agreed . . . they would endeavor to support [the orphans] without drawing from the proceeds of the

Fair, which they succeeded to do."[19] The proceeds were intended for the erection of a house; Catherine walked the city to beg the support.

One event chiefly increased the numbers of orphans and Catherine's urgency in providing for them: the epidemic of cholera that scourged Louisville in 1832. The dates of the orphanage story, when matched with those of the epidemic as recorded in the *Louisville Public Advertiser,* indicate strongly that Catherine, the Sisters, and the local women were racing to keep ahead of disaster. They were planning a fair and a building at the same time that cholera was approaching and even while they were nursing the sick in the face of extreme social and personal upheaval, public fear, and risk to themselves. Contemporary knowledge of the true nature of cholera enables an accurate reading of the challenge to Catherine and the Sisters and the selfless courage with which they met it.[20]

Cholera invaded Europe in 1817. In 1832, it became a pandemic. In February 1832, the *Advertiser* provided a politely worded but gruesomely detailed description of the disease's effects: an "effluvium" with a "peculiar earthly odor," "inexpressible anxiety," "intolerable weight and anguish," and pains unto "agony." Recommended preventive measures (mostly diet, with no mention of filthy environment) bear witness both to the medical ignorance of the time and to the vulnerability of the poor and the homeless, those whom Catherine and her band would be called to nurse. The Sisters' challenge lay in the paper's central warning: avoid contact with the "effluvium," and do not get near enough to "inhale" it. Do not nurse the sick when fatigued or hungry, and do not let imagination dwell on the disease or the dread of it.[21]

Public dread, however, grew into panic as 1832 went on and cholera spread from Canada to cities of the East Coast. Louisville's editor demanded, "Is our city in a condition to encounter the pestilence? Was there ever more filth in our streets?"[22] The city braced itself for impending, inevitable catastrophe. In such an atmosphere Catherine, the Sisters, and the ladies of Louisville planned the first orphans' fair. One senses a determined preparation to deal with the results of the plague, since they had no hope of prevention.

By autumn, the general contagion and filth, contaminated food, and river water had done their work; the menace approached. Successive newspaper reports read like a rising clamor of denial, medical discussion, and death.[23] On October 13, cholera was reported in the city; soon the average number of deaths was ten per day.

Catherine would later remind the mayor what happened next: "At that gloomy period . . . nurses for the sick poor could not be obtained on any terms." Then Father Abell, "in the name of the Society, of which I have the honor to be a member, proffered the *gratuitous* services of as many of our Sisters as might be necessary . . . requiring merely that their expenses should be paid." Who first suggested that the Sisters be nurses is unknown, but Abell could not have offered their service to the Board of Health without consulting Catherine. She would not have agreed without consulting the Sisters and accepting only volunteers. Neither the offer nor acceptance was delayed. Only four days after the first announced cases, the Board solicited the services of the Sisters and agreed to pay traveling expenses, board, and lodging for any who came from Nazareth.[24]

The Council met on October 17 and agreed to send Sisters Margaret and Hilaria Bamber, Martha Drury, and Martina Beaven to join the Sisters already at Presentation.[25] A little drama is in the names. Clare Gardiner, Mother Frances's sister, was one of Catherine's early companions and friends. Apollonia McGill and Martha Drury were among the seasoned members with special and irreplaceable competencies. Martina Beaven was their novitiate companion. The two Bambers were sisters, who had entered and made vows on the same day. They and Serena Carney were young, only two years professed. All knew their lives would be at risk, along with precious relationships and the community's future. It fell to Catherine, the senior member, to sustain her own and her companions' courage and to direct their activity even as she assuredly feared and prayed.

Catherine and the Sisters at Presentation would have known only the descriptions of cholera they had heard or read, enough to know that they were undertaking labor that was exhausting, revolting to the senses, draining to the emotions, and very, very dangerous. Catherine led them first to a service in St. Louis Church, conducted by Bishop Flaget and Father Abell.[26] The bishop invited them, "Come now, my children, offer yourselves to God." After silent prayer and an Act of Consecration, he directed them to an ancient expression of submission to divine will and devotion to a place of service, "Now kiss the floor." From the church the Sisters went with their bags of medical supplies to homes known to be severely stricken and least attended.

Doctors had prepared Catherine and the other Sisters for nursing. But the essential remedy of plentiful boiled water was superseded in common practice by drastic (and probably dangerous) internal medicines and painful external "frictions." Whether these measures did any good, Catherine and her Sisters were *there,* present in homes that friends and even relatives had deserted. By their presence they challenged the fearful avoidance of the neighborhoods and houses of those judged most susceptible and contagious: "the dirty, the immoral, and the poor." Certainly they offered spiritual assistance to the dying without echoing the too frequent public assertion that cholera was divine vengeance on the guilty. They were present to display courage and hope, to give loving comfort in pain, confusion, or bereavement—and to gather the orphans.

The Sisters continued nursing as the cholera raged on through November. On December 1, the *Advertiser* announced that the physicians of Louisville had proclaimed the city healthy. Unreliable statistics allowed dual impressions of the epidemic's severity in Louisville: it was scarcely felt, or scores of people had died. Perhaps your judgment depended on where you had been and what you had seen in those months. Catherine Spalding had seen much.

However many the deaths, they had certainly created more orphans. An image of Catherine during the epidemic created by "a bystander" has become a virtual icon of her: "She came up the street with a small child in one arm, a baby cradled in her apron and a toddler clinging to her skirt."[27] Presentation, closed as a school, was virtually converted into an orphanage. Catherine may have had to give more days to child care than to visiting the sick. Increase in orphans urged the need for the new building.

The NLBI Board quickly responded. In November 1832, with Catherine there to urge her case, Flaget put the question whether the Sisters of Charity should take charge of an asylum and whether NLBI should buy a house and lot. The members decided unanimously that "Sister Catherine Spalding should be authorized to purchase a lot for an orphan asylum"; NLBI would own it and pay for "that portion of the purchase money which is not paid by the contributions of the citizens."[28] The decision signals not only the sense of mission driving the Board but the confidence of the mostly male members in the business acumen of the woman not yet forty years old.

Citizens and Sisters held the first fair that December as soon as the danger was past. The proceeds were $1,150. With that money and that much interest in the Louisville community, Catherine purchased a lot on the south side of St. Louis Church and began construction in the spring of 1833. A second fair in autumn 1833 netted $1,000. Two more fairs and donations brought the total to $5,500.[29] Once again Catherine was building on small sums and huge faith in the Providence that would continue to supply an urgent need.

None of the Sister nurses in Louisville had died of cholera, and as 1833 began, Catherine could feel an immense relief and hope. Orphans there would be, in distressing numbers, but she could now hope to devote herself to their care, to be for them what the Elders had been for her and her siblings. In this, the community would join and support her.

But Catherine had not heard the last of cholera. In the first part of 1833, the disease attacked the Bardstown area with extreme severity. Because Nazareth was a full day's journey from Louisville and one did not leave a busy mission unattended, Catherine could not be directly involved in the struggle at Bardstown no matter how much she may have wished to be. But Nazareth was heavily involved, and the public wagons going to Louisville must have conveyed to her a regular burden of grim news: sick students and two dead; ten Sisters stricken, including Mother Frances, and three dead within five weeks; eight slaves stricken and four dead; Bishop Flaget held in the grip of "my lord cholera" for three days while a grief-stricken David absolved and consoled him. The crisis passed. Flaget and others lived. But at the end of the epidemic, Catherine would hear that enrollment at the academy was down to thirty, and the demise of the school itself was predicted.[30]

Of all the dire news, none could have been more grievous to Catherine than the deaths of the three Sister nurses: June 23, Patricia Bamber, younger sister of the two nursing in Louisville; July 27, Joanna Lewis, Treasurer and only music teacher in the school; July 31, very young Generose Buckman, whose death was totally unforeseen and extremely rapid. If the remembered stories of their courageous and spiritual dying hours were relayed to Catherine, her sorrow would contend mightily with inspiration. But she must have grieved keenly her helplessness to be with and support her Sisters.

Probably grief as well as a sense of justice and dignity prompted one of Catherine's sharpest and best-known letters. In early 1834, she learned of an accusation, "from one of the pulpits of the city," that the Sisters in Louisville were mercenaries, that they had been paid not for their "expenses" in nursing cholera but for their "services." The preacher had cited the city books as evidence. Catherine reacted strongly to this public charge and wrote a stinging letter "To the Mayor and Council of the City of Louisville." She first reminded these "Gentlemen" of the circumstances of the cholera, of Abell's offer of "the *gratuitous* services of as many of our Sisters as might be necessary in the then existing distress," and of the "order from your honorable board, inviting the Sisters." At the time of payment, she said, "I had the mortification to remark, that, instead of saying: the *expenses* of the Sisters of Charity the word *Services* was substituted. I immediately remonstrated against it; & even mentioned the circumstances to the Mayor & another Gentleman of the Council." She had been satisfied by their assurance of a correction. Now she ironically begged them to "pardon the liberty I take in refunding you the amt paid [seventy-five dollars]. . . . Well convinced, that our community, for whom I have acted in this case would far prefer incurring the expense themselves rather than submit to so unjust an odium." She closed with what may be called her manifesto: "Gentlemen, be pleased to understand that we are not hirelings. & if we are, in practice, the Servants of the poor, the Sick & the Orphan; we are *voluntarily* so; But we look for our *reward* in another & a better World."[31] The mayor apologized, returned the money, and ordered the correction.

Catherine wrote this letter just when the new orphanage was being completed, and seventy-five dollars was a small fortune. Grief, anger, and weariness notwithstanding, she had been carrying on the daily care of the orphans in Louisville and the supervision of the building in progress. It had "moderately large rooms, intended for study, work rooms, and dormitories, and refectory, with smaller rooms intended for the use of the sisters." In February 1834, Catherine, several Sisters, and seventeen to twenty-five orphans moved in.[32] Until that date, all had been packed into the "six-room cottage" that was Presentation's convent.

The number of orphans kept increasing. Early Annals said that "no one with sufficient claim upon [the Sisters'] charity was ever refused. Like their Holy Founder [St. Vincent de Paul], they received the orphans and then looked about for the means of support."[33] For a woman like Catherine, feeding this family was probably an energizing challenge to the best of her physical, emotional, and spiritual capacities. She would have to beg, but she knew how to meet people, how to appeal to their better impulses. And her heart was in her requests.

The children needed more than physical basics. They were to be taught academic basics and the skills and habits that would eventually make them self-sustaining. They needed to feel themselves again part of a family, with the mutuality that entailed. Catherine, collaborating with her community, established the pattern of studies; household duties in the kitchen, dining room, and laundry; sewing and knitting; and play. The handiwork of both Sisters and children was offered for sale in a glass case in the parlor. Some was done on consignment for local stores and families.[34]

While Catherine certainly had the enthusiastic support of the Sisters with her in Louisville, it seems that after the first permission to build, the Council at Nazareth could offer very little other help. One reason, surely, was the aftermath of the cholera there; all energies and resources were needed to restore and sustain the school and its environs. Though Catherine surely understood that necessity, it seems that in her efforts to establish the new work at the orphanage, she felt a degree of emotional isolation. Later she would promise her successor there "a heart that will know how to sympathize with you in any difficulty; *which comfort I never had in all that I had to encounter in establishing that house*" (emphasis added).[35] As usual with Catherine, a touch of self-pity was countered quickly with a note of praise of God, acceptance of divine will, and confidence in divine care.

One help Nazareth did give was in the form of several servants from Nazareth. Even slave help, ironically, was not "free" to Catherine. The Council Minutes acknowledged receipt of $700 from Catherine, "purchase money for two Negro girls." One apparent "gift" was a man named Luke. He was evidently showing restlessness at family separation, or perhaps others wanted to purchase him—or both. At the same meeting, the Council resolved that he not be sold but "continue the property of Nazareth" and "remain at the Orphan Asylum in Louisville or any other house" not more than two days' journey from his wife, provided his future conduct should not require a change in the resolution. Only the Council could change it, and none should without "the strongest and most urgent motives."[36]

Cholera recovery was not the only reason the Nazareth Council could not take full interest in Catherine's enterprise. Changes in community leadership, followed by great turmoil, had occurred, and it is impossible to suppose that Catherine did not know what was going on, did not feel it deeply and personally. The facts of this story are hard to specify, but they are enough that the threat to the community and school cannot be denied or underestimated.[37] Since she remained a trustee of the NLBI Board, Catherine was attending meetings where she met and conversed with Angela Spink, Frances Gardiner, and Bishop David. They certainly informed her of and even discussed the conflict in the community. Some official notices had to be sent to branch houses, and private letters surely got onto the wagons to Louisville.

Catherine was undoubtedly informed that in early 1832 a storm had arisen around Sister Ellen O'Connell. Bishop David believed she had excessive influence on Mother Angela Spink, who, knowing her own limits, did depend heavily on Ellen's direction of the school. Some younger Sisters thought Ellen too demanding in her teacher training and had reported to Bishop David their versions of Ellen's remarks and humor. Incensed, David intended to dismiss her from the community. Catherine surely heard about most, if not all, of the ensuing events: that Ellen had pleaded for her vocation and vows; that, when David backed off dismissal, he still insisted, with concurrence of the Council, that she leave Nazareth; and that Angela then insisted on resigning from her office, saying she would not renew her own vows unless allowed to do so. Official notice had to be sent that Frances Gardiner, Assistant Mother, had been appointed to replace Angela until an August election.

Catherine also must have heard that both Ellen and Angela had been sent to White River, Indiana, with Barbara Spalding as superior, to begin again a hardship mission in a wilderness. What must she have thought and felt? Ellen could have been with her, been again her companion, helped her develop Presentation to the level achieved at Nazareth. But Ellen, given a choice of Louisville or the new mission, and motivated by her vow of obedience, had refused to choose. The White River mission lasted only one year. Then Angela was sent back to St. Vincent's in Union County, and Ellen to Scott County. Catherine could hardly have been surprised or less than grieved to hear that the entire episode had split the community into camps.

These changes generated others of which Catherine had to be notified, formally or otherwise. Contention in the community swirled around Bishop David, now past seventy and in poor health. It finally compelled him to resign, first as confessor, then as ecclesiastical superior. His replacement was Rev. Ignatius Reynolds, whose tenure exacerbated the divisions and lasted only two years. (His replacement, most fortunately, was Rev. Joseph Haseltine, a community friend of long tenure.) In late 1833, David withdrew from Nazareth altogether and took up residence in Bardstown, visiting Nazareth only rarely and briefly. And in the course of 1833 and 1834, eleven professed Sisters left the community, about a sixth of the congregation at the time. Many, probably most, of these departures were related to the conflict and discontent. They included Barbara Spalding, who had been appointed first to Catherine's post in Louisville and then to White River as superior.

What did Catherine, this woman of large heart and fidelity, feel for Ellen and Angela, her two early companions, neither of them young, both surely wounded by a sense of rejection and injustice? What did she think of Bishop David's judgment and decisions? What of the Council members who concurred with them by their votes? What of the young gossipers? "The tongue of a third person has cast out valiant women and deprived them of their labors" (Sir 28:15); Catherine knew the fact if not the scriptural verse. What did she think of the "solution" of Reynolds's appointment and David's "exile"? What of the Sisters who left? It is impossible to believe Catherine did not suffer confusion, some anger, deep disappointment, frustration, sorrow, and fear for the future of the community. But from her distance, and without a position on the community Council, she was helpless to remedy anything.

Not all the news from Nazareth was bad. Fourteen women entered during the most troubled years, 1832–1835, and eight of them made vows. Among these was one whom Catherine was called upon to help, and with whom she would have a unique relationship of mutual joys and sorrows—Ann Ross.

The two women met when Ann arrived at the door of Presentation in August 1832, en route to Nazareth, in need of a night's shelter between the boat from Cincinnati and the stage to Bardstown. Daughter of a Methodist minister, a convert despite his furious opposition, Ann was running from home to enter the community. It is not clear that she was expected at Nazareth, and Catherine seems not to have made any particular inquiries about her status. She sent her on, and Ann was accepted in the novitiate. She received the habit in February 1833 as Sister Xavier.[38]

Sometime after that, Ann arrived at Catherine's door again, this time in maximum distress. Her outraged parents had come to Nazareth to reclaim her.[39] Mother Frances had taken her in tears to Bishop Flaget, who sadly told her she was underage and would have to go with them. At the Louisville hotel, however, in a brief absence of her father, Ann had prevailed on her mother not to interfere with her happiness. With her mother's reluctant consent, she ran back to Catherine for help to escape her father and return to Nazareth. Catherine, hearing the dramatic tale, may have felt the power of Providence leading this girl, shaping her for a significant future in the community. With the maternal consent to authorize her, Catherine sent her young Sister back to Nazareth, where Xavier completed her novitiate during the height of the troubles and made vows in March 1834. Catherine may have seen in Ann Ross a reflection of herself at twenty, may have recognized a kinship to her own intelligence, vibrancy, warmth, and passionate determination. In the years ahead, she would encounter these traits unmistakably in Xavier Ross.

Despite disease, death, and dissension, the work in Louisville had to go on, and it was Catherine's comfort and joy. The new orphanage was speedily filled to overflowing. Besides urban poverty and disease, Louisville's location on the river guaranteed a continuing need. Steamboats, sure carriers of infection, unloaded not only supplies but also children whose parents, immigrants or transients, had died on board. The daily paper reported steamboats run against the riverbanks or broken up by ice. Wrecks meant lost passengers and more orphans.[40]

Maternal death left fathers unable to care for both children and business; the children were entrusted to Catherine. One such child was a two-year-old whose father brought her to the orphanage before going to work in New Orleans, agreeing to pay one dollar a week. Seventeen weeks later, he sent twenty dollars "to be paid to Catherine, nun, for boarding my little girl in the nunnery." He asked that the remaining three dollars be spent on clothing for her for the winter, then closed with a plea, "Good Catherine, be so kind as to favor me with a line or two, letting me know how my poor child is, as I am very uneasy about her, and sorry for the loss of her poor mother. Your afflicted, humble servant, James McGloin." Not all parents were that responsible; the paper reported on one "father of two small children, unfortunately both very young, and girls," who had "absconded" from a debt of $1,275 and $300 bail. Catherine, child of a deserting father, had a heart and home wide open to such youngsters.[41]

The children kept coming to Mother Catherine, children of parents deceased, parents unknown, parents gone to other states. With or without connections, children were coming to St. Vincent's from other cities, counties, and countries, in numbers, needing every life resource. Some could not live long; some could be returned to relatives; but most would need to stay in Catherine's care throughout their childhood.[42]

Whether Catherine had not foreseen in 1832 the influx of orphans or had simply built for the emergency as best she could with all she had, in only two years the house on Fifth Street was too small. Trust in the action of Divine Providence was needed again. Divine humor provided a building previously intended for a tavern.

In May 1836, the NLBI Board authorized Catherine, Frances Gardiner, and Fathers Haseltine and Reynolds to inquire about "a certain House and lot in Louisville" and, "should they think it proper," to purchase it. The Council concurred in this Board vote, but the record indicates Catherine had to use some persuasion: "After considerable discussion, the community of Nazareth finally consented to purchase the house . . . then owned by James Marshall." There orphans could be "lodged and accommodated to the number of 50 provided means could be procured to support them." The house, unfinished when bought, was ready for occupancy on October 6, 1836. It had three stories, twelve rooms, and a large wing.[43]

The Marshall house was not the end of Catherine's persuasion. She and her collaborators offered plans that would risk resources but allow for play yards and a vegetable garden and expansion as needed. In October 1836, the Council sanctioned purchase of a lot adjoining Marshall's. They may have agreed to this more readily because the NLBI Board had previously appointed Father Haseltine, Catherine Spalding, and Frances Gardiner as a committee to negotiate the sale of the orphanage on Fifth Street. The diocese bought the property back in May 1837 for $9,000. A majority of the Board then authorized the committee to "close the bargain" for the Marshall house and lot for $7,500, also "two lots of Mr. Wenzel" for $3,030, and the land of the Preston heirs for $5,000.[44] Even with the profitable sale of the Fifth Street property, a total of $15,530 was to be invested in the new orphanage—very big money in 1837. Some fears must have arisen. How much persuasion, one wonders, did trustee Catherine exert to obtain that majority?

Catherine's head and heart may well have expanded in joy that day, in anticipation of years of possible service. A later map locates "St. Vincent Orphan Asylum—Jefferson above Wenzel" midblock of the southeast sector, with the railroad passing in front. The city directory of 1838 would list the asylum, with "Mother Catherine, Principal," as housing forty-two children, infant to fifteen; "the greater portion, however, are infants." In fact, about five hundred orphans would live in that house in Catherine's lifetime. The location on Jefferson and Wenzel would last until July 4, 1891.[45]

When Sisters Catherine, Xavier, Ruffine, and Clementia moved to the new orphanage, four other Sisters moved to the "day school," and Sister Clare Gardiner was appointed its superior. Presentation was also expanding, and Catherine, as trustee of NLBI, was charged with meeting its need for space. As if one house and three lots to buy and one of each to sell were not enough work and worry for one woman, in September 1836 Catherine was singly "appointed with authority" to negotiate the purchase of a house and lot "belonging to P. Macey [Maxcy]" for $5,000, payable in four years without interest. This was the brick house north of St. Louis Church that grew piecemeal into the second Presentation.[46] By the time (1850) the church with its basement classrooms gave way to a cathedral and the frame house became only a foundation hidden beneath it, Catherine saw the Sisters and students lodged in solid buildings.

Catherine's views of possible service in the converted tavern did not stop with the orphans. Care of the sick poor—the first charge of St. Vincent de Paul to the first Daughters of Charity— was her other great desire. Now it could be fulfilled. Orphans were not yet numerous enough to need the large wing on the house. The city's sick did need nursing with real skill and loving care. Some sick would be financially well-off; what they could afford to pay would support the sick poor and the orphans. Catherine had the extensive wing fitted up for two hospital wards sufficient for twenty to thirty patients, and the Council appointed Sisters Appolonia McGill and Hilaria Bamber to "the Infirmary."[47]

Catherine was superintendent of both ministries under the one roof, but here as at Nazareth, she had the wisdom to rely on one more knowledgeable than herself. The Sisters serving as nurses were directed by Sister Appolonia McGill, veteran of the cholera in both Louisville and Bardstown. For many years, she would head the infirmary and be a valued colleague to the city's doctors. Her "great resources in expedients" when means were small, her strength and skill, would in time make her, like Catherine, a household word in Louisville. She was also a valued friend and nurse to Catherine, who was already beginning to have the illnesses that would wear down her strength but not her will to work and pray.[48]

Like all Catherine's enterprises, St. Vincent Orphanage and Infirmary was a collaborative venture, not only with her Sisters but with various laity, Catholic and non-Catholic, in private and public life. Some names appear often in Catherine's story: James Rudd, John D. Colmesnil, Patrick Maxcy, John Carroll, Zachariah Edelin, James McGillycuddy, James Guthrie. Among the men were trustees of St. Louis Church, city councilmen, wealthy businessmen. They sold land and buildings to Catherine, built the first orphanage, and supported it by donations. Their wives were the "Ladies Managers" of the fairs; their daughters went to Presentation or Nazareth.[49]

The men could offer legal counsel, political help, and send supplies or money; their wives and sisters tried organized assistance, with mixed results. As early as 1833, the women proposed to incorporate, to own the asylum and manage the finances. Catherine turned for advice to her experienced Vincentian friend, Bishop Rosati of St. Louis. He counseled that the orphanage should remain under Nazareth's corporation and the management of the more experienced Sisters. Yet he encouraged the women's continued fund-raising and other support. They formed the Catholic Orphan Society and held several more fairs. At least one failed and added to Catherine's debt, but over many years, these women's efforts were a financial mainstay of St. Vincent's, and the women were Catherine's steady and valued friends.[50]

When the 1836 orphanage was established, Catherine collaborated with the Ladies Managers of the Orphan Society on its purchase and future. In May 1838, the NLBI Board passed a long statement of multiple whereases and resolutions. The document acknowledged the financial involvements of the Ladies Managers in the two orphanages and bound the trustees, the ladies, and the Nazareth Council in regard to future locations, improvements, and expenses. The superior of the orphan asylum was "directed to act accordingly."[51] One distinctly senses the tension about who really owned the orphanage property and who was to decide and finance its future. One also senses the wisdom born of experience in Catherine Spalding, that superior who could make friends and collaborators for her community and its ministries yet maintain, by all needed and legal means, their independence.

The women did continue active support, and Catherine welcomed the involvement of such women as Rosalie Mallon Smith, wife of a physician, who visited the orphanage several times a month, helped in the children's studies, conferred with Catherine about needs, and donated. In her will she left a gift for the start of an endowment.[52]

Past connections also helped at times. A long, chatty letter to Catherine Spalding from Catherine Frazer, probably a former Nazareth student, is a clue to Catherine's ongoing relationships with her women supporters. Mrs. Frazer had left a bookcase and secretary in Louisville and did not hesitate to ask Catherine "in [her] leisure hours" to select from the bookcase books useful to Mrs. Frazer's children and send them to a relative in the city to hold for her. She inserts news and many affectionate greetings, then offers the bookcase and secretary as "a debt of truest gratitude." Catherine is to contact Mrs. Frazer's lawyer to obtain the "few dollars [that] might be of service." Catherine's friendship, affection, and patience were genuine but not untried.[53]

A more surprising donation bears witness to Catherine's continued relationships with her cousins in Maryland. She had written anxiously for news of Uncle Hilary's family. B. R. Spalding at

Pleasant Hill wrote back to his "dear Cousin." He supplies ample details of several family branches and asks prayers for his seriously ill brother John. He then says John had written her, giving her permission "to draw on us and our mutual friend Mrs. Elder" for assistance for the orphans she is bringing up in her "universal benevolence and charity." He sends best wishes and a promise of "most ardent cooperation" as long as they are able.[54]

Every few dollars helped, and Catherine was ever grateful to those who gave. By late summer 1838, her life and ministry seemed to be most desirably "in place." She was "Mumsie" to her "Penn baby" and several dozen other children to whom her heart went out constantly in concerned and lasting love. For their support, she was building donor relationships that were both reliable and personal. Her heart was at home in St. Vincent Orphanage and Infirmary.

But Catherine was about to be uprooted once more. Mother Frances's term of office (seven years because of the resignation of Angela) was ending. In April and May 1838, David expressed in letters his sense of needed reform at Nazareth and his hope for it if the Mother to be elected "be such as I wish." On August 23, he reported that Catherine had been elected on August 14, "according to my wishes"[55]—his wishes, definitely not hers. But Catherine was true to herself. At all cost to her heart and will, she would give what the community needed and asked.

Six

Mother and Administrator

1838–1841

I came back from Louisville to take again a burden that I little suited and less desired. My heart clung to the orphans and sick I had left." So began Catherine Spalding's only known attempt to keep a journal, a page or less in each of three successive Augusts.[1] She could not but begin with what was keenest and truest in her feelings, the pain of separation from her mission to the neediest. She underrated, however, her suitability for the office. Probably no one else in the community of sixty-two members could have so effectively continued the communal healing recently begun and still needed, nor dealt so patiently and firmly with the demands of day-to-day administration required to keep the school solvent and growing.

She began her reconciling role immediately after the election on August 14 by dining with Bishop David in Bardstown and inviting him to visit Nazareth after the coming retreat. He reported this invitation with satisfaction to Sister Elizabeth Suttle in a letter written on the same day the Council was appointing Catherine's sister, Ann Spalding, to replace her as superior at the orphan asylum.[2] Catherine herself, however, may not have been able to attend that meeting and certainly could not carry out the invitation.

David's letter adds an alarmed postscript revealing the additional burden that had struck Catherine: "And for a new trial, Mother Catherine is very sick. I anxiously await news from Nazareth; what a loss if she were to die. Pray, pray, pray." Catherine's journal page attests that his fears were not groundless. She says she "was attacked by a most violent form of congestive fever which came very near terminating my imperfect life." The fever, she says, "prevailed throughout the country." In fact, two Sisters did die of it. Catherine must have wondered if congestive fever was about to wreak the havoc of the cholera and this time include her among the victims. She hovered several days between life and death, evoking Masses, novenas, and intense prayers of Sisters and orphans, who wanted daily news of her.[3]

"Congestive fever" was the nineteenth-century term for malaria, still common in the southern United States. Among the variant "malarial fevers," doctors recognized common symptoms: raging temperature, cold chills, and painful, laborious breathing. Quinine was sometimes combined with mercury in a treatment by "salivation." The "superabundant secretion of saliva" thus caused was "accompanied by a coppery taste in the mouth, by swelling of the gums, and sometimes by looseness of the teeth." Catherine was "deeply salivated." This was thought to be the cause of her recovery, but it may have done damage, as excessive salivation is a symptom of mercury poisoning. And it may not have been the only treatment of the era attempted.[4]

In mid-September David wrote that Catherine was "out of danger, but still very sick from the salivation." In December he could say that she "enjoys now very good health." His cheer was premature; in April, Catherine's chills and fever recurred.[5] Eight full months passed before all was over. This long illness, the drastic treatment, and the suffering entailed in both may well account for the recurrent headaches and general decline in health that her letters begin to note.

Once Catherine was well, she renewed her efforts for the reconciliation of Bishop David with the community at Nazareth. He reports visits there in letters that become increasingly cheerful and hopeful. In late autumn 1838, he notes that "Nazareth goes on well. 130-odd boarders. Satan has been trying to interrupt the good work, but I hope all his attempts shall be defeated." He says sadly that the Sisters no longer seek his spiritual advice but admits that his "infirm old head" is little able to give direction, that he is confined to the fireside by asthma and back pains. By spring, Catherine had asked him to give instructions at Nazareth to the novices, then to the whole community, and finally, to preach at Sunday Mass. In November, he reports visiting Nazareth "from time to time" and finding "great peace and union" among the Sisters; the community, he says, "gives me much satisfaction."[6]

The better feelings, however, did not lead Catherine to bring David back to reside at Nazareth or to send an SCN to care for him in Bardstown. He, of course, may not have wanted either change just then. She may have believed that Flaget, who was in Europe, would want to find David in their shared residence. She might well have hesitated to intervene there and try to replace his caregiver, a competent and devoted Sister of Loretto. Most of all, she may have felt that a quick return could revive old tensions, that a gradual pace was best for restoring old affections without implying or encouraging a restoration of old authority. In time she would bring Bishop David home for good. Now she simply extended more and more invitations to Nazareth.

In effecting these visits and the reconciliation with the community, Catherine certainly had the approbation and encouragement of the priest who now held Bishop David's former position as Nazareth's ecclesiastical superior, Father Joseph Haseltine. This priest was of New England Puritan stock, a convert during his residence in Canada, a volunteer for the Kentucky mission. He was David's former student in philosophy, as well as his friend and companion in his Bardstown solitude. Haseltine was appointed to Nazareth very soon after his ordination in 1835. He is variously described as a "perfect gentleman, learned theologian, and pious priest," a "model of punctuality, gentleness and piety," a man of system and interest in details, of "elegant appearance and courtly manner," of "liberal and comprehensive views, sound judgment and great administrative abilities." As a lay manager of St. Joseph College, Haseltine had formerly collected thousands of dollars owed to the college. He would exert himself with equal vigor for Nazareth. During Catherine's last two terms in office, he was her constant and most competent collaborator in all sorts of business, as well as spiritual adviser to her and the Sisters, chaplain of the school, and a beloved friend to all groups.[7]

Community life and relationships could be Catherine's first concern as she resumed office because, despite all traumas of the 1830s, the school had survived, even thrived under Mother Frances's leadership and Columba Carroll's academic direction. An 1834 visitor had written praise of the location, buildings, and curriculum. Rev. George Elder of St. Joseph College had testified in 1836 to examinations that revealed judgment prevailing over memorization of textbooks. Parents wrote of their "implicit confidence" and sent "compliments to the Mother Superior and Sister Columba."[8] Catherine had no reason to worry or need to reform the quality of the education offered.

Compliments, however, had flowed more readily than cash. In May 1838, Catherine had been present at an NLBI meeting at which the Board directed the "Superior and Mother of Nazareth" to make "every exertion" to collect debts and to make no expenses more than "necessary for the support and comfort of the family." The Treasurer was instructed "to exhibit a statement of the affairs of the house" on August 1.[9] Catherine probably recognized an effort to put finances in order before the coming election and knew that a burden might fall on her. When it fell, she was not, fortunately, without support in the decisions and actions that lay before her. She had her Council and community treasurers. She had the acumen and experience of Father Haseltine, as well as her own. And she had her spirit and habit of collaboration.

Illness, death, and debts notwithstanding, school opened on the first Monday of September 1838. Before the end of the year, Catherine notes in her journal, more than 160 pupils had enrolled. In November, the Board approved expenditure of $10,000 to 12,000 for a new building as soon as the superior and Council thought it prudent to begin it. Father Haseltine, Catherine Spalding, and any one other person they chose were to decide the plans. A sense of optimism was evidently pervading the campus. Prudent Catherine, however, noted the prematurity of a building project when so many small improvements and repairs were needed besides the payment of debts. She would begin no new building until the 1850s.[10]

The first necessary improvement was not space for the living but for the number of the dead. As soon as Catherine was able to attend a meeting, the Council decided that the cemetery be enlarged, a "convenient way be made to go to it," and small wooden crosses be replaced by inexpensive tombstones with name, age, and date of death.[11]

Irregular tuition payments meant that the truly indispensable factor in Nazareth's "support and comfort" was the farm. Apparently management had not been good during Catherine's interval in Louisville. Perhaps it could not have been with all the illness at Nazareth. In 1840 Catherine notes in her journal:

> The farm from neglect or frequent change of overseers, had become a mere wreck, and was rather an expense than profit to the community, the stock etc. being reduced to almost nothing, which determined the Council to make the first expenses in adding to, and making large improvements on the farm, the garden, yards, etc., followed by building a good flour mill, raising their own stock beeves, etc, and a good dairy; all of which, with the blessing of God, succeeded well, and the community enjoyed the advantage of having their flour and meal made at home and of a better quality than they had generally purchased, besides having feed for their milk-cows, and always an abundant supply of milk for the school and community daily, and also made a good portion of their butter, while they killed their own beef and other fresh meat.[12]

Catherine's enthusiasm and pleasure in these improvements outran her sentence structures. Collaborator that she was, she credits the Council for the wise decisions and changes. It is evident, however, that she must have led in their making.

The same journal entry notes another change that requires all the understanding history can provide. After noting the purchase of a small adjoining farm, Catherine adds: "We also, in the course of the year, bought five negro men; two women; two girls, and two boys. This year the price of property was very high throughout the country; of course we paid high prices for all they bought; the prices of hire were also very high; and the Council decided it was better to buy servants for the farm etc., than pay so much for hire and then often get bad ones."[13] This is the first explicit evidence of direct purchase of slaves for Nazareth with Catherine's approval. The early annalist cites the passage as evidence of Catherine's "thorough practical mind and wise management,"[14] and that is surely all Catherine intended it to mean—the record of a financial transaction to meet a definite need. The passage, however, opens the way to the necessary consideration of Catherine's attitudes and role regarding the system of slavery and the enslaved individuals whose labor sustained the mission at Nazareth under her leadership. The revelatory data are found in this journal entry, her letters, Council Minutes, the Kentucky Catholic culture in which she lived, and the leaders who influenced any major decisions she might make about Nazareth's property, human or other.

The journal compels a forthright analysis of the cultural assumptions and responses behind what it says—and omits. Five men, two women, two girls, two boys—they have no names. The list gives no hint as to whether any of them were related, bought as family units—or purchased out of such units. The children are assigned no ages, no indication of continuity or disruption in the presence of their parents. Nor does the entry indicate how these people were purchased, privately from someone who knew them, or at public auction by an overseer, with or without instructions to consider their family relations. Despite the euphemism "servant" commonly used by Catholic slaveholders, these eleven people are "property"; the cited concern in the purchase is "price." And the decisive factor is that workers owned are "better," that is, can be trained to the needs and style of the owners. Those on temporary hire may be already "bad," that is, resistant in some way to their forced labor. No awareness of the cause of "badness" is discernible. In the classic phrase of the commodity market, it is better to buy than rent. "We bought. . . . we paid. . . . The Council decided. . . ." Catherine's separate agency, her own voice and preferred action, are not indicated. Yet no Council decisions in her terms of office were made without her participation, almost certainly never over her objection. The paragraph is the impersonal record of an administrative transaction with which she concurred.

The journal, in fairness, must be placed beside Catherine's personal letters. None of these was written to engage the recipient in a moral discussion of slavery, so no such reflection can be expected. But there are many references to individual slaves, and these reveal that Catherine displayed no qualms about owning human persons yet did display much active concern for the general well-being and good feeling of those people, "the servants."

The first mention of a slave is in 1840, ironically in manumission papers for "our negro man" Luke. This was the man "given" by Nazareth to the Louisville orphanage so he could help the Sisters and also be in proximity to his wife. Whether to reward Luke's conduct or to enable his family connection or for some other cause, two years after her return to office at Nazareth, August 15, 1840, Catherine set Luke free.[15]

Nine of eleven other letters also mention individuals by name. The tone is kind, even affectionate; the content concerns their health, maternity, or religious experiences more than their work.[16] But no letters suggest the least reservation about the fact of their servitude. Luke's free papers were to be written by a lawyer over the signatures of Father Haseltine and Mother Catherine because they did "not know the form of such an instrument"; its use was exceptional. No letter mentions either abolition or justification of slavery. If this demonstrably humane and loving woman ever had questions about the system of human bondage and the dependence of her mission on it, they are not to be found in the only documents remaining from her own hand.

Catherine's letters, however, do run counter to the impersonal tone of the journal entry. She sends greetings to or news of particular individuals: Till, whose "fine boy George Washington is dead"; "poor old Aunt Winny," who has died and whose last illness Catherine evidently attended; Uncle Solomon, who is ill; Martha, who must be a good girl; Emily, Ed, and Teresa, who have made their First Communions; Jane, Matilda, and Emily, who have had babies; "big Louise," to whom Catherine will bring "something nice"; "little Louise," who must help more in the kitchen; and

Isaac Bell or Ike, who has been sent to "live with" William Keely, whose "friends feel so much interest in his well-doing," to whom she sends "best wishes and kind remembrance."[17] In no letters does Catherine ever employ demeaning racial terms (not always true in other SCN letters of that time). No letters speak of physical punishment of a slave or of anyone running away. In a surrounding culture that demeaned and all too regularly abused its enslaved population, Catherine displays an atypical and genuine kindness and concern. Yet her tone remains that of both "mother" and "mistress" of servants.

The practical management of the "servants" at Nazareth under Catherine's leadership reflects this mother-and-mistress role. Slaves were viewed much like children, to be cared for materially and spiritually, assigned tasks, supervised, and then trusted, rewarded, or penalized according to performance. This was the norm in the surrounding Catholic culture. At Nazareth the observance was, if not dignifying, at least less demeaning and punitive. The Sisters could not be expected to understand the separate and self-dignifying, self-protecting culture that enslaved people developed within their own community.

The moral distinction, for instance, between "stealing" (from another slave) and "taking" (what was not otherwise paid for their labor) clearly escaped the owners at Nazareth concerned about disappearances. During Catherine's term, the Council mandated that clothes be counted before being distributed to the washwomen and counted again when each returned them to the wardrobe; that Sisters in charge of dormitories, refectories, and infirmaries keep counts and lists of all items and, in case of deficiency, notify the Mother Superior "that she may take her measures accordingly." The Mother was further mandated "from time to time, at least every six months in company with at least one other Sister," to "examine the Rooms, chests, boxes, etc. of all the blacks of Nazareth."[18] If theft was ever uncovered, no evidence exists that Mother Catherine's "measures" were ever physical or verbal abuse. Since examination of the students' and novices' quarters and trunks was accepted practice well into the twentieth century, the remarkable fact may be that the "servants" had even some privacy of rooms, chests, and boxes.

No evidence exists that slaves or their children were educated for literacy or beyond. Like most Catholics of her day and time, Catherine Spalding viewed education as important for one's position in this world, not as a value in itself or a right belonging to one's humanity. She had been taught to focus on life hereafter and on the sacraments that guaranteed access to it. Recognition of the slaves' full humanity is implied in the provision, strictly observed, of religious instruction and sacraments, matrimony in particular. Catherine and other Sisters were sponsors for baptisms and prepared children for First Communion. Marriage ceremonies were performed by the priest. One Sister reports to another that "great preparations" were going on for a wedding; another invites her to a christening at Christmas, to enjoy the "frolic" and plum cake. Catherine's letters note slaves' participation in various religious ceremonies; "all the blacks" participated in a jubilee and "edified us by their pious attention."[19]

Some of the messages in Catherine's letters were intended to give news of a relative to a slave who had been sent with Sisters to one of the branch missions. This practice, an ironic parallel to the voluntary obedience of the Sisters, though it did not separate spouses, did sometimes separate parents and children. Three such "changes in mission" were made just after Catherine's term ended in 1844: Agnes from Union County to Nazareth, Isabel from Lexington to Nashville, and Emily from Nazareth to the orphanage with Mother Catherine.[20]

A few slaves were hired out, especially in Catherine's last term when their number would have been greater. Catherine probably transferred Isaac Bell to William Keely as compensation for the latter's services as architect of the 1850s buildings. In 1855, Edward Miles of New Hope, Kentucky, accepted Catherine's "boy" for a year at her price and asked her to send him on the horse provided. And some persons were sold or exchanged. Sale, however, was clearly not a common practice either with Catherine or with Mother Frances and was done with conditions, such as "to a Catholic who will engage not to send her down the River." The first recorded sale, in Catherine's administration, is of a woman to her husband's owner, "that they, the slaves, may not be separated." No reason is known for a more dubiously humane sale of a mother and son in Catherine's final term of office.[21]

A woman whose letters indicate a strong sense of justice and charity, Catherine Spalding was also a woman of her time, place, and religious culture. In that context, practical considerations would have great power to obscure intuitions of justice and compassion and to overcome objections to slavery, even if any had been offered. The farm needed field workers; in Nazareth's locale, white men tended their own farms or hired out as overseers. If Catherine ever had any secret qualms about slave labor, she would have felt constrained by the milieu, her circumstances, and her clerical leaders to take the workers she could get and incorporate them in some way into "the family." Yet her letters do not suggest that she viewed the "servant" portion of "the family" as on a par with the other members except in access to God's grace, love, and just judgment. In racial and social caste, the Sisters and clergy certainly assumed their superior status and, from it, their obligation to be benevolent.

Beyond practical necessity and reasoning, Catherine was surely influenced by the atmosphere of politics and religious theorizing around her. Controversy over slavery and abolition was raging in public discourse by the 1830s. If she was much aware of it, she would have heard only justifications of the system, with strictures only on its behavioral practice. Students and parents from the Deep South viewed slavery as necessary and abolition as unthinkable. Local newspapers, if she ever read or heard reports of them, condemned abolitionists as rabble-rousers. Louisville's *Catholic Advocate,* begun in 1836 and distributed in Bardstown, which she might well have read, was moderate in tone but no less defensive of slavery and no less opposed to abolition, which was considered the fruit of Protestant individualism. It quoted an opinion that slave states had more "religious liberality" and less "bigotry and narrow selfishness" than nonslave states.[22]

The immediate influences on Catherine's thought and action about slavery were the Catholic leaders of Kentucky and others she would have read or heard cited. It is a fact, appalling to contemporary Catholics, that no Catholic bishop except Purcell of

Cincinnati condemned slavery or advocated for abolition, and he not loudly until the Civil War.[23] The most learned and articulate, such as Kenrick in Philadelphia and England in Charleston, theologized, rationalized, lamented that slavery had ever begun, but saw no ready way to end it, and did not forbid it. They simply exhorted owners to treat slaves with fairness and kindness and to assure them all religious consolations, practices, and sacraments, including stable and sacramental marriage.[24] That was the norm Flaget, David, and their priests taught, that they practiced as owners of slaves and maintained at Nazareth Council meetings where slaves were discussed. Even Father Haseltine, for all his New England origin, saw no problem in owning his valet, Henry Haseltine. Catherine Spalding, Catholic woman of her times, could not follow leadership that was not there.

Catherine, of course, was demonstrably able to challenge episcopal authority when she was sure of a wrong or inadvisable practice. She simply did not see the radical injustice of slavery. Yet her manner of participation in it was generally better than that of her leaders and the general population. She may, in fact, have been somewhat ahead of the common attitude and practice of her time and place. Now one must ask, in justice, what a woman of her moral caliber would have thought, said, and done had she lived in a later century, with its theology of social justice, its communications, examples, and incentives. With that question, her twentieth-century Sisters have grappled in her name.[25]

Slaves indeed ate the hard crust that enabled Nazareth Academy to live and grow. But not even that economy could or was expected to alleviate the monetary struggle that was Catherine's portion throughout this term of office. On her return as Mother and administrator of the academy, she had found not only the wrecked farm and outstanding debts but also a full school of more than one hundred young women. By selecting the "common branches," or "Other," and such extras as French, music, or dancing, a parent could educate a daughter at Nazareth for about $300—or less—per year.[26] Parents appreciated this education; some of them viewed it as a gift—literally.

In 1839, Flaget noted with pleasure that "the richest and the most distinguished families in our regions eagerly entrust their children" to Catholic schools.[27] Some parents may have fit this description; more likely they were small planters or businesspeople trying to climb. If they were rich, they were not invariably responsible or ready to pay. Catherine deeply believed in the mission of solid education of young women and did not spare her energies to maintain and advance it. But to do so, she who loved to be with orphans had to give inordinate amounts of time to reading and writing letters or consulting with and directing agents, who were mostly seeking money for a just and overdue tuition.

All through this period, Catherine was reading the letters sent to her, her Sister treasurers, or Father Haseltine.[28] These letters record a sorry history of delayed or partial payments attributed to bad health, hard times and failed crops; credit given or merely assumed; estates not yet settled or executors retaining the money; bankruptcies; scarcity of ready money; or problems with the forms and banks of transfer.[29] In every mail, Catherine received apologies, thinly veiled demands, promises made but not kept, or simple, sheer resistance. To sample these letters is to know that Catherine's third term was not one of exciting expansion but of daily, tedious, even irritating efforts to maintain a mission. Only occasionally an excuse might offer some amusement, as when J. S. Silsbee wrote that the Democratic Convention in town had held meetings at night instead of attending his theater; he hoped that ten to twenty thousand Whigs coming next month would enable him to pay and that Catherine would not humiliate his daughter by dismissal.[30]

Some examples reveal the cultural gender expectations that impacted a school for women. A father in Mississippi could not make the requested "immediate payment" of his daughter's account because money was needed for the claims of St. Joseph College in Bardstown for her brother. A mother in Louisiana, awaiting her own remittance, could not borrow money "on any terms whatever." In 1843, a married alumna wrote Catherine that she was surprised to receive a bill because her mother had forbidden her to pay for herself and kept the bills. Her mother was now remarried and unlikely to pay, but Catherine should write her and let the daughter know the result.[31]

Collection of debts was a collaborative enterprise of Mother Catherine, Father Haseltine, and their agents in several cities. They seem to have divided tactics as well as labor. A pleasant letter from Catherine with a health and progress report and praise of his daughter brought a cordial reply and money from a father in New Orleans. At times she seems to have appealed through students' relatives. Father Haseltine and the agents used the rougher tactics, such as lawsuits. Still the excuses and delays went on and on: "in two weeks," "next month," "next summer." Yet somehow Catherine and Haseltine managed to keep the school solvent, to remit tuition deliberately for a parent "in difficulties," or to accept payments in such kind as "bagging and rope."[32]

Money was urgently needed to meet Nazareth's debts. Father Haseltine was often Catherine's mediator in dealing with creditors. One man instructed him to tell Mother Catherine he could not accept any more small payments; she might pay one note at a time but not less. Other demands were more serious. Mr. Wenzel, seller of the orphanage property, wrote asking for $3,000. Almost simultaneously, the Trustees of St. Louis Cathedral asked for a reduction in their debt to Nazareth for the Fifth Street property. Catherine, Council, and Board bargained shrewdly. The trustees could pay Wenzel's note and another for $1,000. Then the balance of their debt could be put into six yearly notes with interest. To justify this firm dealing, Haseltine explained that Nazareth was "really poor" from losses on the school, and the Sisters were suffering for lack of room: "They are obliged to make every shift possible to get a place; some sleep in the upper story of the washhouse, always comforting themselves with the hope of one day being able to make a convenient building for their accommodation."[33] None held that hope more strongly than Catherine, still uneasy in a better-than-common bed.

Mother Catherine not only was the lead voice on the Council and a member of the Board but essentially was in control of all the business Father Haseltine did. He contributed to decisions and wrote many letters, but he got the money from her. Letters cite payments from her to him of $1,020, $300, $845, and $200, all for notes due on Nazareth.[34] She knew her business, and she knew how to collaborate to get it done.

With the money Catherine did receive, she conducted her principal financial occupation, purchasing and paying. Francis McKay was Catherine's agent in the city. His letters to her in the 1840s cite shipment of students' trunks and boxes, and numerous purchases of food and supplies, from sugar to mackerel, nails to mops, stoves to "sundries." Catherine had to specify kinds of goods (a "description of the pipes") and decide values: should McKay buy a certain candle for $.25, since it never sold for $.16 or $.18? Should a mangle be repaired or a new one bought for less? He purchased and sent bills; she struggled to pay them.[35]

Besides all the ordinary business, Catherine and Haseltine together dealt with numerous "occasional" problems. One was contests with Sisters' siblings who maneuvered to deprive their sisters of their share in the family legacy and thus to prevent its eventually going to the community on the Sister's death. Haseltine wrote some biting or blunt letters to agents, lawyers, and brothers about justice.[36] As long as Nazareth was not cheated, Catherine and her collaborator may have found diversion in some of the requests and offers they received. A Mississippi editor wanted $84.93 for ads he had run for the academy; he explained at length his lack of authorization but hoped they would "contribute" twenty-five or thirty dollars. Mrs. Love was told "a mortgage on your land does not suit us" as payment for three years schooling of her daughter, who had "profited so little from our efforts" that more would be a waste of time and money. She would be sent home. A governess in a Mississippi home had claimed to be a former student of Nazareth and given Mother Catherine and Father Haseltine as references. She was now rumored to have been a New Orleans prostitute; information from Nazareth was urgently sought.[37] The variety of issues, at least, might offset Catherine's annoyance at the demands on her time and acumen.

Parents may have paid reluctantly, but some quite readily demanded for their daughters services well beyond the academic. The more sensible and courteous letters to "Miss Catherine Spalding,

Lady Superior" or "Mother Superior" show a reliance on her judgment mixed with very specific wishes about selection of studies, time to be spent on music and dancing, cultivation of virtue and religion, singing style and sitting posture, and visits to relatives or friends. Discipline was expected; one father requests Catherine to "be more strict even to chastisement if found necessary" (a means never known to be used). Further directions include receiving a shipment of bed and bedding and later shipping the bed back. The most frequent request is that a girl's clothes be purchased or made in Kentucky, "leaving it to the taste and judgment of Mother Catherine to select them." Few seem to have considered whether the "good Mother" had the time for all they required.[38]

Catherine, raised with the Elders, may have guarded her own thoughts about what constitutes a spoiled girl. One Mississippi parent admonished Catherine to curtail his daughter's purchases, as "many children sent from this country to school in Kentucky have imbibed expensive habits and run into useless extravagances." But another wrote detailed instructions "indispensable for [his daughter's] health and comfort": a fire in her room night and morning in winter, an agent to supply her needs, holiday visits to the agent's home, and a "more able" physician if she were sick. The agent would pay. One mother ordered that all necessary articles be gotten for her daughter, as "I would rather send for her home than have her want for anything or to be in the least uncomfortable or unhappy."[39] Catherine may have remembered her begging trips to meet the basic needs of impoverished and homeless children. She may also have thought of the Sisters sleeping uncomfortably above the washhouse.

Yet Catherine's loving-kindness for the students remains as legendary as that for orphans. The girls were far from home for one or several years, and letters from parents often indicate respect and gratitude for Catherine's motherly attentions to their daughters. Some later letters from students indicate how fondly and appreciatively they remembered her. One came from a student of this period whom Catherine had sponsored in Baptism. The style is ridiculously effusive and full of "poetic" images and diction to express her "glowing emotions of love and friendship" and her mem-

ories of Nazareth's "groves of the bee-haunted locust," the parlor
and chapel, and "'Mother's Room' where I listened to thy gentle
teachings" on religion. She recognizes that Mother will think her
"extravagant in my expressions." Catherine's own simplicity and
directness were known. Yet the girl has an obviously sincere and
deep love for the one who instructed and sponsored her.[40]

Not all Catherine's days were spent at a desk. She was in and
out of classrooms as she had been in Eliza Crozier's time and memory. She had to be in the parlor as primary hostess to greet guests
and new students, and out on the property as its primary overseer.
At Council meetings she presided over decisions about Sisters' acceptance (or refusal) for the stages of novitiate, profession of vows,
and assignments to missions. She attended the daily Mass and led
the community prayers, her chief support and refreshment "in the
burden of the day and the heat." She would seldom allow herself
to miss the community recreation periods. Her humor, affection,
and personal interest would have appeared there as spontaneously
as they do in her letters to Sisters (in the extant collection these
begin to appear during her third term).

Catherine could not always be at Nazareth. As Mother Superior,
she was responsible for promoting community and mission by visiting the branch houses. Just how often she was able to make the
trips, most of them several days by horse or wagon, cannot be
ascertained. At the time, the branches included four academies:
St. Vincent in Union County, St. Catherine in Lexington, Bethle-
hem in Bardstown, and Presentation in Louisville. At St. Joseph
College in Bardstown, Sisters maintained the wardrobe, infirmary,
kitchen, and refectory, and in Louisville the orphanage/infirmary
was a constant concern. Council minutes of these years suggest she
was not able to give the branch houses much financial assistance.
More often they got permission to purchase slaves or make physical improvements if they could raise the money themselves.[41] But
her presence and concern for the Sisters' total welfare were surely
a source of encouragement in their mission and especially in their
spiritual and communal lives.

No branch house could hold a more special place in Catherine's heart than the orphanage, but she could not give it more help than she had. In 1839, Sister Louisa Dorsey, then superior at the orphanage, sent a begging message by Sister Ambrosia Foy. From Nazareth, Catherine replied, "I laughed when she told me. I replied that you would have to do as I did, & turn about and get funds—(This you know was a mere joke), yet rest assured you will always find in me a heart that will know how to sympathize with you in any difficulty." She added one of her most self-revealing lines: "If your heart beats friendly toward my dear orphans, be assured it is a new claim you have on me & an additional tie full as strong as the one that unites us in the sacred bonds of religion." She enclosed ten dollars.[42]

Because the orphanage was so dependent on donations and collaborative assistance, Catherine's heart was not her only dictator of efforts to meet its special needs. She went frequently to see and advise with the Sisters there. In her absence and illness, some of the "Ladies Managers" had evidently attempted to turn collaboration into control. They made some resolutions that the Council rejected as "highly offensive and in every respect objectionable and insulting to the whole Society of the Sisters of Charity." The Council petitioned the coadjutor Bishop Chabrat, who was in charge during Flaget's absence in Europe, for "his interference that the peace of the Sisters and Orphan Asylum in Louisville may not in future be molested or troubled in the Management of said Asylum." Catherine went to the orphanage. Chabrat joined her there "to console, help, and direct" her.[43]

Whether the problems were financial or procedural, who was embroiled in them, and whether or not Chabrat exercised his own controlling style, Catherine was grateful enough to send him a warm letter of New Year's wishes. He replied with thanks and equal cordiality, wishing for "you and all under your care all kinds of good success and prosperity, but above all an increase of zeal and fervor in the discharge of your religious duties." If Catherine could win Chabrat's respect and maintain cordial working relations with him, she was perhaps unique in the diocese at that time.[44]

Still another concern for Catherine was the number of Sisters available for the growing ministries. The significant losses of the

1830s had been somewhat recouped by new and persevering members. But in these middle years of her term, both departures and deaths continued to strike at community and mission. Four professed Sisters left the community early in 1841. One was nearly twenty years professed, while the other three left together in what must have been an ominous instance. On February 13, 1841, Catherine and the Council judged it "expedient that Sisters Cornelia, Ambrosia, and Ignatia be sent from the City as soon as possible on account of the excitement they cause in the House." Records do not clarify the nature of the excitement that provoked such a speedy reaction. All three, however, left the community three days later. Cornelia had previously been the elected Treasurer. She left behind, ironically, a debt of $260.52 for clothing furnished her niece, a free boarder. For Catherine, the sting of her departure must have been especially sharp.[45]

The four departures in midterm were matched by five deaths. Catherine had special cause to grieve each one.[46] The first, in 1840, was Pulcheria Wathen, still a young teacher, seven-year sufferer from ruinous doses of calomel administered in the 1833 cholera. The last, within two months of 1842, were Mildred Stuart, pioneer of St. Thomas years, and Mary Catherine Cox, who made vows on her deathbed. Between them, in 1841, went Sophia Carroll, Columba's own sister, one of the era's all too numerous victims of consumption; she was thirty. Mildred Stuart's death would disrupt an old relationship, while the young deaths would challenge Catherine's sense of responsibility for the Sisters' well-being and her confidence in the future of the mission.

No news of death, however, could have been more wrenching to both Catherine and Columba than that which reached them one week before Christmas 1840. Ellen O'Connell, Catherine's friend, soul mate, and earliest support in the mission of education, had died suddenly in Lexington. The story transmitted was awesome enough to be preserved in its details. At her last recreation, Ellen, typical humorist and storyteller, was the source of lively enjoyment. As one burst of laughter subsided, she suddenly remarked, "See now we are all in great glee, I perhaps more than anyone; yet who knows but by tomorrow night, I may have received my death summons?" She became sick that night and died two days later, December 18.[47] One must imagine the mix of Catherine's emotions at this report: sheer personal grief; deep regret that she had never been able to bring Ellen home from her exile, as she must have hoped and intended to do; gratitude that she had permitted Columba Carroll to go to Lexington to visit her beloved teacher; appreciation, both awed and amused, of Ellen's blend of earthy wit and realism with prophetic spirituality; and a powerful sense of the gradual ending of the era of her pioneer companions and friends.

Even as Catherine mourned Ellen O'Connell, she anticipated the death that, more than any, would mark "the end of the beginning." Ever since Catherine's return to Nazareth, Bishop David's health had been declining. His last years had been spent in Bardstown in spiritual direction, writing and translating, and musical work. He wrote freely to Sister Elizabeth Suttle of his increased infirmity, of his affection for her and the pain of separation by distance, offset by expectation of eternal reunion in "a few days, or at most a few years." He does not mention Ellen O'Connell or leave a record of his feelings at her death in the exile to which he had sent her. Yet his letters all sound the theme of reunion of spiritual and cherished friends in a "society without interruption and without end," as well as his loving interest and inquiries for various Sisters. Age, illness, and prayer were healing the scars of the 1830s.[48]

In April 1841, David had a stroke, fell, and dislocated his shoulder. From then on, his mind and speech wandered between short prayers and the memories and desire expressed in "Nazareth," "dear daughters," and "home." Catherine heard of his condition while visiting branch houses. She hurried back, went to him, listened and wept, and promised to take him home. Next day, she sent ten servants in white trousers and black coats with a curtained litter to carry him to Nazareth. A crowd of Bardstonians followed. Sisters led by Catherine lined the Nazareth road. David was heard to say, "O thank God! I have come to die among my daughters!"

For eight more weeks, Sisters in relays of two cared for him.

On June 4, he reached eighty years. The next day Flaget gave him the last sacraments. On the morning of July 12, 1841, Catherine recognized the approaching end, dismissed classes, and gathered the Sisters to his bedside. In a final effort to bless them, Bishop David raised his hand, then dropped it in death.

Catherine notified the branch houses immediately, using the windowsill of David's room as an improvised desk. We cannot know whether she felt a fresh access of sorrow and self-questioning that only his last weeks were or could be at Nazareth, or perhaps a depth of consolation that he had died there, had experienced at last the Sisters' full love in their attentive care and presence. For two days Sisters kept vigil in a draped church. Then Flaget, two other bishops, clergy, community, and laity performed the funeral rites and laid Nazareth's founder in its cemetery. The reconciliation was complete.

Any expressions of Catherine's grief in conversation or letters have been lost. One indicator remains. After Bishop David's death, she moved a picture of the Madonna and Child from his room to her office. Before she left the office of Mother, she wrote on the back of the picture:

> This picture hung many years in the room of our
> venerable Father & founder Bishop David. I now beg as a
> favor that it may always hang in the room of the Mother
> Supr as a remembrance of his many virtues & his zeal for
> the Spiritual & temporal good of Nazareth.

>   July 1844
>
>   Pray for
>   Sr Catherine Spalding
>   Mother of Nazareth[49]

Whatever Catherine felt, she had to know an era in the community's history had ended, but a call to deep spirituality had been left as its inheritance. Whatever trouble David had caused or himself suffered, his essential spirit and character remained. The es-

sence of that legacy remains in one of his hymns, still sung often
at Nazareth:

> My God! My life! My Love!
>   To thee, to thee I call.
> O come to me from heaven above,
>   And be my God, my all.
>   And be my God, my all.

Seven

Community Life-Giver

1841–1844

One month after burying Bishop David, Catherine was reelected to another three-year term of office. It could hardly have been otherwise. The previous April, she had been plunged into the center of a storm raised by Bishop Flaget's intent to merge the SCNs with the Sisters of Charity in Emmitsburg. This crisis would be the greatest of her leadership, and it had come to its climax even as David was dying. Its impact could have been the death of the community or at least of its distinct identity. Before it was over, Catherine would be stretched to her limits of talent and emotion.

From April to July 1841, one might suppose Flaget would have had little on his mind other than David's decline and a new, demanding issue, the impending transfer of his see city from Bardstown to Louisville.[1] But in those months of 1841, he was also deeply engaged in the Emmitsburg project and was forcing it on Catherine's attention. To be fair to Flaget, one must note that his Sulpician brothers were forcing it on him.

For more than ten years the Sulpician superiors in France had consistently pressed their American confreres to give up all works except seminaries (their particular charism and ministry) and especially to end their direction of religious communities of women. Flaget had long thought a necessary and desirable beginning of that end would be the unification of the two communities of Sisters of Charity in the United States, the Kentuckians with the older and larger community in Maryland. When Emmitsburg Sisters replaced SCNs at Vincennes, Indiana, Flaget expressed his thought that Providence might be working "sweetly and forcefully" to advance the former and diminish the latter community until the desirable union could be effected.[2]

As for David, the troubles at Nazareth in the 1830s rekindled his belief that the community would be improved by union with Emmitsburg. He wrote frantically to Bruté of expenditures going out of bounds and of divisions that "have led our community to the brink of ruin." The Emmitsburg Sisters, by contrast, were everywhere "an object of admiration, veneration, and gratitude." A union, by the mercy of God, might remedy the evil. "Oh, when," he lamented to Elizabeth Suttle, "will the little drop of Nazareth have the good sense of merging itself in the vast sea of Charity?"[3]

Flaget undoubtedly shared David's concerns about the SCN "troubles." These became personal when Flaget's niece, Sister Eulalia, abruptly left the SCNs in 1833, after conflict with Mother Frances and other Sisters. In 1835, Eulalia accompanied "mon oncle" to France, and in 1836, he requested through Chabrat that she be received back into the community. The Council refused—a rather bold decision, given that the bishop was the highest superior of the congregation, with expectation of command and submission.[4] The refusal could hardly have sweetened Flaget's taste for SCN independence.

When the bishop returned to Bardstown in 1839, still accompanied by Eulalia, it was Mother Catherine's task to receive him at Nazareth—without her. Catherine welcomed him on October 9, with bishops, clergy, Sisters, and students, at a ceremonial banquet. Before his arrival, however, the Council had resolved "that the Superior or Mother be authorized to say to the Bishop that— \—\—\—\—\—\"![5] Whatever had been said but not recorded probably referred to Eulalia. However Catherine had to fill in those startling blanks by her powers of diplomacy-with-firmness, Eulalia did not again become an SCN.

Before he left for Europe, Flaget had proposed the merger with Emmitsburg but found a majority of Sisters so strongly opposed that he desisted—at least for the time. In Paris, however, he learned of clerical plans to affiliate the Sisters of Charity in Emmitsburg with the Daughters of Charity in France. He was much interested. Perhaps Nazareth could be part of one grand scheme that would commit all Sisters of Charity to the care and direction of the Vincentian Congregation of the Mission. When Flaget returned to Kentucky, despite all other pressing matters, he resumed his project.[6] A simple first step would be to link the American communities by uniform dress.

At first, Catherine may have thought the bishop was renewing the 1829 tempest, a minor harassment over clothes, this time the cap. In April 1841, Flaget proposed or ordered the change of Nazareth's white cap to the black one worn in Emmitsburg. Catherine responded:

Rt. Rev. dear Bishop & Father,

I do not know that you required any answer to your letter of yesterday.—I have read it with all the attention of which I am capable—& I have spent not only 1 qr [quarter hour] before the adorable Sacrament where in fact I find my only comfort, but quarters have been spent there.—& I feel now as I did at first.—I can only say to the best of *my* power I will endeavor to comply with your orders—If you believe that Almighty God will be more glorified by our wearing a black cap instead of a white one—I hope you will do me the justice to believe that I attach no importance to those little articles of our clothes—If we have worn the white head dress for these 25 years, we have done so by the decision of the Council & that of our revered founder & 1st Supr & one among the reasons that then decided this was this, that white was the color worn by the Sisters since the days of St. Vincent.—But this matters not—white or black is the same to me.—& for anything further, I forbear to make any remark.[7]

This paragraph, in its thought and style, shows Catherine stretching toward her peak ability to handle a man like Flaget, to negotiate a solution that would both respect his authority and withstand the threat he represented. Whether her words came simply from her wearied, spontaneous thought and emotion or also from a canny intuition, she registered between the lines challenges about Flaget's awareness of the distress he was causing, his own degree of prayerful reflection, his priorities and values, and his conception of the divine will and glory. She also implied quite clearly that she could not or would not try to coerce the Sisters into compliance.

In the same letter, Catherine went on to remind Flaget that he had visited Nazareth and found the community happy in the observance of their religious duties, thus underscoring what really mattered. She also noted indirectly that Chabrat must have been involved in this proposal and pressure. Evidently his prickly nature had taken offense at some of her words. For these she offered the expected humble apology, but added, "I know I have sometimes spoken jocosely & perhaps too freely with Bishop Chabrat, but as all was in joke, I thought it no harm." This offers an insight on her humorous nature, as well as on her memory of Ellen O'Connell and the need to manage episcopal sensitivities.

Catherine may not have known at this writing just how far beyond the cap Flaget's project extended. He was conducting the whole business in great secrecy, communicating only with Father Louis Deluol, the Sulpician ecclesiastical superior at Emmitsburg. But sometime in May, Flaget must have taken the next step and announced his wish to abolish the role of Nazareth's ecclesiastical superior. The loss of Father Haseltine and the probable increased influence of Chabrat as spokesman for the aging bishop were prospects totally unacceptable to Catherine and the community. In this dilemma and tension, she sought another collaborator whose sympathy and influence she knew—Father Badin.

On Catherine's call, Badin went to Nazareth, met with the Sisters, and, as he wrote Flaget on June 1, "heard what they had to say, as charity dictated." He summarized his "observations": (1) that the Sisters were happy, doing good, and desired to be left under their present constitution; (2) that the bishop is acknowledged as their first superior but, given his many "necessary engagements," they need and want their secondary superior (Haseltine); and they "think and flatter themselves that the Reverend Bishop Flaget, left to his own reflections and natural mildness, will not insist" otherwise; and (3) that a notable change in the cap would elicit "public remark and probably ridicule"; its "forms and colors might be let alone without criminality." Some simplification of the design would suffer no opposition—"to satisfy the Bishop." Badin could resist neither occasional bites of irony nor the barb at Chabrat as the voice behind the throne. But he reasoned from his knowledge of ecclesiastical discipline and from common sense.[8]

Catherine's efforts at best stalled Flaget's action. He was still concerned about the cap. On June 6, 1841, he wrote Father Deluol, noting that three other prelates had been "almost scandalized by the elegance of the round white bonnet" and that he had given the order to make the change in August. The Sisters' "beautiful white heads will appear publicly in complete mourning to the great displeasure of several members of the said community."[9] His order would be changed only if he was assured by Deluol that Emmitsburg would adopt the white headdress of the Daughters of Charity, which Flaget was sure the SCNs would prefer. History, soon and later, would tell how little Flaget understood the wishes of either community.

Flaget also asked Deluol for the rules concerning the superior appointed by the bishop. He was genuinely puzzled about the proper authority of various superiors of religious communities. He then urged Deluol to press on the "important affair" without mentioning the SCNs, who were "entirely unaware of what I am writing to you." Flaget would have thought this secrecy entirely appropriate and within his right.

David seems to have had Flaget's confidence—and perhaps Catherine's as well. Though David had formerly so desired the union with Emmitsburg, by 1841 he had changed his view, whether from age and illness or from a new insight. He evidently knew what the issue was costing his friend Catherine; he said she was "having her trials, but she will come through."[10]

By late June, Catherine knew exactly what she had to go through. Flaget, accompanied by Badin, had made a formal visitation to Nazareth, met with each Sister, and suggested the advisability of the union. The Sisters were unanimous in their wish to remain a distinct congregation. Catherine would have to struggle for the community's existence now as never before, but she would not struggle alone.

Catherine drew her Sisters into an informed union of prayer for light and grace and the accomplishment of the divine will in regard to the community. She was unquestionably sincere in that prayer. She also remained sincerely convinced that the community's mission depended on continuation of their communal identity and way of life. Sure of the Sisters' loyalty and united will, on July 6, Catherine marshaled all her forces of mind and spirit and wrote the most important letter of her life and leadership.[11]

Beginning with the assurance of united and repeated community prayer, Catherine proceeded straight to her "thesis": "We have come to the conclusion to lay before you, our Bishop and Father, our humble and earnest entreaty, that we may be allowed to continue unchanged, in the manner in which we have been established in your Diocese." She promptly followed this direct request with references to David, St. Vincent de Paul, the "court of Rome," and Flaget's own solemn authorization and approval of their "practices, rules, and constitutions." She stressed at some length David's opinion in favor of a "separate and distinct body" and supported it by Flaget's own recommendation of David as "one of the greatest divines and holiest clergymen." Catherine's "entreaty" was thus embedded in a supportive structure of all the names Flaget could least contradict, including his own. Nor could he very well forget that David lay dying even as he was reading.

The following nine densely packed paragraphs cover four main topics:

1. a review of SCN history from St. Thomas onward as an unbroken, scandal-free succession of services to the diocese and its institutions; a building up of the church in Kentucky by education, alms for the poor, and care of orphans—all of it "only our duty" but accomplished by the "untiring exertions and labors of the Sisters" and by their monetary resources;
2. a quiet defense of the community against the charge of numerous defections and small membership, and assertion of its

spiritual health—"never happier, more orderly, more united, or more zealous . . . all most desirous to live up to the spirit of their state";

3. an assertion of the need for the ecclesiastical superior, with full acknowledgment of the bishop's primary role and right of visitation and correction;
4. a summary of reasons against "so remarkable a change" in the cap after twenty-five years.

This content largely echoes Badin's "observations," but the tone and technique are uniquely Catherine's.

Besides repeated references to David and St. Vincent, Catherine regularly cited Flaget himself: David is "*your* co-laborer," "whom *you* have so frequently and so warmly recommended to our confidence." He believed "we should exist always as *you* and he thought proper to institute us." We are thankful to "*yours* and our revered Founder's protection and instruction." "Permit us to recall to *your* paternal recollection" our labors "in *your* diocese"; it was "*your* most ardent wish" to have the orphanage "(all who do justice must acknowledge)" (emphasis added). The barrage of "you" and "yours" went on. The bishop was, in effect, challenged to contradict now his past history and all his praises.

The one missing pronoun is "I." Flaget was not up against Catherine but the community: it is *we* who labored, *we* who have read the discourses of Vincent de Paul, *we* who want to remain unchanged, *we* who "have concluded" and now entreat you. Catherine had to be very sure she was writing so strongly both for and with her Sisters.

Assertion and entreaty alternate throughout the letter. *We* can assert what we believe to be necessary for us and our mission, what we were promised in the beginning, "the interests of the Society, and our constitutional rights," which we "do urgently and humbly implore" as vital to our happiness. In the best practice of persuasive writing, Catherine repeated her thesis in varied words at least five times, ending with the conviction that the changes ordered would "be the laying of the axe to the root of the tree, which *you* and *we* equally believe to have been planted and watered by the hand of God," which our holiest Sisters also believed and asserted when dying.

As forcefully as Catherine styled her argument, she cushioned each blunt or direct challenge by expressions of "deepest respect, and true filial regard"—sentiments she repeated in varied ways, along with addresses to him as "beloved" or "cherished Father" and references to his "paternal heart." Her words were not mere flattery or political maneuver. Catherine deeply admired and respected Flaget, even as she challenged his judgment. His authority was for her a matter of her faith in the church. Pushed to the limit, she would have led in obedience, not in a public protest or work stoppage. But she also believed firmly in her cause and in her Sisters' rights, including their right to speak up for themselves.

Tradition tells that Catherine assembled the Sisters, read her letter, invited all who wished to sign it, then left the room. The letter carries the signatures of twenty-eight other Sisters, most or all of those present at Nazareth. A later addendum carries signatures of the Sisters in Louisville, Lexington, and Union County.

What this letter cost Catherine in emotional stress and in hours of prayer, reflection, and composition may be imagined. But its effect was not immediate. Flaget was still puzzling over the status of both Emmitsburg and Nazareth as religious bodies and the identity and extent of authority of their superiors and local bishop. On July 20, he again wrote Deloul asking about those questions and the headdress.[12] Catherine and the community had to spend an anxious month or more.

But Flaget, according to his biographer Lemarié, was apt to capitulate to feminine will definitely expressed, and Badin and Catherine had convinced him "he was wasting his time in struggling against a regiment of women armed to preserve their autonomy and convinced of their right." On another occasion of surrender, he had written, "What woman wants, God wants."[13] After a few weeks, he conceded, asking only minor changes in the habit. What he wanted then, the women gave. White cuffs became black; the white cap was changed from a double bow to a single knot with shorter strings, and wider plaits around the face, stitched down. These alterations satisfied all parties enough to last until the 1960s.

Flaget and Catherine both lived to hear of the eventual union of Emmitsburg with France. When that occurred by clerical orders, over the stunned and distressed opposition of many of Mother Seton's Sisters, the SCNs may have realized how nearly they had been caught in the avalanche, how much they owed the preservation of their distinct identity to Catherine Spalding's mode of collaboration, her understanding of what constituted obedience in action and appropriate involvement of the community. Columba Carroll had Emmitsburg's experience in mind when she wrote to Frances Gardiner, "Oh! How we should cherish union among ourselves. Had they been united, such a measure would not have carried."[14]

When the long struggle was over, Flaget may have been disappointed, but he retained to the end his warm feelings for "those holy Sisters whom I call my well-beloved daughters." He must have realized his end could not be far in the future. He was almost eighty and in poor health. New bishops and sees had shrunk his diocese to Kentucky alone, thus lifting his burden. But he needed all his energy for the new era he now had to inaugurate, even as he saw another long era ending.

On December 23, 1841, Flaget moved to his new see city, Louisville. He said Christmas Mass at St. Louis Church, now his cathedral, then resided at the orphanage until his new rectory was ready. He said Mass for "the orphan girls and their adoptive mamas" and was cared for in illness by the Sisters. In January 1842, he wrote "my very dear Catherine" his thanks for her New Year's greetings, news of his health, and his prayer for her to have the abundant spirit of St. Vincent so she might communicate it to her "dear daughters . . . scholars and servants." He signed himself, "Your old friend and very affectionate Father in God."[15] In the nine remaining years of his life, Flaget had no known conflict or disappointment with Catherine or her community.

Catherine must have felt the community crossing with the diocese into its own new era. The missions, their needs, and her required tasks would remain unchanged for several years. But with assurance of the community's stability and with new freedom of leadership, she could now expend fresh and concentrated energy on leading the spiritual and communal life.

A meditation from a "small booklet belonging to Mother Catherine," dated 1842, offers a clue to the impact on her of the 1841 events. It is also a key piece of evidence about Catherine's own developing spirituality. The "Meditation on St. Catherine [of Siena]" has three "points" for consideration:

1. the saint's spirit of prayer; in constant union with Christ, she "referred all her actions to the divine Glory";
2. the saint's devotion toward the Holy Eucharist, by which all Christ's friends may be daily replenished;
3. the saint's devotion to the sufferings of Christ; "if I wish to be crowned with Christ, I must learn to suffer with him."

The conclusion notes that these virtues made St. Catherine "in the hands of God, an instrument for doing so much good in the church. She composed differences, reconciled dissension, promoted the peace of the Church . . . and wherever she appeared was the angel of mercy, and the messenger of peace."[16]

Whether Catherine copied these reflections or composed them herself is unclear. Her preservation of them indicates their importance to her, and her letters echo the same themes: God as reference for all action and feelings, desire for the Mass and Eucharist even though she could not receive daily, and the unitive and ministerial value of suffering.[17] The concluding description of Catherine of Siena is echoed in reminiscences of Catherine Spalding's personality and actions.

The spiritual welfare of each Sister was, of course, Catherine's principal ongoing responsibility as the Mother Superior. She exercised it primarily by example. What she urged on the Sisters she strove to practice: prayer, charity to one another and one's neighbor, faithful observance of rules, and management of duties so as to participate in communal prayer and other events and observances.

Practical management of time was surely Catherine's challenge as she balanced duties of administration and community life with acts of charity, her most enduring legacy by example. Since Sisters typically went out in pairs, one was almost always companion and witness to Catherine's outreach to the sick and poor. In summer 1842, a lay professor at St. Joseph College was so ill that Father Martin John Spalding prepared him for death and asked the Sisters at Nazareth to pray for him. In January the man wrote that "Mother Catherine and one of her sisters walked in one evening to wait on me. I never before met with such kindness among strangers as I have in this community."[18]

Catherine's enduring reputation as community leader rests on early testimony to her blend of warmth, compassion, and firmness. A sheet of notes, probably composed by Marie Menard from memories of the Sisters, is worth quoting at length. It summarizes how Catherine's authority was exercised and experienced on a daily basis:

> Mother Catherine gave admonitions freely. . . . yet she was never rash and was always guided by a sense of duty. She had a peculiar way of removing the sting of a rebuke, always closing her admonitions by a few kind, encouraging words, so that one felt strengthened and urged to cheerful, renewed efforts by her reproofs. She knew how to forgive and forget, so that once a reproof had been given, she never again referred to the fault.
>
> She wanted to know the Sisters' sufferings. She wished them to come to her very freely. They were always sure to find her ready sympathy and assistance. She supplied all she could for their comfort, and was especially kind to the sick. There flowed from her heart beautiful words of encouragement. If a young girl received into the novitiate was delicate but good she was never in a hurry to dismiss her, but thought of every possible means to improve her health.
>
> She noticed everybody, had a kind word for everyone. On Christmas morning, she had a little present for everyone in the house, personally selected—every Sister, each child and servant was remembered. . . .

She always gave an instruction to the Sisters the day they made their first vows. It was a day of Jubilee for her. She seemed to enter fully into their joy. Each postulant had a private interview with Mother on her arrival. Mother questioned her, putting her quite at her ease and giving her correct ideas about the religious life. . . . Her aim always seemed to be to promote piety, union and charity among the Sisters.[19]

Encouragement, compassion for suffering, piety, and universal charity—the citation of these hallmarks of Catherine's leadership testifies that her aims were her character traits as well.

Yet Catherine had some abrasive edges revealed in occasional spurts of sharp response. One story records that she gave a young Sister a little alabaster vase, saying it would serve nicely for her to keep some holy water. A few days later, when Catherine saw it in a decorative use, she summarily reclaimed it. Petty exercise of piety or authority was not, however, Catherine's characteristic. In that time when correspondence was subject to inspection, Catherine once sent for a postulant, saying, "Now, my child, here is a letter that I would much prefer your not reading," at the same time handing her the letter to give her freedom of choice. The girl threw it in the fire. She was a convert, and the letter was from a vehemently prejudiced friend. The same postulant went to Catherine with a stream of complaint about some vexation. Catherine heard her out, made no comment or rebuke, smiled, and asked her to oblige her by doing an errand—a rebuke the Sister subsequently recalled as more effective than a lecture.[20] Catherine's love in leadership was genuine, pervasive, and influential. Her regular reelections were no merely polite or charitable gestures by her community.

Given the losses of members and the needs of the missions, temptation must have been strong to recoup the numbers by too ready a policy of admission to novitiate or vows or by too great tolerance of erratic behaviors. Catherine and her Council firmly resisted that temptation. The only recorded concessions for admission are for a greater than usual age or inability to provide the customary dowry as means of initial support. Some postulants and novices were dismissed or postponed from reception of the habit or profession of vows. Even a professed Sister might be postponed from the annual renewal of vows in order to "reform her conduct." Or approval might be conditional: "if she engage to correct herself in receiving company"; "if they make public acknowledgment of a fault they had committed."[21]

This discipline was designed to prevent a repetition of the troubles of the 1830s and their near destruction of the community from within. Fortunately, firmness did not prevent new growth. During this six-year term, Catherine presided over eleven "days of Jubilee," receiving the first vows of twenty-one novices. She welcomed thirty-seven postulants, of whom twenty-eight received the habit and twenty-five eventually made vows. Until 1851, none failed to renew.

To receive and affirm new life is one great good; to maintain life in the face of poverty, hard labor, cold, and contagion is an immense challenge. In face of youthful deaths, Catherine repeatedly insisted on practical care of health. One early remembrance is of a Sister working outdoors on a very cold day:

> Her feet were cold and damp, the bell was rung for adoration, she went to Church thus, and was sick. Mother reproved her. "I like punctuality in attendance to the exercises," she said, "but I also like prudence and common sense in the care of the Sisters' health. We cannot expect God to work miracles on our behalf to preserve our health. If we lose it through our own fault and carelessness, we deprive ourselves of a powerful means He has given us whereby to serve Him."[22]

Catherine's letters to Sisters almost always report on the general health of the family, noting who is or is not sick. To the last, they reflect her concerns and affliction at deaths "in the prime of life." She asks about Sisters with persistent coughs and urges care, "for once the lungs become diseased there is no stopping it."[23]

By 1843, the community life had been renewed enough in numbers and in spirit that Catherine could again seriously consider expansions in mission. On April 29, 1843, the *Catholic Advocate* announced that a "Female Catholic Free School" was to open in May in the basement of St. Louis Church. Parents who lacked means would now be able to give children "a good common education" with special attention to religion. Non-Catholics were welcome but must attend instructions. One dollar was charged in each of two sessions to pay for fuel.[24] Before she left office, Catherine had again devised a ministry for the poor of Louisville. It grew to have more "day scholars" than Presentation, its predecessor in the church basement.

A much more risky expansion was then to be tried—another mission out of state. Even before the independence crisis, Richard Pius Miles, OP, bishop of Nashville, Tennessee, had written Catherine of his eager wish to have a colony of SCNs in his new diocese. Two years Catherine's senior, Miles had grown up in the same Fairfield area and had been ordained in the Dominican community at St. Rose in 1816, the year she made her vows. In the diocese, he was known as a devout priest and effective teacher, pastor, and administrator. He was also known for kindness and good humor, quiet strength and prudent tact, had nowhere been "accused of an unjust or even an uncharitable deed."[25] Thus, his past actions and reputation could have predicted to Catherine only sensible and helpful collaboration, even if the new mission would be a geographic and financial challenge.

Catherine, some Sisters, and 130 students from Nazareth had attended Miles's consecration in the Bardstown Cathedral in 1838. Catherine was certainly sympathetic to whatever she heard of his experience in Nashville. He began ministry there with no Dominican community in a diocese with no money, no priests at first, no religious women, and one small brick church in disrepair. In 1838, while Catherine was first struggling to do repairs at Nazareth, Miles was riding circuit and battling loneliness, poverty, and illness. He and she could hardly have collaborated then. But in 1841, with the Dominican nuns too few to help him, Miles turned to SCNs and "met with a charitable response."[26]

Catherine's response actually was neither rapid nor easily gained. She had too much else to deal with in 1841, and Miles's urgency may have given her pause. Letters in November and December pressured her to send the preferred SCNs before he accepted other offers, to send Haseltine to buy a fine farm or a city lot and house, to open a school in spring, to match her speed to the demands on all sides. The letters abound in such phrases as "at latest," "soon," "very soon," "sooner the better," "as soon as possible." And she might also make a foundation in Memphis.[27]

Catherine was prudent as well as daring. Nashville was several days' journey into a territory with few Catholics, plenty of anti-Catholicism, and still almost no priests. She may well have wondered if the bishop's urgent enthusiasm could be relied on for the long haul. She would find out, but much later. On August 17, 1842, the Council took the risk and voted to open St. Mary's Academy in Nashville with six Sisters, including Sister Serena Carney (pioneer of Presentation) as superior.[28]

St. Mary's Female Academy did succeed. A Protestant paper, in a diatribe described as "absolutely furious in the expression of its malignity," had objected to the presence of nuns. But Miles was patient, the Sisters gained esteem, and in two years the school enrolled a hundred students, many non-Catholic. The Council sent more Sisters, and the bishop began to urge purchase of property.[29]

Catherine went to Nashville herself sometime in 1843, but she objected to the first suggested property. In October, Miles assured her he had found another house one hundred yards away. He had simply forgotten to tell her during her visit! Faced with an auction two months earlier, he had bid on the house and obtained it for $11,050, payable in three years. The Sisters, he said, were all delighted. Now he was delighted Catherine had agreed to the "most important part"—helping to pay for the house. Catherine's degree of delight is suggested by the notation that the SCNs became property owners in Nashville "reluctantly."[30]

One additional gift to Nashville Catherine evidently made reluctantly yet generously. In January 1844, during her final year in office, she concurred with the Council to send to Nashville Sister Claudia Elliott. This decision would make a contribution to community history that Catherine could not have foreseen or intended. Claudia Elliott was one of those women who spread vital energy and good feeling around her. Sisters loved her and wrote to her from Nazareth and the branch houses, in letters full of affection and local news. While she was missioned at Nazareth (August 1839–January 1844), she became Catherine's close friend and unfailing support. Catherine wrote to her at Nashville, and Claudia, one of a very few among the Sisters, preserved Catherine's letters.

These letters are the best evidence of Catherine's personality and powers of relationship. From Nazareth she laments "Oh! It hardly seems right for me to be here without *you*. But so it is.—But in my heart and soul we can be united." In February 1844, she assures Claudia, "I am glad to hear you are so pleased with your new home, for you know, dear Sister, that my desire is to see you always happy." But by May 1844, she begs: "I think indeed that you have enough to keep you very busy. Still you must try & find time to write me a little letter sometimes. I wish I could give you gumalastic legs or some kind with which you could step even back to Nazareth for I assure you I never did miss anyone so much in my life, & if the thing were to do over again, I believe I would *not* consent to it. But I suppose others are gratified, & it does not matter for me."[31] Claudia's absence clearly did matter greatly to Catherine. Her letters to Claudia, more than any other, reveal her capacity for deep, enduring individual friendship in balance with the common interest.

Catherine, however, was soon to leave Nazareth herself. In August 1844, her third term ended, and she wrote to Claudia, "I can read your letters with great ease & always with much pleasure. But don't write to me any more until you hear where I am stationed, for at this time I am but a loose piece of furniture. But I am truly glad to be so.—I never felt so much relieved in all my life." She sent the stockings she had been making for Claudia, love to all the Sisters in Nashville, and the assurance that "I am not changed but for *you* I will ever be the same old friend."[32]

Her "loose" interval for rest from six years of heavy labor and stresses was short. She left Nazareth a few days after the election of Frances Gardiner. A witness to her leave-taking wrote Sister

Claudia that "I never saw anything so much like a funeral in my life. The novices grouped in her room in tears, and followed her to the stage." Catherine's own feelings were surely more mixed. The Council had appointed her to follow her heart back to the only place she said it clung to, St. Vincent Orphanage.[33]

Eight

Louisville's "Mother Catherine"

1844–1850

The Louisville to which Catherine returned in 1844 had been booming in her absence. From her initial residence in the 1830s, the population doubled every decade, from ten to twenty to well over forty thousand by 1850. The residents then included 5,432 slaves and 15,782 foreign-born.[1] Given the issues of labor, health, and distribution of wealth engendered by such a population explosion, the number of orphans could not fail to boom as well and to create related issues of their welcome and support in the city. As leader of St. Vincent Orphanage, Catherine came back to a task requiring all her skills of management, relationship, and persuasion.

The first great influx of the foreign-born consisted of Germans. Because they were generally skilled and apt to contribute to society, their coming was not at first felt to be a threat. But the Irish pouring in after the Great Famine of 1845, though still fewer than the Germans, roused great concern among the "cultured" native citizenry that both economy and culture would be overwhelmed by this horde, poor, unskilled, uncouth—and Catholic.[2]

More than labor, religion became the immigration issue in Kentucky. It would touch Catherine in both her urban ministry and community leadership. The original French, two-thirds of the

Germans, and virtually all the Irish were Catholic. The church in Louisville grew rapidly, and its mission blossomed. Catherine saw parishes opened for all three groups. The Jesuits, Sisters of Loretto, and Sisters of the Good Shepherd all began serving in the city in the 1840s, but for their initial safety, the immigrant Good Shepherd Sisters were advised to arrive in secular clothing.[3]

With the waves of Catholic immigrants came also a wave of virulent anti-Catholicism new to Louisville and new to Catherine's experience. The usual tolerance of the 1830s yielded to old perceptions of Catholicism: bizarre doctrines, worship in a foreign language, hierarchical governance, allegiance to a foreign potentate, and opposition to Protestant liberty. To offset misconceptions and instruct the faithful, a diocesan paper, the *Catholic Advocate,* was initiated in 1836. The Louisville Protestant League, initiated in 1844, published pamphlets and held lectures on the "startling doctrines of the Church of Rome," to which the cathedral priests and layman Ben Webb responded with lectures and essays in the *Advocate.* Catherine surely would have read that paper, thus increasing her own religious and social awareness.[4]

The Protestant League feared that Catholics might take over the country by educating the children of the affluent and influential, especially by "female education" in the growing number of Catholic academies. Given female influence on family religion, one converted girl could lead to a whole Catholic household. Catherine and her Sisters would now have to conduct their mission amid political and religious maneuvers that fanned the fires of bigotry throughout the rest of the 1840s. Just after Catherine's return to the city in October 1844, the anti-Catholic Millerite sect announced the end of the world; for the event, they set up an assembly ground three blocks from Presentation Academy.[5]

Catherine probably did not read the *Louisville Journal* and the infamous rhetoric of its editor, George D. Prentice, but her many contacts would let her know that fear of the Catholic vote was rousing even the church's most lethargic opponents. Whigs blamed Henry Clay's defeat for the presidency in 1844 on the "overwhelming immigration of hordes of Catholics to our shores." Because Clay was the idol of Kentucky, adored in Louisville, anti-Catholicism rose in proportion. Whigs, on the decline, became the nucleus of the nativist American Party. They held a huge organizational meeting in Louisville in 1845. Catherine, observer of what was going on around her, knew that factions surrounded her home and her charges, making her task of protection and nurture all the more risky and difficult.[6]

St. Vincent Orphanage, with its immigrant children, could not afford to seek safety in obscurity. Catherine had to make her mission well known and generously supported in Louisville. The institution had a reputation for "good and wholesome regulations, and . . . liberal charities to the orphan." Catherine knew the value of such public repute. She had to use it for the needs of the "near sixty beings who have few to think of or love them," for whom she was content "only [to] be useful."[7]

The orphanage received girl children from around Kentucky and beyond. These girls were abandoned or committed by a parent, by citizens, or by a court because they were "without home and protection, and without moral or religious training."[8] They included one taken from "her poor unfortunate mother" and placed with a poor woman of Nashville who could not keep her; another "—— born [whose] relatives wish to get her out of the way"; three girls of a mother who died leaving seven children and their father, poor, sickly, and a drunkard; children of widows; also the daughter of a divorcée, "*in all things,* a correct woman, now very poor, supporting her children by hard labor." "Sophie Ann, child of Frederick Siepness, who died in the night after arriving here in town, [was] found clasped in his arms"; he was German, his American wife and other children had died in New Orleans.[9] For all the children Catherine accepted so willingly, she had to provide all necessities of body, mind, and spirit.

Letters of appeal to Catherine usually preceded the children but sometimes arrived with them. Priests especially presumed on her known charity and urged her concern for children "ere the peachdown of innocence fades from their cheeks." The priests sometimes sent clothes or money or promised to preach sermons on charity ("in about two months"). Well might Catherine write pointedly, "Altho' our number is considerable for our means . . .

I trust Divine Providence will provide for them all." No one, it seems, appealed to Mother Catherine more often than Rev. John Quinn of the cathedral. Her "sincere friend in Christ" spoke truly enough: "I suppose there shall never be an end to the applications made to you. . . . but you are our only refuge under such circumstances. . . . Every orphan in the city claims you as their mother."[10]

Father Quinn may be "John," author of a long article in the *Catholic Advocate* about "the warm-hearted daughter of St. Vincent de Paul," the orphanage, and the ways a girl there was "acquainted with whatever is necessary to qualify her for her calling in after life."[11] Catherine must have promptly established a program of daily life in the home on Jefferson Street. Ever open to collaboration and advice, in 1849 she wrote to Sister Margaret George, SC, at St. Peter's Orphanage in Cincinnati, asking her mode of management.

Sister Margaret's reply gives a daily schedule from a 5:00 A.M. rising to the end of the school day about 5:00 P.M. Each day included Morning Prayers and Mass, Dinner Prayers "same as the ones which, of course, you know," meals, hours of classes and homework, duties in the dormitories and dining room. No school on Saturdays, but a "general review of the dormitories," bathing, sewing, reading, and so forth. Sundays included two visits to the cathedral; this kept the orphans before the public and encouraged their support.[12]

How much St. Vincent's resembled St. Peter's cannot be said; probably both schedules included sufficient indoor and outdoor play. Catherine definitely shared Sister Margaret's struggle with contagion and also her view that "the only chance these poor children have for education is while they are with us, therefore, we should do all we can for them." She undoubtedly resonated with her counterpart's abrupt closure: "My time is not my own just now, opening of schools, new work, mechanics and all the etceteras of our Martha life . . . you know and can feel for us—pray in union with us all for accomplishing the will of our one Supreme and only good."

Admiration and contributions, however, did not relieve the

orphanage's persistent and severe poverty. Catherine and the Sisters bore all the hardship they could in order to spare the children. During evening recreation, they sewed and mended their own and the children's clothes and altered them for size to make them last for a long time. Only for that hour did they light a fire in the community room. Otherwise, the Sisters' rooms were without heat.[13]

Providing adequate nourishment for the "family" was Catherine's principal challenge. Her begging tours became legendary. The best-known story is from this period. She called on Mr. Mc-Gillycuddy, businessman and former guardian of Sisters Columba and Sophia Carroll:

> After a short conversation the gentleman said: "Mother Catherine, how about your little family? What can I do for the orphans today?" With that pleasing smile, the charm of which all have felt who knew her, Mother replied, "Very much indeed, Sir; we are in want of everything but potatoes, which have constituted the sole diet of the orphans for more than a week. Many of them are sick and require other food." The gentleman flushed as if rebuked and exclaimed, "Good heavens, Mother! Why did you not send to me sooner?" The result of that day's call was a bountiful supply of groceries for several months.[14]

Obtaining food was the largest shared labor of Catherine's "Martha life." Her main responsibility was governance.

Though the asylum had a Board with some rights of visitation, its "interior government" was "entrusted to the Sisters of Charity." As superior of both Sisters and mission, Catherine had to be the primary arbiter of policies: minimum age for admission of full orphans "except in extreme cases," payment by the surviving parent of a half orphan, recommendation by a pastor, admission of non-Catholics, and the distance from which a child might be accepted. She welcomed 215 children to St. Vincent's during her terms there, nearly all between the ages of one and ten.[15]

St. Vincent's was every girl's home until she was eighteen, but the overcrowding of the house and the need to admit very young children created some urgency to "place out" the older ones. For this, Catherine had to collaborate with the Catholic Orphans Board and make or approve placements. She arranged free tuition for some at the academies; they worked in return for board. She sent Barbara Dosh to St. Vincent's in Union County so that she might receive a musical education proportionate to her obvious talent. Other girls returned to their relatives or went to "positions" in families. Catherine either initiated or confirmed the policies designed to prevent a girl being proselytized by employers or shuffled about as temporary help. Any employment was continued by mutual consent, and a girl could return or be returned to St. Vincent Orphanage "as her proper home."[16]

Most of the young women who called the asylum home and Catherine mother went on to establish their own families. Several became religious, others nurses, governesses in "respectable families," or self-supporting seamstresses. In a society not yet committed to assist young women without family, Catherine's "changeless vigilant love" is cited, the gilt of rhetoric not obscuring the core of fact: "She never forgot one of her orphan children, and to the period of her death, continued to feel the greatest interest in their welfare. This interest, so far from ending with their removal from her care, followed them to distant states, rejoiced in their prosperity and deeply sympathized in their misfortunes, endeavoring upon all occasions to infuse into their minds her own perfect resignation to the divine will."[17]

People—orphans, young women, the poor and sick, Sisters, servants, lay collaborators—people were the focus of Catherine's activity in mission. But people live in buildings, and she had once more to raise funds and to supervise maintenance and new construction. An early, "very convenient addition" to the asylum was "a neat little chapel," then an addition to the house, allowing more rooms for children and a separate kitchen and cook for the infirmary. It was characteristic of Catherine to begin with a chapel as she had at Nazareth and to invite Sister Claudia's brother, Father James Elliott, to celebrate its inaugural Mass, attended by some of the Sisters missioned elsewhere in Louisville.[18]

By 1848, both orphanage and infirmary had grown so much that Catherine hoped the time would not be too distant when they could be separated.[19] Until that division could be accomplished, Catherine had to remain superior of the infirmary and involved in creating its policies. One decision, remarkable enough for its time, and indicative of both her leadership and her expansive charity, was to undertake care of the mentally ill.

The one case recorded was a Mrs. Gray from St. Louis. From March to May 1845, her husband, H. H. Gray, exchanged letters with Mother Catherine. Catherine was involved with both interpretations and decisions in the case. Doctors believed that Mrs. Gray "had some sorrow of long standing on her mind"; Catherine thought "the subject of her parentage had something to do with it." Gray believed early indulgence of her demands and "ungovernable temper" had initiated her present condition. Unhappy and powerless, he put his hopes in Catherine's "experience in similar cases," her advice to himself, her "motherly care and advice," and her "kind offices" for his wife.[20]

Catherine mediated the relationship of husband and wife in the situation. She wrote him details of Mrs. Gray's state of mind and her own fear that no further service would help her. She suggested Gray visit his wife. He did so in early April, and Catherine agreed to keep her longer and try further. But in early May, Mr. Gray was pleading with Catherine to "do all in your power to reconcile her to me" before he brought her back to St. Louis.[21] This episode was the start of a tradition of mental health nursing among Catherine's Sisters and of care for those least able to help themselves.

In a city without structured public assistance, Catherine combined institutions like the orphanage and infirmary with her own personal outreach and appeals to private charity. She became known on the streets of Louisville as the visitor to the destitute. Reputation and her manner protected her in the roughest urban areas. The "lowliest and most degraded were sure of nothing but aid and sympathy from the friend of all. . . . the more worthy the sufferer of reproof, the less of reproof was in her gentle words." She was said to have been one in "perfect command over self, in whom passion or anger never had a moment's victory," who therefore had "remarkable influence over others."[22] The words suggest an exaggerated aura that grew around her. She certainly could yield at times to anger and pain. Yet a few specific stories from those who knew her preserve both the heroism and the humor of her deeds.

Mother Frances Gardiner wrote Claudia that Mother Catherine had taken in a "family of seven of the poor sick Irish." One child had since died, and the old grandmother was dying. "The boats bring them into the city. Some have been assisted on carts, others on landing under the sheds. Poor creatures! They have nothing but the clothes on their backs."[23] The letter supports the community's tradition that Catherine frequented the docks to rescue such families and their children.

Another story concerns a visit in severe winter to a sick woman "at some distance from the Asylum." Catherine

gathered a portion of her own flannel, and not asking how the woman came to her sad condition, hurried to her poor excuse for a home, accompanied by a sister. It was only after she had walked several blocks that Mother remembered that her name in full was on the clothing. She mentioned the dilemma to the sister, who fortunately had her scissors hanging at her side. They stepped into an unfrequented path and ripped the tell tale marks from the garments, but this is only one instance of the daily acts that made up her noble Christian life.[24]

As much as humility and selflessness, the story also instances Catherine's practical humor.

If destitute citizens, orphans, and the sick poor were all to be assisted out of the means of the Sisters, it was necessary that Catherine be a very busy fund-raiser and public relations person in this new and volatile Louisville. She had to tap the city's booming economy and win over its citizens of all ethnicities and religious persuasions. She needed to renew and strengthen her old friendships with the people who patronized Presentation, who could afford the cultural events in the theaters and halls that had sprung up during her six years away. On her walks, she could see new factories making steamboat parts, machinery for mills and gins, ornamental and architectural iron, stoves, wagons and plows, paper, pianos, and organs.[25] She needed to know and win respect from the owners of these plants, from "liberal Protestants" and such Catholics as the trustees of St. Louis Cathedral, from city councilmen and politicians, all prominent men of means—with wives. If her renown in the city could not rival that of the famous visitors of the 1840s, she nevertheless became a resident of sufficient importance to earn "many presents, testimonials of affection and admiration . . . from wealthy friends who admired and loved her." These were "all made to serve the cause of Charity in some way."[26]

The testimonials came in many forms. The city donated coal. Clergy in Louisville, Bardstown, and elsewhere preached on special occasions for the orphans' benefit. Among the immigrant Irish, the "Panegyric of St. Patrick" on March 17 was especially effective. Patrick Cavanaugh had a stable built at the orphanage; Catherine witnessed his statement of payment and donation. An old, nearly blind man, out of the church, heard of the orphanage and the number it supported entirely by charity and sent fifty dollars, explaining, "My Church and conscience called louder than aught else." Several gentlemen made St. Vincent Orphanage the beneficiary of their wills, asking the prayers of the Sisters and the "female innocents."[27]

Like any fund-raiser, Catherine sent out seasonal letters of appeal—with typical mixed results. One donor on Christmas 1844 sent her twenty dollars and good wishes for the "benevolent Asylum over which you preside." Another gentleman sent warm approval of her appeals, elaborate praise for the Sisters' work, and assurance of the highest heavenly reward. But being in a "load of debts," he must send "the unadulterated will for the deed."[28]

Private donations, however generous, could not be Catherine's sole reliance. St. Vincent Infirmary in 1848 gave to the asylum $1,171.85, a quarter of its total revenue. Only one annual fair netted more ($2,000).[29]

In these years, the fair grew into the major fund-raiser that it remained long after Catherine's lifetime. Because it was aimed at Christmas, preparation went on from spring to late autumn. Despite all the work of the ladies, or because of the need to assist them, that preparation grew into a heavy demand on Catherine's days and energies, requiring a volume of contacts for petition and persuasion—in this era, by handwritten letters and personal visits. Sisters helped all they could, even if only concern was possible. One reported to Claudia Elliott that "Mother had a great many articles prepared" for the fair. Another wrote from Nashville, "O dear Mother, how much I wish I was with you . . . that I might assist you in preparing for the fair. I would most gladly do it where I am if it were in my power."[30]

The fair was held in a large public hall; it lasted six days and evenings. If Catherine's presence was expected some part of this time as walkabout hostess, she would have paused at tables managed by ladies offering "fancy articles of the most exquisite manufacture . . . , from the most magnificent to the plainest" and refreshment tables serving "delicious viands . . . the most refined and exquisite." The young could be entertained by a "very witty, fascinating" fortune-teller or leave a "perfumed billet" at the "Post Office."[31] Whatever Catherine thought of all this elegance and youthful absurdity, she could not but be grateful for the enormous labor and the generous donations and purchases that went into this appeal by "the Ladies of Louisville" to the "benevolence of fellow citizens." In 1851, the fair netted $2,500 for the 112 orphans Catherine had just left at St. Vincent's.[32]

Fairs were seasonal, but Catherine's labors went on every day, all year, punctuated by single events demanding prudent management. A Mr. Laughlin, apparently by trickery, got or withheld $100 from Mother Catherine. He seems to have been formerly a workman at Nazareth, then at St. Vincent Academy in Union County, with his child at the orphanage. Sister Elizabeth Suttle wrote to inform Catherine that man and money were both gone. In another episode, Catherine had apparently been accused of holding the trunk and possessions of a dead man. Regarding this matter, Father John Quinn wrote, "I am more than conscious you would do nothing wrong under any circumstance." He advised her to hold the trunk until the wife in New Orleans had been heard from. "In the meantime pardon them for the fault they have committed in doing or saying anything to one who deserves every mark of affection and gratitude from their hands."[33]

Episodes like these were time-consuming annoyances. Other events were far more challenging and consequential. One that brought Catherine to the city's attention in 1845 was the legal contest of the will of Miss Polly Bullitt. Catherine became a star witness in the court, possibly the key to the trial's outcome.

Polly Bullitt, of a prominent local family, had severe cognitive and emotional limitations. Both her parents had children by first marriages. Both died when Polly was eight, leaving a fortune for her care. Her guardianship was eventually given to her maternal half sister, Eliza Prather Guthrie. For kind care and whatever education was possible, Mrs. Guthrie sent her to Nazareth, where she resided eleven years. Catherine, consequently, knew her well. When Mrs. Guthrie died, Polly remained devoted to James Guthrie and her three nieces and continued to call their home hers. For the last three years of her life, she was resident at St. Vincent Infirmary. Shortly before her death in 1843, at thirty-five, she had a will made, leaving all her fortune to the Guthrie girls. The Bullitt half siblings contested this will on the grounds that Polly was incompetent to make a will and was manipulated by the Guthries. Two rich and famous families were thus pitted against each other, with the Sisters of Charity in between.[34]

Twenty-seven Sisters of Charity, Catherine among them, all who had dealt most with Polly at Nazareth or the infirmary, were deposed for evidence of her mental capacity.[35] Catherine's testimony was evidently extensive and cross-examined in the courtroom. She cited Polly's ability to remember names and degrees of relationships of family and acquaintances, to recall conversations and give the substance in her own words even days later. On May 2, 1846, in his charge to the jury, Judge S. S. Nicholas quoted Catherine especially, adding:

There was then the possession of a powerful memory—Mother Catharine almost startled me, when she said Polly's memory was *better* than her own. . . . You remember upon my inquiry of Mother Catharine; whether if a fracas had occurred at the school, at which Polly was present & after the lapse of some days it had come up for her investigation, she would have relied on Polly's statement of facts and conversations in relation to it, she said she would, that she would have placed the same reliance as upon the statement of one of the sisters.[36]

The point was that Polly could also remember who had been kind to her, could know she had money, and could decide who should receive it.

Judge Nicholas discriminated carefully between the capacities to manage money and to choose a legatee. Polly could not manage property, he conceded, saying that most females could not. But, he allowed, there were exceptions: "This mother Catharine who appeared before us is also an eminent exception. They tell me she has the capacity to govern a state." The weight of testimony reiterated in the judge's charge (in truth, not a wholly unbiased document) was enough to convince the jury, which rapidly returned a verdict sustaining the will.

The Bullitts appealed, and Catherine found herself in court again, this time eyeball to eyeball with their new attorney, Henry Clay. His public stature created immense excitement and a crowded-to-overflowing courthouse for more than a week.[37] The statesman who had given the first diplomas at Nazareth now had the task of cross-examining Nazareth's Mother. One of William Bullitt's daughters wrote to a brother in Philadelphia, gloating over Clay's grilling of "some of the catholics . . . Mother Catherine especially" and the priest who witnessed the will.[38] She pronounced him successful in confusing witnesses with hooked questions and creating laughs at their expense.

Courtroom performance notwithstanding, to the extent that this second round was a contest of Clay versus Catherine, he was defeated. The "honorable and honest men" argued over three hours and finally were discharged as unable to agree. The will of Polly Bullitt stood. For Catherine, the event was not only priceless experience but also a public relations coup. She could not have paid for the publicity that enhanced her and her community's reputation for integrity, charity, and good service in their school and infirmary.

One suspects Catherine may have enjoyed some of this challenge and victory, at least the first time around, when other sorrows had not yet intervened. But losses of real importance dogged the years between the two trials. The *Catholic Advocate* of August 2, 1845, gave notice: "Died . . . of Typhus fever, Sister Regina All, in her 26th year." Catherine had admitted her, received her vows only a year and five months earlier, and missioned her to Louisville. No doubt she was with her often before death and probably accompanied her remains back to Nazareth, grieving yet another loss of youthful zeal.[39]

February 1846 brought two losses of very different kinds. Sister Pelagia Vallée had been Catherine's elected Assistant at Nazareth, superior of the orphanage, and a member of the NLBI Board. Obviously she was one of the particularly competent community women, and she was devoted to Catherine. When she returned to Nazareth, battling the constant enemy, consumption, Catherine promised to be with her when she was dying. She did make the trip, but Pelagia lingered so long that Catherine felt she had to return to Louisville yet dreaded to wound the dying woman's feelings. When she gently spoke her dilemma, Pelagia responded, "Go, Mother, where your duties call you."[40]

Catherine had barely turned from Pelagia's grave when an arsonist struck at the asylum and infirmary. The stable burned down, destroying a pony and two cows—a "great loss to them."[41] If Catherine ever knew the perpetrator or motive, she needed all her capacity for charitable pardon, given the loss of much-needed milk for her children.

Help came from Nazareth within a month. On March 3, 1846, Mother Frances wrote to Catherine assuring her that Nazareth's overseer would load the wagon to Louisville with flour, middling, potatoes, soap, and a cow. Because of the cold, the marketing people had not come in, so she could send no butter or eggs. But Catherine's mended shoes were included. Catherine was to send back with the overseer the boilers for the cooking stoves previously sent for repair. Nazareth and Louisville were in an ongoing exchange of messages, services, and goods, for the benefit of both places.[42]

Some losses cannot be compared to those of stables and animals, nor even to the natural deaths of beloved companions, however saddening. In 1848 Catherine faced possibly the greatest grief, anger, and moral demand that any loss ever created in her life. Two Sisters at Lexington were poisoned by a slave girl. One survived with damaged health, but Catherine's own sister, Sister Ann Spalding, lingered a few days and died on May 15. Catherine might have been able to be at her deathbed.

The fact of this murder is well attested.[43] Although Catherine was not on the Council, by virtue of her kinship she had to be fully informed and consulted about action to be taken. What she knew about the circumstances and motives would certainly have affected her reactions. The Lexington Annals say only that Sister Ann "cared for and protected" the servant girl and that "jealousy prompted this child to put poison in buttermilk."[44] No information is given about the nature of the "protection" or the "jealousy." Ann Spalding's personality and attitude toward slaves, in contrast to Catherine's, are not known well enough to provide clues. She was a successful teacher and twice superior (thus mistress of the slaves) in Lexington. In letters, Ann refers to the servants in tones that are primarily light, interested, and even affectionate, though tinged with the oblivious racism of the "good mistress."[45] Given the era, nothing recorded of Ann and the slaves would have surprised Catherine, dismayed her, or prepared her for so shocking an end to her youngest sister's life. When it occurred, she was inevitably involved in the response to the horror.

Catherine's response, also the Council's, was directed by Ann's. Before her death, Ann discovered the identity of her murderer but refused to prosecute and requested that nothing be said about it.[46] Community tradition says she asked that Catherine protect the girl.

Protective concealment, with Catherine's necessary consent, began in obituaries that spoke of "lingering illness" and death "perhaps hastened by over-exertion."[47] A fair trial would have been impossible. Black persons could not testify in court, so the girl's story could never have been heard. Releasing her identity would only have exposed her to the gross public penalties that the law or lynchers would have visited on a slave who murdered her mistress, a well-known Catholic Sister and schoolmistress at that. In this context, the mercy reportedly given by Ann and ratified by Catherine takes on its full value.

The Council at Nazareth, however, had to deal with the chaos in the community house at Lexington. Again, Catherine, whether consulted or not, had to know the decisions. In quick succession, the Council appointed a new superior and shifted Sisters and servants from or to Lexington.[48] Mother Frances was authorized "to dispose of Mary, servant at Lexington or otherwise remov[e] her off the place with her child." This suggests that Mary, possibly Aunt Mary, the cook, or more likely, her daughter (the "child"?) was the killer. Two or even three people could have been kept together or separated in this "disposal" of the slave, not legally punished but probably sold to a distance. Whatever occurred, and even if Catherine consented to it as the necessary and best possible solution, it had to run counter to every better feeling and action typical of her in relation to slaves.

Beyond the circumstances of the death, Catherine had to deal with her personal loss. Ann was the baby sister she had played with, the youngest, who had grown with her at the Elders' and followed her to St. Thomas. Ann was the only sibling who seems to have remained actively connected to her. Four months after Ann's death, in answer to a letter from Claudia, Catherine first gives ordinary news, then almost cautiously touches her pain: "Good Bishop Kenrick & two others all said Mass in our little chapel for poor Sister Ann. . . . I thank those who said Mass for her in Nashville & hope you will continue to pray for her poor soul—pray also for me, my good Sister."[49] The poignancy of the last phrase is in its brevity.

One of the great gaps in Catherine's history is the apparent absence of her other siblings, who might have shared her grief. Yet she may not have lacked all family comfort. Besides the relatives in Maryland with whom she had correspondence, the local Clark family kept their connection.

A year before Ann's death, Rev. William Elder Clark, Catherine's "affectionate cousin," wrote that his "Brother Edwin wishes to send for Laura," whose mother sends "sincere respects and many thanks" for Catherine's kindness to her daughter. The letter includes references to Edwin, their parents, Grandma, Uncle John Horrell, Cousin John Elder and his two daughters at Nazareth, and Uncle B. Wight—all obviously known to Catherine. While the network of relationship is now partially obscure, the binding thread is Clementina Elder Clark, Catherine's cousin and Father Clark's mother. "Grandma" was therefore Elizabeth Spalding Elder, who died at age ninety-four in 1848, the same year as her niece and foster child Ann Spalding.[50]

Father Clark, born in 1808, would have been a small boy during Catherine's girlhood residence with his parents, a child she played with and cared for. Later she would have seen him often at Nazareth, where he served as confessor for eight or nine years and continued to visit while teacher and pastor in the vicinity. She may have assisted at his grandmother's funeral and then had to console his mother only two years later, when a "malignant fever" caused Father Clark's own death on March 5, 1850. The personal and community ties that bind are witnessed by his burial at Nazareth.[51]

Probably in attendance at both Elder funerals and, one hopes, consoling Catherine's sorrows were two other clergymen and more distant cousins, the brothers Martin John and Benedict Joseph Spalding. During these years of Catherine's service in Louisville, they were successively pastors of St. Joseph Church in Bardstown. She maintained ongoing cordial connections with both of them. They appealed to her to accept the parish orphans. To Martin John, in 1844, she wrote acceptance of an orphan. In 1849, she called on practical experience to tell Benedict that she had to guard space in the orphanage for the care of older children, "for anyone else can nurse & feed an infant just as well." The large child she would take.[52]

Catherine's contacts with the Fathers Spalding seem to have been collaborative and solicitous for their concerns. When Martin, then pastor of the cathedral, was seriously ill at the infirmary, she wrote Benedict accounts of his progress. She wrote in haste to tell him of the impending death of John M'Atee, probably his parishioner, only two days at the infirmary. "We sincerely sympathize with his friends but fear it is now too late. . . . Please convey this news to his friends as soon as possible.[53]

In these Louisville years of labor and sorrows, Catherine received letters from associates at Nazareth, a welcome consolation and assurance of friendship and affection. Father Haseltine seasoned business with news: money to be sent by the "first safe conveyance," and accounts of Sisters, students, servants, and other friends. Columba Carroll, directress of the academy, wrote "My beloved Mother" her congratulations on the success of the fair and its testimony to the love of former students; she sent news of Sisters (all healthy except a novice) and present students (Jefferson Davis's nieces were to be baptized). As requested, she was sending pens and stockings for Sister Philippa. "My thoughts and affections were often with you. Ever truly your devoted . . ."[54] The tone is chatty and warm, not quite casual but very loving. These letters testify to Catherine's ongoing cordial interest in people and desire to maintain contacts with friends, as well as their eager concern not to lose touch with her.

Letters must have been especially welcome as Catherine seems not to have gone to Nazareth very often during these years. She was present at only three sessions of the Board of Trustees. Her final one held an embarrassment: John D. Colmesnil and his wife, prominent Catholic Louisvillians, had been early promoters of the orphans and fairs. Now the Board resolved that Colmesnil "be required to pay the amount due by him to Nazareth, either by property or by a joint note of himself and wife."[55] Even from her most supportive friends, Catherine had to exact firm justice. It must have been painful to return to Louisville and meet them there.

No letters reveal Catherine's state of mind and feelings in this period better than those she wrote herself. Few are extant, but the recipients and topics are varied enough to indicate the complexities of her personality.

The extent and cordiality of Catherine's friendships with lay-women are evidenced in an 1845 letter to Mrs. Maria Crozier. Because this must be the mother of Nazareth student Eliza Crozier Wilkinson, the friendship was of at least twenty years' duration. Catherine conveys to her "own dear & esteemed friend" her continuing "most cordial sincere regards," her wish to enjoy her visits again, and her gentle distress ("pardon me") "that I scarcely ever receive even a kind message from Mrs. Crozier" when she is in town. To this friend she can safely be a bit reproachful and also release her perceptive, slightly caustic humor mixed with compassion: "Today I had a call from Mrs. Judge Marshall & an hour's conversation, or rather I listened to her for that length of time. . . . poor lady, things are different with her from what they were in times of yore." As the letter goes on, Catherine asks about and sends remembrance by name to eleven other friends and some of their children—"in a word to all who may ask for me." A very few sentences suffice to account for the general good health of her "little family of charity" and her own contentment in being with them.[56] The letter is an expression of deeply felt personal friendship.

The letters that most reveal Catherine's capacity for such friendship and her ability to balance it with the priority of community are the six messages (at least) which went from the orphanage to Sister Claudia Elliott in Nashville. Three motifs run through these letters, revealing significant aspects of Catherine's personality and experience.[57]

Claudia evidently expressed some diffidence about her own ability to write well, to please, or to be remembered by her busy friend. One motif running through Catherine's replies is reassurance of her satisfaction and pleasure in receiving Claudia's letters: "I know it is harder for you to write than me; & it is always a pleasure for me to write to you, or to hear from you"; and again, "You must continue to write to me for two reasons, your own improvement and my pleasure.—I see you improve in every letter. Do then continue to write."

Evidently Claudia did continue, and another motif, fidelity in friendship, echoes throughout Catherine's replies, revealing more than Claudia's need. Catherine cites her own unchanging affection and, all too often, a poignant gratitude for Claudia's fidelity to her:

> Why could you think for one moment that I could be tired of your letter?—No, Claudia, if you do, it only proves that you do not know me,—for I do not change.
> . . . you have been too faithful and untiring in your many acts of kindness to me for me ever to forget you. & so far, I have never been deceived in you.
> I know you could never do me the injustice to suppose that I could ever forget you or your many kind attentions for me; you are one of the few that always seemed to understand my feelings & sentiments, & you never changed.

The iteration of these "leaks" of pained feeling exposes some damaged trust or lost affection. The praises heaped on Catherine cannot conceal that she must have had the experience of most leaders—fondness or adulation turning to criticism or condemnation when a decision did not please, or simply the distancing of old friends as a result of lost interest or differences of expectation or opinion.

Catherine's third motif is simply the difficulty of being at a distance from so good a friend and confidante. It is no little feat for a superior to maintain her authority and required confidentiality yet retain a confiding, casual, light-toned relationship. With Claudia Elliott, Catherine seems to have been able to keep the balance, and that made it all the harder to accept the separation imposed by mission. Every letter expresses in some way "how sincerely I love you & how often I think of you.—& I almost begin to despair of ever seeing you." In the days of long distances and slow travel, Sisters did stay on missions a long time; Catherine's dread was realistic and understandable. She seems to fear emotional distance even more: "I suppose you have become quite attached to Nashville. Do you remember old times and how we used to talk over everything?—Well, I hope you will ever be happy.—I am still plodding on as best I can." As the six years go on, Catherine's expressions of affection grow more spontaneous and intense: "Oh, I do value your letters highly. . . . Oh, I can never forget you."

These letters are not merely outbursts of emotional need. They are also casual conversations of one close friend with another about common interests and friends. Knowing the distance to Nashville and the infrequency of communication, Catherine loads even briefer letters with news Claudia will like to have and thanks her for sending the same. Her subjects are the various Sisters, their relatives, mutual friends, Bishop Flaget, Father Martin Spalding, and, in every letter, some notice of Claudia's brother James. She gives accounts of the orphanage, its expansion and that of Presentation and the school in Lexington. She hopes the infirmary can soon be separated from the asylum and a day school for the poor be opened in that part of town. Every letter includes greetings, messages, and love sent to the Sisters, to clerical and lay friends in Nashville, to a servant, "to all acquaintances."

One letter of this period stands in sharp and surprising contrast to all others. In late May 1848, Catherine received and answered a letter from her niece Juliann Pierce Skinner, child of her sister Louisa Spalding Pierce's youthful marriage. Juliann had been registered at Nazareth Academy in 1824 at the age of eleven, during Mother Agnes's term. In May 1829 she entered the community and received the habit in December as Sister Olivia. Catherine was thus the Mother who received her, affirmed her progress, or at least consented to the Council's favorable vote. But she must have had concerns, because Juliann/Olivia did not make vows after the usual one-year novitiate. She left the community in April 1831 and subsequently married B. Skinner. At some point Juliann was left to support two children, and she seems to have done so by "roving from place to place," calling on the resources of relatives, and "getting a start." One of these relatives was her Aunt Catherine.[58]

Catherine had tried to help. She had written to her cousin John Spalding, son of Basil Jr., at Pleasant Hill, Maryland. He offered Juliann a place in his home "as long as agreeable to her," and a position teaching his and his sister's children.[59] But Juliann passed up a chance to live with extended family in the ancestral home, a choice that could hardly have earned Catherine's approval of her judgment. By 1848, she had spent a "few days" in Louisville, with some bad effect to which Catherine refers. She had migrated to Lexington, where Sister Ann Spalding was superior, and then to Bardstown. From there she wrote Catherine, asserting that Father McMahon, pastor in Lexington, had advised her to return to Louisville and asking Catherine's advice about a place with a family.

Juliann seems to have been hopelessly immature and unstable, unable to profit from good counsel or practical assistance, no matter how often sought or given. Catherine was quite capable of frank impatience with odd or parasitic types like Juliann and of blunt speech when confronting them. In this case, she was severe indeed.

In an abrupt opening, Catherine asserts that she has no advice to give, for Juliann had never followed any that she did give her—"& I know you never will." Catherine never advised her to go to Bardstown but now is certain she should stay there. Louisville is "no place for you . . . rest assured if you were here, in one month the Gilchrist family would be tired of you & shun you & soon you would be a public pauper.—This I am determined on, if you do come here, I never will see you nor have anything to do with you.—I will not."[60]

Catherine goes on to tell Juliann that she has the ability to support her two children, that prices in Bardstown are much less for the "advantages" she seeks, "vegetables, rent, shoes, hat trimmings &c, &c," and that if she would "sit down to work" she would get through initial difficulties and earn people's confidence. "But No, you have no perseverance, but perpetual change." She dismisses Father McMahon's advice as not candid, with no motive "but to get rid of you." After a paragraph concerning Sister Ann, she closes with the repeated warning, "If you ever attempt to live in *Louisville* from that day, never think of me again."

In no other extant letter does Catherine release such anger or threaten outright rejection. If she was often so angry, she characteristically kept control. This severity seems to exceed the firmness required and expected in dealing with someone like Juliann. Catherine was not a psychologist, could not have discussed projection of fear and anger, but she was wise, experienced in the ways of the weak, and known for her compassion. She must have known her niece's unstable early life. Juliann could not have been altogether unlike the orphans "with few to love them" to whom her own life was devoted.

But there is found the probable first explanation: Catherine's orphans were in genuine need, unable to care for themselves until the Sisters had taught them—at which point most of them did become self-supporting. Juliann, with her actual ability to support herself and children, threatened to become a leech on the always scarce resources of the orphans, and Catherine would prevent it by whatever severity-in-truth was required, even by rejection. In this letter, she resembles nothing so much as the biblical "bear in the wild" defending her cubs (2 Sam.17:8; Pr 17:12).

Yet the final paragraph of the letter reveals a cause much deeper than exhausted patience or even defense of the orphans' livelihood. Juliann's request, her concern for shoes and hat trimmings, had coincided with the death of Ann Spalding. Ann had died on May 15. Catherine's letter was written only nine days later, in the hour of bitterest loss and grief. News of the death had reached her niece. Catherine confirms it: "Yes, poor dear Sister Ann is gone! & you can't forget all that she has suffered on your account. These sufferings have no doubt done their part in hastening her to her grave." That accusation truly was unfair; Catherine knew Ann had not died from her niece's behavior. All the turmoil caused by that death was in progress when Catherine wrote this blistering letter to Juliann. Whether it severed their relation permanently remains a question.

A year after Ann's death, Catherine is again writing to Claudia in Nashville, acknowledging that she is indeed very busy and writes few letters, but asking her friend to believe that writing her is one of her "sweetest occupations." "I am getting old now & ought to begin to die to this world before it dies to me.—Still I can't feel willing that my best friends should change or forget me." Near the end she adds, "My best love & kindest wishes for dear Sister Xavier. I will write her as soon as I can, but she must write to me."[61] In light of all the year's losses, the plaintive personal note in this letter is readily understood. In addition, the letter reveals a special interest in the mission at Nashville, now in its sixth year, and in its young leader, Xavier Ross.

Having initiated that mission at some risk, Catherine might well maintain her concern for it. In 1845, Sister Scholastica Fenwick had written her that the school was progressing well and could do much good, but it required much humility, devotion, and unity of action to run it in a place of "so much pretension, so much aristocracy, and so much indulgence" of the young. Four months later, Rev. John McGuire wrote that the school was still well patronized, but the "policy pursued by its Head will ruin it for a certainty. It sinks fast."[62] In these letters from Nashville, Catherine might hear the rumbling of a conflict to come.

The "Head" was not the Sister Superior but Rev. Ivo Schacht, the priest appointed by Bishop Miles as director of the Sisters. Schacht was a man of his own adamant ideas and at this time strongly supported by the bishop. Perhaps it was with this problem in view that Sister Xavier Ross was sent in 1847 to apply her strong mind and will in leadership. In 1848, cholera and Father Schacht conspired to create a hospital and orphanage. More Sisters were wanted, and he wanted to select them. In August 1849, the Council resolved "that the authority of the Motherhouse be sustained over the Branch house at Nashville and if it cannot be done the Sisters to be called home as soon as it can be properly done."[63] All this presaged Catherine's first crisis when she would be recalled to office as Mother.

In Catherine's last year in Louisville, the social and political challenges to both mission and community increased with the issues debated at the Kentucky constitutional convention. The conflict over slavery was heating up. Louisvillians conducted slave sales in front of the Jefferson County Courthouse, where Catherine would have seen them on her walks, and also held "respectably attended" emancipation meetings there, including a huge one in February 1849. Voters split along pro- and anti-slavery lines in selecting delegates to a constitutional convention, where abolition was defeated.[64] Catherine leaves no record of her sense of the future or of her opinion. Slavery or abolition would affect her mission chiefly in affordability of servants.

The other burning issue, immigration, she would consider for its effect on community membership. Naturalization was still a state function in 1849, and it was proposed that the new constitution require a wait of twenty-one years, so as to prevent those "tainted with the Romanism of Europe" from getting control of the ballot box "by slow and cautious movements." Once again Catherine's good Protestant friend James Guthrie led the emphatic defeat of the proposal.[65] Had it passed, it might not have slowed immigration, but it could well have discouraged commitments of new SCNs subject to deportation for scant reason except bigotry.

Before she left Louisville, Catherine had to experience one more closure in her own history, one more transition to a new relationship that would deeply affect her and the community. From 1843 on, Bishop Flaget had been declining. He was now past eighty, nearly deaf, and unable to preach. Rome appointed Martin John Spalding as coadjutor despite Flaget's reservations about his health, numerous relatives in the area, and possible lack of independence. Flaget's last public function was the consecration of Spalding on September 10, 1848.[66] Catherine was certainly present, and she may have spent some thoughts on her own probable future with this active and firm-minded relative at the head of the diocese.

Bishop Spalding was essentially the presiding bishop for Flaget's final months. He began plans for a new cathedral and laid the cornerstone on August 15, 1849. From the balcony of the rectory, Flaget gave his blessing—his final public appearance. From then on, he was weakened in body and memory but cheerful in spirits, saying, "I forget everything; could I but forget myself I would be a perfect man." On February 11, 1850, he quietly ended his service, sixty-two years as a priest, forty as a bishop.[67] An era for the diocese, for the church in the West, had ended. One who had to feel it was the woman who had been his collaborator during the thirty-seven years since they met at St. Thomas Farm, who now attended his elaborate requiem in the cathedral and led her Sisters and orphans in the long procession to his resting place.

Catherine's own time with the orphans was about to end once more. On August 21, 1850, she was again elected to leadership as Mother Superior at Nazareth. Behind her on Jefferson Street she left four Sisters; four laywomen helpers, ages nineteen to thirty-four, two of them from Ireland; ninety-four orphans, ages nine months to fourteen years, three of them males, originating from Kentucky, New York, Indiana, Ohio, Missouri, Ireland, and "Unknown"; two priests from Ireland and France; and twelve others designated as laborers.[68] She did not want to leave them. But she was not one to deny the community voice. New issues were looming, and the "time to build" had come again.

Nine

Builder for a Future

1850–1856

In August 1850, Catherine wrote to Claudia Elliott: "Well, my dear good old friend & Sister, here I am again, seated at the old place writing to your own dear self.—But you know what it has again cost me to be torn away, as it were, from my poor, dear children. . . . How glad I would be to see you once more—but we must wait the disposition of Divine Providence. If we live, all things will come around."[1] She had written prophetically. Her final six years in her old place as Mother would nearly complete both her own spiritual character-building and her labor as builder of her community, its mission, and its physical home—but not without painful cost to her health, her heart, and her hopes.

Returning to office in 1850, Catherine found a much larger and more varied community at Nazareth than she had left in 1844. During the interim, forty-three women had entered, seventeen in 1845 alone. One Sister wrote Claudia that the refectory would hardly hold the many new Sisters. Another noted that almost all were "New Yorks" (immigrants), and that "one might suppose they are real beauties," but "some of them make the *big rats* run." The native-born Kentuckians of English ancestry had met their intercultural challenge in these mostly Irish and immigrant women. Another hint that the spirit of nativism had to be dealt with even at Nazareth is found in an 1855 letter of a Jesuit stating that "a certain number of *natives* have performed at Nazareth. If the

thing depended only on me, I would 'knock them off' very gladly."
Catherine's policy was to accept all and make room, "if they be
only good subjects to make true Sisters of Charity."[2] Her challenge
was now to unify this growing, diverse community and enable its
members to live together in St. Vincent's spirit of charity.

The physical environment of Nazareth had also changed. To
accommodate the expansion, a building of four stories had been
erected and existing buildings enlarged to include a new bakehouse and washhouse, Sisters' room, dormitory, and wardrobe
connected to the academy.[3] But the growth of the academy and
the lack of any truly sufficient, unified, and homelike space for
the Sisters would force Catherine again and more than ever to develop and use her acumen as a builder, to employ it at Nazareth
even as crises and needed expansion were demanding her response
elsewhere.

For this last and most stressful era, she still had a variety of
helpers. Sister Columba Carroll, elected Assistant and Directress
of the Academy, continued to offer her skills as teacher and administrator, as well as her intelligence, deep affection, and good counsel. Father Haseltine, ecclesiastical superior, ever the good friend,
pastor, consultant, and collaborator, would share the burden of
difficult decisions and communications, while encouraging the
spirituality of both Sisters and students.[4] And, as a touching encouragement, Catherine found still in her place the one remaining
pioneer friend, Teresa Carrico. The elderly Teresa, wrote Mother
Frances, stayed "up over the wash room . . . always mending . . . ,
Mother Catherine's old blue bed screen around her to make a cell.
. . . And many a holy prayer, no doubt, does she send up to God
during the day."[5] There Catherine would find her when in need of
her prayers, her reassuring faith, and her unfailing friendship.

The pioneers Catherine and Teresa could have rejoiced together in an immediate call to mission—a return to St. Thomas to help
open an orphanage for boys four to ten years old, "really destitute,
and exposed to loss of their faith." The Sisters of Charity were
asked to manage the kitchen and dining room, wardrobe, and infirmary. In December 1850, two Sisters moved into the old Howard house, the log house where the pioneer Sisters had entered.[6]

Catherine offered the bricks of the 1818 school to Father Francis Chambige for the new orphanage and went with two Sisters to take a last look at the building that had given so much joy and cost so much grief. She renewed her vows in the chapel adjoining the church and went to the spring. After that she returned often with young Sisters to drink of the spring and tell the story of the beginnings there. Whatever glow time has cast around the story, Catherine's transmission of this early history enabled others to pass it to the first annalist, and the tradition of "Mother Catherine's spring" survives in the community.[7]

Some of the original poverty accompanied the new mission, but this time Catherine and her Council thought a just support from the diocese was appropriate. They compromised on the annual forty dollars but resolved bluntly that Father Chambige "be required to hand to Sister Clementia twenty-five dollars for each sister at St. Thomas—she to use it to purchase articles of clothing." If the sum was insufficient at the end of the year, "he will make up to her the amount."[8]

Some Sisters did not find the aura of history enough to content them. Catherine and her Council had to make a number of changes in the staff and working conditions. Nevertheless, the orphanage grew to nearly seventy boys by the end of Catherine's term, and the Sisters' service continued well into the next century.[9]

No problem near home, however, could compare with what Mother Catherine had to face immediately at the most distant mission in Nashville, Tennessee. The conflict there was near to explosion when she returned to office, and it would test her leadership and spirituality as nothing else had done.

Despite the success of the school, the relations between Nashville clergy and Nazareth superiors were never really smooth. Developing the diocesan mission was the priority of Bishop Miles and his close helper, Father Ivo Schacht. For this, they understandably wanted to conserve and enlarge all financial resources and especially to have competent and stable personnel, dedicated to diocesan goals. With those aims Nazareth was in sympathy, yet the Mother, her Council, and the ecclesiastical superior had the collaborative duty of maintaining the community's rules and rights in the conduct of mission. Tension had built up very early.

The bishop had objected to a compensation of fifty dollars per Sister per year; moreover, he wanted the Sisters to sing in the cathedral choir, contrary to Nazareth's custom and rule. Father Haseltine had reminded him that fifty dollars was no more than was needed for Sisters' clothing, personal necessities, and some advance for their "worn out" years. And if more Sisters were to be sent for a hospital and orphan asylum, the Rule of St. Vincent would be sent with them and observed.[10]

The climax approached when the bishop expressed his wish to designate which Sisters would be appointed to or removed from Nashville. This was a violation of the core procedure by which the various missions were staffed, and Nazareth would not yield. Father Haseltine communicated firmly that if the authority of the motherhouse could not be maintained and the bishop be satisfied, "we will make immediate arrangements to free you from embarrassment."[11]

Perhaps if all the Sisters in Nashville had been of one mind on the controversy, the bishop might have accepted Nazareth's authority. By 1850, however, Sister Xavier Ross and some others thought the bishop should have his desires. They were close to the situation, and they either really agreed with him or thought acquiescence necessary to maintain the mission.

From this point, episodes and dates must be pieced together. In the summer of 1850, perhaps to resolve the issue of loyalties, perhaps simply to give Sister Xavier both a healing rest and some distance at which to think and pray, she was brought to Kentucky, probably to Nazareth. On August 1, she wrote to Claudia Elliott in Nashville a letter very like some of Catherine's, revealing the same qualities of loving leadership, good management of resources, and prudent directions. But other parts of this letter suggest the lines of the struggle to come:

> Have you heard from our good Bishop since I came away? I feel twice as strong as I did in Nashville, but something whispers to me daily, that I am recruiting to go elsewhere

to labor. Well, God's holy will be done. I do feel resigned, the more so, the more I think of it.

We will return week after next. . . . We will wait until Mr. Schacht returns.

If my darling Bishop gets home before I do, give him my best love, for I do love him and ever shall. I wish all the world were like him. But then, I would be too happy and would perhaps forget my home in Heaven. Had I remained in Nashville, I should have written to him before this.

The letter ends with a touching apology for "being so cross to you the night before I left. I was so worried."[12] Whether Xavier returned to Nashville in mid-August is unclear.

This was the unresolved state of affairs when Catherine returned to office on August 21, 1850. She wasted no time. The very next day the Council met and appointed outgoing Mother Frances Gardiner superior at the Nashville Academy and Sister Xavier superior of the orphanage in Louisville. Five days later and again in the autumn, various changes were made in the staffs of both St. Mary's Academy and St. John's Hospital. Nazareth's authority and the Sisters' loyalties had become burning and divisive issues. Gentle Mother Frances, "little Moses," it was hoped, could mend the breach at Nashville while Catherine firmly gripped the helm.[13]

But by then, the thought in Nashville had gone beyond choirs and assignments. The new project was to make the Sisters an entirely separate community under episcopal authority. Bishop Miles was certainly aware of the precedents with Sisters of Charity in New York and Cincinnati. Why not in Nashville? One of his priests (probably Schacht) said it would be a "great consolation for the Bishop to have . . . a Sisterhood which he could control without foreign interference of any sort."[14]

How much of this plan was Miles's and how much Schacht's is debatable.[15] This much is certain, that by 1851, ten years after the independence crisis, Catherine Spalding's most pressing obligation was yet again to maintain Nazareth's membership and mission against "foreign interference." In June 1851, Schacht wrote to Bishop Spalding, urging him to visit Nashville: "The Bishop

[Miles] desires that the house of Nazareth would be kind enough to furnish him with five or six Sisters to commence a Novitiate with of our own. Our . . . circumstances render this an imperative duty on our part. I consider a refusal almost certain, because I could not take any other but such as I would name myself. Moreover, *the thing is to be done*. I want to do things amicably, and find myself without such counsel as I need. Mother Frances most pressingly invites you too."[16] This letter strongly suggests that Father Schacht saw himself as the prime mover, the one who would determine the event. Mother Frances probably saw Bishop Spalding as the only one who might halt both Miles and Schacht, the one who could take a clear account back to Mother Catherine and the Council.

Sister Xavier, meanwhile, was performing her office in Louisville and keeping in touch with Nashville. In the winter of 1850–1851, she wrote Claudia a simple cordial letter, asking about the illness of the bishop, who had written on her feast day, and sending love to all the Sisters, "Mother first, though she never thinks of me now. I wonder what I have done to her."[17] The startling final line must refer to Mother Frances, her replacement in Nashville. What later Sisters in the two communities of Mother Catherine and Mother Xavier have long wondered is how this painful drama was playing out between *them* in its final months.

The two women were undoubtedly in communication and mutual struggle. Xavier was seriously and sincerely questioning if God was "recruiting" her for a new enterprise whose value she could see, and Catherine was urgently wishing to prevent departures that she could only envision as defections from community. Some measure of conflict and much personal grief for both cannot be doubted.

Catherine and Xavier had a long history in common since their meeting in 1832, when Ann Ross had sought shelter with Catherine in the Louisville orphanage. Catherine had received young Sister Xavier on her first mission and for two years mentored her in religious life and the care of orphans. As Mother, Catherine had brought her back to Nazareth to teach and then made her superior at Presentation and authorized her taking music pupils.[18] When

Catherine returned to Louisville in 1844, the two superiors were in cordial contact and collaboration.

This collaboration is reflected in letters Xavier wrote to Father Ben Spalding in Bardstown. When she could not take a poor girl to work at Presentation, Mother Catherine agreed to take her at the orphanage for six months of instruction in literacy and religion, after which she might be situated at Presentation. At Father Spalding's request, Xavier took a suggested prescription for his brother to a doctor at the infirmary and reported, "Mother Catherine declared that in proportion as his form dilated mine contracted—but in this she must have been mistaken, for the only emotion I felt was a strong inclination to laugh at the doctor's evident pique."[19] Clearly, the women's relationship included casual good humor and teasing. It could not be severed without great pain to both.

Mother Frances had sent Xavier to Nashville. When Mother Catherine's Council decided to remove her, she was not "demoted" but returned to the orphanage as superior. Xavier's love for orphans seems to have matched Catherine's. So did her ability to manage and direct an institution and to deal with a variety of persons. Facts support the opinion that Catherine nurtured Xavier's leadership and hoped to see it exercised in the community's future, perhaps as her own successor.[20]

In the effort to understand what both women experienced in the Nashville crisis, it is instructive to look at analytical studies made of them.[21] These trace two personalities so alike as to make for powerful union if the goal and methodologies are the same, and painful rupture if they diverge. Both Catherine and Xavier were emotionally responsive to a high degree, "heart over head" people, controlled by proper pride and dignity. Both had to grow in intuitive awareness of others' feelings. Their decisions could be quick, influenced by feelings and by confidence about an issue; yet they were balanced by fine analytical, critical thinking. Neither was highly imaginative; both preferred action on facts as they saw them. Most significant for the situation, both were women of strong will and determination, both assertive, even aggressive on occasion, frank, yet capable of diplomacy. Xavier, it was said, would not give up a project halfway nor in the face of defeat;

Catherine had "some reluctance to loosen the grip on what had been achieved."

Loosen it, nevertheless, Catherine was forced to do. Whatever passed between these women in the winter of 1851, by summer, Xavier had made her choice. On June 26, 1851, she severed her tie to the Sisters of Charity of Nazareth.[22] To Father Ben Spalding she communicated her decision:

> Did you know how long—how thoroughly I have revolved the matter in my own mind—how composedly and *peacefully* I take this step, it would appear to you, as it does to me, the necessary result of causes which have produced it. I have not done it hastily but have reflected on it long, and constantly prayed that I might do *only* God's holy will. . . . I leave in peace with all and I hope my leaving will disturb the peace of none. I shall not cease to be a Sister of Charity.

She adds a postscript, "Of course I have informed my Superior of my intention."[23]

How soon Xavier returned to Nashville is unknown, but her communication to Mother Catherine precipitated action. On July 2, 1851, the Council resolved that "Mother Catherine start tomorrow for Nashville" and that "she be and is hereby authorized and required by the Council of Nazareth to order home . . . in the manner she may judge proper" the Sisters at St. John's Hospital. She was to "ascertain the present dispositions of the Sisters at St. Mary's Academy" and, if she thought changes were needed, was "authorized and requested to send such Sisters home."[24] The language is legal and decisive. The intent is obviously to end the mission of the hospital and, if possible, to save that of the school.

It was all too late. Whatever Catherine thought and prayed on her long journey down, whatever she said in conversations described as "amicable but unbudging," this time she was unable to persuade either the bishop or the Sisters. Three Sisters from St. Mary's and two from St. John's joined Sister Xavier to form the Sisters of Charity of Nashville. In community age, they ranged from Xavier's seventeen years in vows to Jane Frances Jones's eighteen months. One would like to credit fully the later assertion that "throughout all the negotiations the most kindly feeling was manifested. Mother Catherine only attempted to dissuade them from precipitancy" and "trembled lest their courage might lead them into peril." She may well have credited their concern for the mission of the struggling diocese and their long and hard discernment of God's will for them. But later documents suggest a depth of wounding and disapproval that could hardly have been concealed even by heroic kindness and concern.[25]

Mother Catherine managed her farewells as best she could and returned to Nazareth. With her went eight Sisters, including Mother Frances Gardiner, Sister Margaret Bamber, heroine of the 1830s' cholera, and the ever faithful Claudia Elliott.[26]

Catherine had just endured the huge failure of an effort in community leadership. She had to deal in her own prayerful heart with the questions and feelings such an event must have created: all the "might-have-beens," her level of responsibility for the outcome, the possible impact on the community's future in membership and mission, the welfare and future of those she had lost. It was not in her character to lose care for them, no matter how disappointed or even angry she might be with their choice. No doubt she found support in her faith in Divine Providence. But neither she nor the Sisters in Nashville could have any comfort then in knowing or even imagining how Providence would carry the severed branch to the West and plant it where Nazareth could never have gone.[27]

Catherine had to deal immediately with the disposition of the community property in Nashville. The hospital belonged to the diocese; the Nazareth Council accepted an offer of $12,500 for the academy. The note was finally paid during Catherine's last year of office. The great break was concluded—officially.[28]

But the end was not reached without interim annoyances and further losses. Bishop Miles was a hard man to discourage. Seven months after the separation, he sent Mother Frances a letter he had deferred "lest I should give offense to some that might feel concerned" (obviously Catherine and Haseltine). But he assures Frances the Sisters in Nashville are cheerful, happy, and successful;

"we only want a few more such spirits to bring us through triumphantly. . . . Could you not send us some postulants?"[29]

Two more SCNs did go to Nashville. In a reverse move, Sister Baptista Carney appealed to return to Nazareth; the Council allowed her "if she will enter the Novitiate and make such reparation for her fault of leaving the Community as the Council may direct." The wording reveals the pained judgment of the separation. But Baptista (renamed Julian) spent only four months in the novitiate before being allowed to renew her vows.[30] The softening and healing had to be also Catherine's.

Just after the Nashville crisis subsided, Haseltine wrote Mother Frances, now superior at St. Vincent Academy, Union County, reminding her that if she had trouble there, it was "nothing to what you left here for your successor [Catherine] in the Mothership of Nazareth."[31] That successor, moreover, being on the Council and Board, had to be involved with Frances in the troubles that had simmered at St. Vincent's since the 1830s. Most of these were dealings with the powerful pastor of Sacred Heart Church, Father Elisha Durbin, who was much too eager to manage the finances of school and convent and direct Nazareth's purchases. Some Sisters also gave trouble about rendering financial accounts to Nazareth on time, resistance to rules, dissension in the local community, and resultant frequent changes of assignment.[32] Haseltine was helpful, but it fell to Mother Catherine, then immersed in construction at Nazareth, to make the long trip to Union County in late 1852 to negotiate with Father Durbin. He was building a new Sacred Heart Church and wanted Nazareth to buy the old one adjacent to the academy. Catherine and Council met continually through 1853, to bargain, concede, and refuse land dealings.[33]

As for community life at St. Vincent's, in 1855 Catherine wrote a revealing letter to a Sister there. She assures her, "No, my very dear Sister, I am not displeased with you nor with anyone on the place. My heart yearns for you *all* with maternal interest." Then she launches into one of her most often quoted statements of principle: "Oh, if you *all* have hearts as devoted to all the *interests* of the Community as mine is, there would truly be but one *common* interest, and self would be laid aside.—No one should be anxious to appear as having done more, nor others less. Our Community must be the centre from which all our good works must emanate and in the name of the Community all must be done.—Then let none of us be ambitious as to who does more or who less.—God will judge it all thereafter."[34] One might hear in her words echoes of the experience of Nashville.

One trouble that would have deeply distressed Mother Catherine is hinted at in various references to Sister Angela Spink. After the trauma of her resignation and the year at White River, Angela was at St. Vincent's at least until 1839, along with Sister Elizabeth Suttle, to whom Bishop David was writing criticisms of Angela and the community at Nazareth. Soon after returning to office in 1838, Mother Catherine brought Angela back to Nazareth, where she seems to have stayed until 1848, when Mother Frances sent her back to St. Vincent's. First builder and superior of St. Vincent's, once so regarded as to be elected trustee and Mother, Angela was now in some painful dark night of her life. In 1852 and 1854, Council references to her annual renewal of vows indicate unexplained confusion and incapacity as part of Mother Angela's inner life. Mother Catherine's role in the decisions affecting her early companion could hardly have created less pain for her than for Angela. On August 8, 1854, Angela Spink died and was laid to rest in the land she had tilled more than thirty years earlier.[35]

Angela's death was probably the most personally saddening of the seventeen that occurred in Catherine's final term. But Angela was aging; most of the seventeen were less than ten years in vows. In a small community, one death a year may be borne, nine in two years just barely. A postulant died, a novice two days after she made vows on her deathbed, and in one month, two Sisters only four and six years in vows. Catherine was simultaneously building for the future and burying the youthful hope for it. She lamented, "It afflicts me to see so many of our dear Sisters dropping off in the prime of life. But God knows best." Resignation did not mute her repeated calls for proper care of health: "The Sisters should all be very prudent about their health, for once the lungs become diseased there is no stopping it." "Tell Sister Humbeline she must not neglect her cough.—We have buried Sisters enough now. . . . I do think everyone is bound to be prudent about her health for without it the work of God & the neighbor could not be carried on."[36]

All through this term, Catherine was experiencing her own declining health and the increasing effects of age and stress. As early as 1849, when she was fifty-five, she had written, "I am getting old now & ought to begin to die to this world before it dies to me." Three weeks before the losses to Nashville were finalized, she told Claudia she had a severe headache and had to stop writing until it got better. Columba Carroll reported that continuous neuralgia tormented Catherine through most of 1854 and left her "greatly debilitated." In early 1855, Catherine pleaded, "Now, my good Sister, don't be too particular with your poor Mother. You know it is rather hard for me to write since I have suffered so much severe pain & I never expect to be entirely well again."[37]

Burgeoning life, however, strove with death to claim Catherine's spirits. In early 1856, she reported happily the excellent health at Nazareth and the presence of sixteen or eighteen in the novitiate with "still room for more." In her final term, seventy-six women entered, and fifty-six received the habit. The numbers suggest that the novice director, Catherine, and the Council carefully tested the postulants' motives and stability and affirmed only those likely to "make true Sisters of Charity." Of the fifty-six novices, fifty-one made first vows, thirty-six while Catherine was still in office.[38] Perhaps she came from Louisville in her final years to see the remaining ceremonies. Catherine's "days of jubilee" far outnumbered the funerals.

Many letters of this last term are to the young Sisters in the branch houses to whom Catherine looked for prayers, support, and the fidelity that would give continuity to the work of her life. To these "dear absent Sisters," she sent encouragement to observe their rules and duties, to persevere in commitment and in the spirit that gave their life its meaning. She assured them of her willingness to support and comfort them in struggles. Sister Baptista Walls had been accepted for vows only with the Council's notation, "she to be admonished previously by Mother Catherine." A year later,

Catherine sent (unopened and uncensored) a letter received for Baptista at Nazareth, and wrote her own gentle advice not to be too independent and cause herself trouble, but to take counsel with her superior and another older Sister. All these letters include expressions of warm, sincere, deep love and good wishes for the Sisters' life and mission.[39]

The mission, indeed, was alive and growing throughout Catherine's final term. Both Louisville and Nazareth greatly needed larger spaces for their ministries of health care and education—and as quickly as possible. Expansions began almost simultaneously, and however severe her headaches and neuralgia, Catherine Spalding had to focus and expend enormous energy in the 1850s on planning and building.

The first project was to separate the infirmary from the orphan asylum and find a larger space for it. For this purpose, Catherine had to rouse her energies for repeated meetings and trips to Louisville—one day each way—to view property, to negotiate with Bishop Spalding and property owner James Guthrie, to purchase and report back. In the end, the Council decided not to build but to lease diocesan property vacant on Fourth Street just north of Prather (Broadway) and to send Mother Catherine to Louisville to put the new hospital into operation as soon as possible.[40] This she did, with her supporter Appolonia McGill and eight Sisters collaborating with twenty-one physicians. St. Vincent Infirmary was officially closed in 1852. At its new location, it was named St. Joseph Infirmary. In the heart of the city until 1926, it served all creeds, colors, and classes; it remains a chief part of Catherine Spalding's history.[41]

The idea of building a hospital or something else persisted, it seems. In May 1854, the Board of Trustees decided that Catherine Spalding should enlarge the Guthrie lot by further purchase "to the center of St. Catherine Street." That name is the only lasting interest this acreage has in Catherine's history. No SCN building ever stood on it, but the "country road" to the south of the lot was widened, and James Guthrie put on his deed the name that the street still bears. Shrewd businessman, lawyer of national reputation, and devoted father of Nazareth graduates, he chose to honor a woman who matched him well in mind, heart, and civic accomplishment.[42]

Relocation of the infirmary allowed Catherine to think of her other concern for the poor, namely, education. A free school had succeeded Presentation in the basement of the cathedral. Now she could serve the eastern part of the city by initiating a day school in the orphanage. The usual pattern was developed: payment by those who could afford it, free offering to those who could not.[43]

Education for the poor in the east end of town was soon to be matched in the west end. In 1854, at Thirteenth and Market Streets, SCNs and Xaverian Brothers opened St. Patrick Free School for the children of Irish immigrants. But in July 1855, the Council declared that the Sisters could not return "under the arrangements of last winter." Living conditions apparently had been intolerable. Catherine had known plenty of cold, insecurity, and unavoidable hardship, but she was not letting the Sisters' health or lives be needlessly endangered. Something must have been improved. In October, the Council decided to pay the rent of a house near St. Patrick Church and to support the poor school "for God's sake."[44]

Catherine's last new establishment was in the new diocese of Covington in northern Kentucky, separated from Louisville in 1853. The Council's intent was "to teach the poor," and Catherine notified diocesan officials that the school was to be "only a common school, common branches." Bishop George Carrell, however, told the vicar general, "You had better write Mother Catherine about the pay school, music, embroidery, etc. Without a good school the Sisters will not make money to buy bread, much less to pay the rent of a house, etc." As before at Nazareth, Catherine faced the need to provide refinements for young women in order to provide basics for the poor. She also faced the risk of another Nashville episode in a new diocese. Catherine relayed to Sister Clare Gardiner the financial conditions concerning support for Sisters, house, and school. Clare signed for her, and LaSalette Academy and St. Mary's Cathedral School for the poor opened in 1856. Catherine accompanied the pioneers there, and Bishop Spalding voiced the hope that there would be no "Secession."[45]

All these years, poor health notwithstanding, Catherine was frequently on the road, doing business for the schools, infirmary, and orphanage. From Nazareth, Sister Columba Carroll wrote that Catherine had gone to Louisville but was far from well: "There is so much depending on her, and her presence and active influence are always necessary but especially now, that it is doubly painful to see her sick and suffering." Columba was trying to help by doing a great deal of the business writing.[46]

While these branch house projects were requiring attention, Catherine was supervising the largest, most demanding project of her career as builder: a new church and academy at Nazareth. The Council had determined in 1849 on a church, true to the earlier priority of building a chapel before other new construction. Catherine had been back in office only a month when the cornerstone was laid, in September 1850.[47] For the next five years, in collaboration with Father Haseltine, she supervised massive construction, even as the work of leading the school and community went on.

William Keely, architect for the Louisville Cathedral, was engaged. Probably in a bartering of labor, Catherine sent Isaac Bell, slave at Nazareth, to live with him. Referring to Bell, Catherine wrote Keely, "We sincerely hope he may prove to be all that you wish him, & that his friends who feel so much interest in his well-doing, may not be disappointed." Later, she sent "Best wishes and kind remembrance for Ike." It is likely that some of Ike's fellow slaves remaining at Nazareth helped erect the new buildings.[48]

In that same letter to Keely, Catherine reports stonework ready to begin and the foreman's need of Keely's presence and direction. Then she adds, "Now, please, don't think me importunate in saying I would be very glad to see the general plan you have made for carrying out our own buildings here.—as I would prefer to have nothing done or commenced, nor even decided on; but in view of, & in accordance with that plan.—Still we are greatly in want of some little arrangements & even of more room."[49] Shrewd businesswoman and diplomat, she conveyed her right to be consulted and decisive, as well as her urgency about the task.

Urgent as the convent seemed, by the end of 1851 Catherine knew the plan to build it had to be abandoned. A larger academy was needed first. The school had 154 boarders, "almost a pity to have so many," wrote Haseltine. The Council faced priorities; Catherine with Keely should travel to St. Louis to examine academic institutions there and, if necessary, go to the Convent of the Sacred Heart "on the coast" (perhaps New York) before a new plan was made. They decided eventually to renovate the 1825 academy building into a motherhouse—after all else was completed. Until then, the Sisters would continue to sleep in cabins, over work areas, or "where we may find most convenient."[50]

By the middle of 1852, church and academy were being built simultaneously. In May, Catherine wrote of having "very heavy undertakings . . . which give us a good deal of trouble" and of being "surrounded by work and workmen besides our very large family." A June letter to the Sisters at the infirmary and orphan asylum reveals the pressure, her exhaustion, and her true preferences: "I have just been away from you long enough to make me think a great deal about you all." The buildings are "getting along very well," and she hopes soon to begin the hospital for "the poor and suffering members of Christ." Then she makes a poignant reflection: "But, dear Sisters, what will all that profit us if we should neglect the spiritual building of our own perfection by a faithful observance of Rules & the true spirit of religion." As if in self-examination, she comments on "poor human nature's" tendency to contract the *habit* of neglecting attendance at religious exercises, even though it is merit to postpone them when *duty* requires: "Oh! Let us be watchful on ourselves in this. . . . It is the only way to secure the blessings of God on our labors for His glory. . . . You are particularly blessed in that house as all your labors are for those immediate works of charity." Catherine Spalding would always do the labor required; she would also yearn to exchange construction for care of children.[51]

Year by year, the walls continued to rise. Supportive structures were put in place and a road laid out, presumably to link the building to the outer edge of the property. The road created some controversy that cannot be fully explained but that reveals Catherine's ability to combine hard business decisions with good relationships. In May 1854, the Board appointed Catherine and Father Haseltine to a committee to confer about executing the road "without sacrifice of the interests of Nazareth, and as far as possible to accommodate the neighbors." At least one neighbor, it seems, could not be satisfied and pulled his daughter out of school. Undaunted, in September, Mother Catherine wrote to "my dear Kate," her godchild, a very loving letter sharing her regret at "the necessity that compels you to stay from school." She assures her, "I fully appreciate your pa's good qualities, and as for that affair with regard to the road . . . I say nothing about it. We pray to Almighty God for everyone." She intends to see Kate and her mother at their home, urges her to visit her friends at Nazareth, and sends love to her mother and grandmother, "respects to Ma and Pa." Catherine maintained her relationship with Kate. A later sympathy letter says Catherine had also sent a promised "pretty little present . . . without alloy and as pure as the love I bear you."[52]

In the midst of all the activity, in February 1854, the school was attacked by typhoid fever. Students were sent home or to an SCN house, yet two died. Both Catherine and Columba Carroll recorded their grief, the "sad void" and "bitter tears," their empathy with a mother's loss. Both wrote alumna Eliza Cook, Catherine particularly to assure her that her younger sister was in no danger of the typhoid. Most but not all students returned.[53]

As Catherine looked forward to the completion of the church, her spirits brightened. In April 1854 she wrote, "If you could only see how fast the walls of the new church are running up.—The tops of the window frames are already above the roof of the Sisters' house, and where will it be when all is finished!" Although all was not finished, the consecration of the new church was set for July 19, 1854, feast of St. Vincent de Paul. Columba Carroll conveyed to Mother Frances the exciting preparations and Catherine's invitation for her to come from Lexington, but also the distressing news that Catherine's continuing and unrelieved neuralgia would probably preclude her attending the six-hour ceremony. Columba feared she could not recover. "But God gives her the grace of perfect submission to His Holy Will." She suggests that Frances come after retreat when a more peaceful visit would be possible because "it would do her good to see you."[54]

Whether or not Catherine was able to enjoy the climax of her achievement, she had long mulled her motives for the labor that so drained her basic health and energy. She records her core desire that "the finishing and fixing" would contribute to "completing all as a real Community establishment." The church would be "an edifice to the honor of God, not indeed as fine and rich as the one built by Solomon, but as fine as his poor daughters of Nazareth could build to his honor for future generations." The former academy would become a home "for the Community where they may live as a *regular* Community should live."[55]

As for her personal hopes at this time, Catherine voices them rather plaintively: "Oh! How I long to see all fixed as a Community should be & then I may lay me down in peace.—Pray for me, my dear child, that God in his own good mercy may give rest to my poor soul in a better world, for in this life there has been little rest for us—& indeed we should not seek rest here—for here is the time for labor and sorrow."[56] High spirits do not easily survive extreme fatigue. Yet if the young woman's buoyancy is depleted, the wise woman quickly asserts her acceptance of fact and controls self-pity.

Use of the new academy in the summer of 1855 would complete the construction project. All through it, Catherine had still been the principal manager of the academy. Although the school was so much larger than in her previous terms, parents expected her to provide no less care, education, discipline, and service for their daughters. Numerous letters remaining from this period suggest how great was the actual volume received and answered, what a load of tasks Catherine had to perform or delegate to others.

Catherine the headmistress was still asked to provide clothes and books and specific amenities, to regulate visits to "a few select families" off campus, control the girls' personal expenditures, convey messages to them from relatives, arrange their summer trips home or their profitable activity during vacation at school, and report the "pleasing intelligence of their progress." She had to approve each new prospectus for the school, including terms of payment, and invite the guests to and attend the annual public examinations, three long days, 8:00 A.M. to 5:00 P.M., in the heat of July. Echoes of the many letters requesting Catherine to select and provide dresses can be heard in a decision in 1856, based on "experience of many years," to adopt "a *fixed Uniform,* to be worn by all the pupils."[57]

Catherine the administrator made yearly contracts with a baker. She more than once sought a French teacher. One lady from New York, after agreeing to take the position for $500, mentioned that she had "failed to tell you that I speak very little English" and could neither converse in it nor translate to it.[58] Small wonder that Columba Carroll took over some of the business letters.

One hopes Sister Columba assumed the onerous task of answering at least some of the letters Catherine received concerning tuition and other bills due to Nazareth. The same problem that had dogged academy management in Catherine's earlier terms remained a daily nuisance, an irritant to her sense of justice, and a threat to her ability to sustain the school and community. Parents politely, apologetically, or belligerently delayed or refused to pay: Catherine should predate the bill for a year in the deceased mother's lifetime so it can be an estate account; "you will please do this soon." A ten-dollar music book is "exorbitant"; the father had been led to believe that Nazareth was not only a good school but "a cheap and economical one." It was "not convenient" to pay an entire balance and "very inconvenient" to provide the daughter's clothing; but she will need to remain at school through vacation because she needs Catherine's "parental care." Catherine had an agent for the South; it may have been he who left two unsealed bills in a doorway, causing a Mr. Montgomery to send Catherine a blistering refusal, insulting in tone and diction: he will not pay "what I do not owe, what I never had anything to do with." Mrs. Montgomery is the responsible party. And unless Catherine explains the letters "underhandedly conveyed," he will pay nothing or, if he pleases, "a donation."[59]

Catherine somehow retained her patience and her faith in the

mission and future of the academy. Faith and her progressive fore-
sight are registered in her Council's decision to take twenty-five
shares in the proposed Louisville and Nashville Railroad, provided
it would pass within a quarter mile of the Academy. Just after the
new building began use, the NLBI Board constituted Catherine,
Columba, and Haseltine a committee with "discretionary power"
to subscribe to a branch railroad from Bardstown to the L&N.[60]

The Nashville break, St. Vincent's problems, a new hospital and
four new schools, leadership of community and academy, construction of a church and school, and renovation of a motherhouse—all
were managed despite headaches and neuralgia. One might suppose Catherine Spalding had had sufficient occasions to live by her
norm to "suffer and meet with some trials" so as to "be followers
of Christ."[61] She needed no new trouble or troublemakers with a
bishop. But even as she was preparing for Bishop Spalding to con-
secrate the church, history was repeating itself.
      Catherine's relationship with her distant cousin Martin John
Spalding remains something of a puzzle. The bishop was amiable
and approachable, generally tolerant, also imbued by his training
in Rome with a deep respect for ecclesiastical authority. When he
himself was vested with it, he found it limited chiefly by religious
orders. In his dealings with Mother Catherine, genuine and mutual respect was jarred more than once when his idea and exercise
of authority collided with her Council's respectful assertion of its
right to make decisions.[62]
      The rise of real tension is first hinted in an 1852 letter from
Catherine to Bishop Spalding. Sister Gabriella Todd, daughter of a
prominent Frankfort judge, had presented to the bishop her desire
to visit her father during vacation. The bishop wrote to Catherine,
who replied, "I don't think there will be any difficulty made"; Gabriella need no longer be "restless" about it. Then to a few lines of
pleasant news, she added, "I sometimes think I would be glad to
have a conversation with you."[63]
      During the next year, Catherine and the Council had to deal
with Gabriella three times. She was obviously "restless" about
renewing her vows and was to do so only if she could "express

herself disposed to persevere."[64] Gabriella did not leave, but she may well have been one of those who reported to the bishop their dissatisfaction with Catherine's administration, specifically of the novitiate program.

That such complainers existed and were having an effect on Bishop Spalding is certain. Early in 1854, Columba Carroll, Catherine's Assistant, informed Mother Frances that on a recent visit the bishop was "gentle, amiable, and almost as of old. I hope he will retain his former, truly paternal manner; 'tis sad to see a change in one so loved and respected." A month later, Columba writes again:

> I hope there will arise no ill will between the new Bishop [Carrell of Covington] and Nazareth; for bishops are human, and unfortunately act from feeling and prejudice as well as other people. The evil most to be deplored is when they express their disapprobation to members of the community who thus feel themselves justified in failure of duties, throwing the censure on the community, not on themselves, and deeming themselves supported by high authority. . . . I dislike any contest, particularly of a pecuniary nature with bishops or priests. But still I am not disposed that Nazareth be imposed on.[65]

What Columba Carroll knew, Catherine Spalding knew and felt.

Whoever the troublemakers were, they precipitated a letter from Catherine to Bishop Spalding that exudes barely controlled anger and pain, in words as close as Catherine ever came to pure defensiveness. She begins "with a sad heart and much hesitancy . . . in the presence of my dear Redeemer," hoping to speak "with due respect, sincerity, & humble submission" to the bishop, "who has a right to know things as they *are*." Then, with biting irony, she disposes of the accusation by "informers" that she had "given a Sister a tremendous scolding for having spoken to you disapprovingly of the Novitiate!" After a positive denial, she points out the obvious: "even common sense and policy" would prevent her from giving such a Sister a second occasion to complain to him.

As for the novitiate, she describes its observances and the competency of the director. She invites and challenges: "If you, dear Rev. Bishop, will give us a better and more efficacious plan, I promise most faithfully to have it carried out."[66]

A clergyman had quoted the bishop as saying there was a "*falling off*" at Nazareth. The basis for this seems to have been "temporalities." Catherine refuses reproach on this score; temporalities are only "a *means* to do good—and that in your own diocese." She does reproach herself that "I *had* labored harder for this diocese and my Community, for spiritual and temporal, than I had done for my *own* sanctification." This fault she will now amend and leave all else in the hands of God.

The accusations to the bishop had included quotations of Catherine herself. To these she replies that he is "perfectly welcome to know whatever I may have said, provided it be *understood just* as I said and meant, for I have made it a rule through life to say nothing to *others* that I *cared* for being repeated, though I might not wish it. & few in this world have ever had my confidence in that respect." She cites an occasion when, "perplexed, embarrassed & unhappy," she had confided in a spiritual adviser and afterwards found she "had not been understood . . . & this I think, dear Father & Bishop, is at the bottom of your soured feelings toward me." In blunter terms, the adviser had betrayed her confidence. The letter implies that the betrayal concerned her insistence on observance of the constitutions as "necessary for permanency, peace, and good understanding of the Society." But her contention for that observance "was *never* meant with a view to curtail *our* contributions to good works."

Finally, she comes to "the point that weighs heaviest on my simple heart: If I am the cause of so great evil as you believe to exist . . . I most humbly beg of you to devise some plan for having me removed." While this offer is a challenge, one may believe her assurance that she would "cheerfully take any corner & in any kitchen" and concentrate her energies on her own soul. Well might Catherine Spalding, at this time, have envied Teresa Carrico her quiet, prayer-filled kitchen ministry.

While not incoherent, this letter leaves its reader still somewhat uncertain what Bishop Spalding's real problem was. As bishop, he had a right, perhaps felt a present need to concern himself with a "falling off" of religious observance or readiness to serve in his diocese. And perhaps a too busy Catherine had been unable to keep aware of all developments in the community. Yet she seems to say clearly enough that his specific concerns, whatever they were, were unwarranted and roused mainly by discontented Sisters and clergy. By contrast to her 1841 letter to Bishop Flaget, this one is far less organized and shows her exhausted from labors, the betrayal of her trust, the misrepresentation of her opinions, motives, and actions, and the need to defend herself. The style suggests rapid writing and the intensity of emotion discharged in multiple heavy underscorings.

At the end of 1854, a weary but yet determined Catherine met with her Council to discuss all the subjects the bishop had raised either to her or to Sister Columba. They noted his concerns for nursing and education of the poor and cited the community's intent to expand both public and private charities as soon as the motherhouse was out of debt.[67]

With one final threat to her mission, Catherine could not deal directly. By 1855, half of Louisville's sixty thousand people were Irish or German, and the anti-immigrant, anti-Catholic sentiment had risen in proportion, fanned by Know-Nothing, American Party politicians and the vituperative editorials of George Prentice. A Know-Nothing mayor was elected in April; that summer Catholic teachers were dismissed from public schools, and in July, St. Patrick Church was searched for munitions. By August 6, 1855, the day of elections for governor and representatives, the city was ready to explode, and did. The rioting of "Bloody Monday" in the German and Irish neighborhoods left at least twenty-two people dead, many injured, and extensive properties burned.[68]

How much news of the rising hostility reached Nazareth before that election day cannot be ascertained, but surely enough to cause genuine concern. There is no evidence that Catherine was in the city on Bloody Monday. But word must have reached her speedily that rioters assembled around the orphanage, that her Sisters and children huddled within, that several hundred terrified refugees from the mobs were in the yard and house, and that only one bold leader would have been needed to start a rampage through the plank fence. A year later, Catherine writes from the orphanage to Lexington, asking for a daily litany to be prayed in common by all the Sisters until November, "to obtain a just and *peaceable* election. . . . we poor orphans will join."[69]

Through all the years of this final term of office, of large and lesser crises, of daily cares and her own illness, Catherine Spalding had what most upheld her spirit and gave her joy—her relationship with her God. Her letters register the fidelity to prayer, the submission to and trust in Providence, the awareness of the divine love that called her into mission and would sustain it, would sustain her until her part was done. She had also an abundance of earthly relationships, the love and fidelity that are reflected so strongly in letters she exchanged and in the reminiscences of her that were sent to Nazareth.

However many unfortunate letters from parents that Catherine had to read and answer, she had also many other expressions of respect, gratitude, and friendship, occasionally spiced with teasing humor. In a letter concerning his daughter, W. C. Peters voices regret that he failed to see Catherine when she was in Cincinnati "as it would have given me much pleasure to have played the beau in her train." Ann Baxter in Alabama may represent the alumnae who wrote warm, chatty, trustful letters to their "dearly loved Mother," citing the "deep interest" they knew she had in them and their families. Mrs. Baxter sends news she knows will please Catherine: of her husband's return to her and to religious duties, of common friends, their health, family visits, the weather. Clara Bowen recalls waking in the night during a serious illness and finding Catherine by her bedside. Before that time, she had been afraid of her but now knew Catherine loved her. Mary Linton recalled to Haseltine how Catherine had instructed her, then brought her to him for her first sacraments; she had written to Catherine and sends her "best love." Julia Sloan Spalding reminisced about many of Catherine's specific acts of personal interest, guidance, and kindness, beginning with her greeting "on the threshold of my school days." In the hall to welcome returning pupils, Catherine "clasped my hand warmly saying: 'Here is our little Julia come at last. Welcome to Nazareth, my child.'"[70]

As the summer of 1856 closed, Catherine readied herself to leave Nazareth, the buildings she had erected, the grounds, the school, and the students she loved. Her final term of leadership had expired. To her "dear Baptist" she wrote, "I am still here, neither one thing nor another, nor have I any idea what is to be my future destiny, nor do I care. God's holy will be done. If I can save my soul, all will be well." She was to be missioned once more to the orphanage, but as if she sensed how short a time it would be her destiny, she had focused herself on the "one thing necessary."[71]

Ten

Final Harvest, Global Legacy

1856–1858 and Beyond

When Catherine Spalding returned to Louisville at age sixty-two, she almost certainly knew her leadership of the entire community had ended. Age and health would preclude another election six years hence. She also may well have felt leadership of the orphanage to be heavier as she picked it up again. She speaks of "taking my chance" there. But the load was light compared with what she had just laid down, and she could anticipate happy years where her heart was ever at home. Her love for the orphans, her managerial skills, and her connection and influence with so many Louisville leaders—all of whom she knew—are cited as the Council's reasons for her reassignment.[1] What neither she nor they anticipated was that her tenure would be less than two years.

Whatever Catherine felt about her responsibility, she followed her own counsel to "cheerfully exert yourself to fill the duties of your situation." In essentials her duties were what they had been before: admission of orphans according to the conditions she laid out to applicants; maintaining support from citizens, especially the Ladies Managers; directing maintenance and expansion of the buildings; directing the staff and the daily program; and, above all, knowing, nurturing, and loving individual children. She asked her lay collaborators to visit her at St. Vincent's, and she became an increasingly recognized figure on the streets of Louisville as she visited affluent donors and ministered to the poor.[2]

But other elements of Catherine's situation were different now. As she had found a change in the community at Nazareth six years before and had furthered it by accepting many immigrant women, so now she found that change at the orphanage. Several Sisters of ten to fifteen years' profession and experience were there, with at least three who had less than four years in vows. In the following years, the pattern of assignment would increasingly involve the very young and Irish-born. Catherine's first essential duty was to inspirit this group with a religious and communal unity that surpassed any national or sectional boundaries, and then to develop in the less-experienced members a proper knowledge of the care and education of the children and a devotion to duty, however demanding.[3]

Catherine had also the management of their lay assistants—laborers, domestics, and seamstresses—persons of similar youth and origin. All these people she had to try to instill with her burning care for more than a hundred orphans from nine states and four foreign nations. She had to make more room for their work. A new washhouse and bakehouse were built and a clothes yard paved between that and the main building.[4] She had to pay for construction and salaries, and to feed, clothe, and warm the children.

Chiefly as a result of nativism and Bloody Monday, Catherine's financial task had become a severe challenge. Removal of debris and cleansing of the streets had by no means wiped out all local hostility. In 1857, the Ladies Managers decided that "the present state of public feeling & the general depression in money matters" made it inadvisable to hold the annual fair. They determined to apply to the clergy and diocesan institutions for help. At their request, Mother Catherine wrote letters of appeal to potential benefactors.

The one extant letter is to her counterpart, Mother Josephine Kelly of Loretto. Catherine asks "in the name of those dear destitute little ones to lay before you their humble petition" for a "benevolent and charitable offering." It would establish a claim to the daily prayer offered "to Him, who deigns to call himself the *Orphans'* Father." The formal begging language (probably used for all potential donors) is balanced by a very personal closing expressive of a sentiment and principle that infused Catherine's sense of mission: the "cordial & sisterly affection that should ever exist among the communities of our holy religion:—for after all, we should make but one common family to carry on the different works of our common & divine Master."[5]

Yet one more public remnant of the era's anti-Catholic sentiment appeared in 1857, and one more intervention by Catherine in public response is hinted at in a letter of Mother Frances Gardiner to the notorious George Prentice, editor of the *Louisville Journal*. She says that "a friend" sent her the issue of March 12, containing the "Exposition of Roman Catholic Persecution of a Protestant Scholar at Nazareth." This "friend," if not Mother Catherine, was certainly one of the laity who kept her well informed and sent the *Journal* issue with her encouragement.

The "Exposition" was by Miss Mary Miller, who had run away from Nazareth and claimed as her reason that Sisters tried to force her into Catholic practices and confined her for days without food when she would not go to confession. Frances Gardiner responded with the facts of Miss Miller's enrollment, behavior, and disappearance. The "Protestant Members of the Senior Class" wrote a lengthy exposition of their knowledge of Miss Miller and their contrary religious experience at the academy, while "K.C." of the *Louisville Courier* gleefully cudgeled Prentice for "the disease apparent in his editorial sanity."[6] Catherine probably enjoyed the failure of Prentice's attack. No doubt she was also grateful that the necessary response was not, as in 1834, hers to write.

In her last years, Catherine did find time for a good deal of personal correspondence. These letters chiefly document and reveal the relationships and concerns that filled Catherine's mind and heart during her last eighteen months of life. Of thirteen extant letters, eleven are to her Sisters; they are revelatory by both their recipients and their content.

Internal references make clear that Catherine exchanged letters with a variety of Sisters, but only three recipients seem to have preserved their treasure: Claudia Elliott, the faithful friend, and Baptista Walls and Cleophas Mills, both very young in community.

Both had received the habit and made vows during Catherine's last term and by her authority. They were obviously devoted to her and eager to maintain the mutuality of affection and correspondence. Catherine's letters to them differ notably in tone and in the concerns expressed from the notes sent to Claudia.

To her "dear good old Sister" left behind at Nazareth, yet "always the same" to her, Catherine now wrote short notes that read like one side of rapid dialogue. In tone they are informal, teasing, occasionally even annoyed. They carry assurance of remembrance and affection, bits of news of the city Sisters and the orphanage, and notation of items sent: coffee and a coffeepot, soft kid gloves "for your poor chapped hands," and rosin soap because "some of the Sisters used to want it." Catherine evidently wanted the "Muly Cow" from Nazareth because milk was "mighty scarce for so many babies." She did not receive it as expected. Claudia did not report reception of the gloves or account for the cow, and Catherine demands, "What is the matter with you? I have sent you several messages & I never get a word from you. . . . you are as dry as ever." She quickly reverts to business: jog Sister Margaret to send back the beer barrels, "as they are not worth paying for," and tell her whether Nazareth may lose employee Thomas Wathen. The central theme of each letter is her constant remembrance of Claudia's past kindnesses and her repeated request for her prayers. In the grateful remembrance of those who care for Catherine Spalding, Claudia Elliott remains as the one above all who left the evidences of her friend's varied, human, and humorous personality.[7]

The letters to Baptista Walls and Cleophas Mills are hardly less informal and newsy but are longer and more revealing of Catherine's deepest concerns and hopes for the future community these young Sisters represented. The letters mention by name twenty-six Sisters, only five of them "senior," and fifteen in the novitiate during the term Catherine had just ended. It seems that at this time, she was very conscious that the harvest of her life's work was not in buildings, or even in the institutions they housed, but in the younger members she had influenced and would leave behind.[8]

Catherine's concerns were both practical and spiritual. She

wanted these young Sisters to work to improve their knowledge, to experience assignments appropriate to their abilities, and to have "agreeable & efficient help." Practical and unpretentious as she is, she offers that help: "If a few hints from me will do any good, they will be given. . . . you will ever find in me a mother's heart & as far as I can ready to render you every possible service." She, who had herself grappled with sorrow and bouts of self-pity, wants them to learn to live with the inevitable "contrarieties of life" and so to attain cheerful contentment, to control sadness by steady and selfless occupation.

Repeatedly Catherine expresses her wish that her young Sisters strengthen their bonds with community through letters and visits: has Cleophas, on her first mission, received many letters from Nazareth yet—and has she written? At least she must write to Catherine. She sends best love to Sister Gabriella Todd and will "always be glad to get a letter from her" (a significant message, given Gabriella's recent history of correspondence with Bishop Spalding). Baptista is asked to pray for her and "please write often." Catherine encouraged visits among the houses. She invites Baptista to spend time at the orphanage after her examinations. She reports a visit to St. Patrick's on Market Street, and Sisters there had come to St. Vincent's. Two newly professed Sisters had stopped by en route to their first mission.

In Catherine's view, the interactions of community life were necessarily part of the members' spiritual life. In these letters, as before, she repeatedly stresses—and exemplifies—the heart of charity: genuine interest in each other and sisterly affection free of personal ambition or jealousy. She wants letters herself, acknowledges that one Sister seldom writes to her "tho' I hear of her writing long letters to other places.—But believe me, Sister, I am not jealous in that, I wish all to follow their own inclinations.—I have lived long enough to take all these things just as they come. & whether I write or not, the Sisters are always the same to me, dear to my heart, & my best wishes are always for each one of them."

Realistic leader, Catherine urges the patient, even cheerful endurance of hard circumstances: "We must suffer a little here." She and the Sisters can afford a fire only by day in the Sisters' room, the schoolrooms, and nursery, but not at night "not even to sleep by." From her own long and still continuing experience, she has found the core meaning in such trials and the key to enduring them: "We should not be followers of Christ if we did not. Let us be *humble* and we can do all things and bear all things."[9] Her statement is direct and simple but no mere platitude. She has known the difference between those who can or cannot surrender comfort and a proud exceptionalism for the sake of community and mission. She can speak as one who has done so.

These last letters of Catherine's are not deeply reflective. Their simplicity differs sharply from the eloquent, exhortative style common in letters by nineteenth-century authority figures. They do not allow a reader to describe fully her spirituality, much less to plumb its depths, yet they do reveal its core traits. She who had lost her human father expressed the hope, "may we deserve to have God for our Father"; God was "Father of Orphans." Catherine's spirituality could hardly have been scriptural, for at the time, neither custom nor finance would have provided a Bible for each Sister as the basis for her meditation. However, she had learned her Bible history (from Ellen as well as David), may have had a New Testament, did have the medieval classic Thomas à Kempis's *The Following of Christ*. In any case, through liturgical readings, sermons, and instructions, she had absorbed the life and spirit of Christ enough to make echoes heard in her own simple comments, however casual they seem. Her center of meaning and of all action is the following of Christ. And the sustenance of that relationship is prayer. Her repeated requests for or promises of intercessory prayer spring from an inner well, as do her references to the Mass and the annual retreat. The Eucharist, in liturgical celebration and communion and in hours of personal prayer, kept Christ before her as the goal of her love and the model and support of her offering and her trust in Divine Providence.

Catherine had encountered and reported many deaths in her life as an SCN, but her emphasis in letters had always been on prudent, preventive health care rather than reflection on mortality itself. Ten months before her own death, she speaks plainly to an unidentified Sister of her own feelings: "A death is always gloomy to poor mortals; still one that you speak of has too much consolation in it to make us sad.—There is so much to suffer in this life, and so little to live for, that I can't grieve to see anyone leave this world well-prepared,—and then so many dangers and risks for us in this life,—and some so blind as to their real God."[10] The letter suggests a period of low or struggling spirits. It is hardly characteristic of Catherine Spalding to find "little to live for" or to shrink before suffering, dangers, and risks. She was transitioning to advanced age and the loss of vital energy that confronts every mortal who lives long enough, sees enough trouble, and loses some health and too many friends. But her recovery, in the letter and perhaps in her psyche, is characteristically quick and spiritually grounded. She asserts her readiness to meet trials and be a follower of Christ.

Catherine's last extant letter, written only two months before her death, shows a resolution of any inner struggle and an instinctive, future-directed wish for all her Sisters, especially the young. It is a typical, cheerful letter, written to Owensboro, where her dear Baptista had been transferred in company with four other recently professed Sisters. Catherine is glad she is pleased there, encourages her renewal of vows, reports on other schools, on the fair for poor children in western Louisville, and on Mr. and Mrs. Keely (he is ill and she "so much confined"; Catherine has been to see them). Louisville is threatened with scarlet fever, but the new mission in Newport, Kentucky, is doing well, while the new house at the orphanage adds much to appearance and convenience. St. Patrick's Sisters have visited and are well. She asks about others by name and sends them love. All this is vintage Catherine. Her opening and closing, however, are a kind of testament and legacy of faith, love, and good counsel:

And you want a long letter, do you dear Sis.—& what shall I say in a long letter, just keep repeating: that I love you, wish you every happiness: that I feel the deepest interest in your well being & well doing: & finally: that I ardently desire to be eternally united with you in another & a better world in the mansions of our Heavenly

Father? And all this depends on ourselves. . . . You must
forget all the last year times & only labor more for the
present & leave the rest to God.

> Always your friend & Mother
> Catharine[11]

God would lead Catherine to that better world sooner than
she or anyone else seems to have anticipated.[12] In mid- or late
February 1858, she went on one of her typical errands of relief for
a sick and destitute family. The streets were worse than usual in
the area because of winter rain and melting snow. Her feet inevitably were soaked while she attended the family, more so by the
time of her return to St. Vincent's. She took precautions against
illness as soon as she reached home, but that night symptoms of
pneumonia began and gradually worsened through the week. The
annalist says Catherine would have called the doctor at once for
someone else but was inclined always to make light of her own
ailments as sure to pass. When the doctor was called at the Sisters'
urgent pleas, he saw the gravity of the case, applied "the most active remedies," and called a specialist in lung diseases. It was too
late. Perhaps, given her age and fragility, the call could never have
been soon enough.

The end was not rapid, however. In the early stages of her
illness, Catherine spent much time in spiritual reading and meditative prayer. Opening *The Following of Christ,* she came on the
passage "Quickly shalt thou be gone hence, see how matters stand
with thee." She applied it to herself. When Sister Appolonia had
to tell her that her end was near, she immediately resigned herself
and began to "put her affairs in order": directions on management of the orphanage, asking and giving forgiveness wherever it
seemed called for, distribution of gifts to the Sisters from a box of
small gifts given to her, and urging on them the concerns that most
held her mind—"more devoted attendance on the sick, and more
perfect charity to the poor."

Word of Catherine's perilous condition reached the Sisters at
Nazareth, the local clergy, and lay friends. Mother Frances came
from Nazareth, and the Sisters there waited in pained anxiety and

hope for bulletins that only reported "worse, worse, or no better." Father Walter Coomes, chaplain of St. Vincent's, administered the church's final sacraments. Bishop Spalding and other priests came daily with their prayer and blessing. Catherine had said often that she would like to die among her orphans. On her last day the "Penn babies," now married but still the "grateful children of her love," were with her.

That day, Saturday, March 20, 1858, was one of excruciating suffering. Mother Frances reported that it was inconceivable to one who had not been there. Catherine's sight was gone, her hearing impaired, and her breathing so terribly labored that she could not lie down but remained propped up by pillows or the arms of a Sister. She had frequently been delirious, but most of that last day was herself and spoke clearly. Late in the evening, the Sisters yielded to her repeated requests to be put on the floor.[13] Shortly before midnight, after an agony of about twenty minutes, she surrendered the life she had first given as a nineteen-year-old girl.

Citizens came throughout Sunday to see and honor Louisville's Mother. Frances Gardiner said she looked "beautiful and natural, such a sweet smile on her countenance." The telegraph was now available to carry to Nazareth the news that created "grief and consternation" among Sisters, awestruck students who whispered around the news that "Mother is dead," and servants who "wept bitterly." Preparations were made for transfer of the body. The scene at St. Vincent's, the "uncontrollable wails" of the orphans as the procession began to move, were said to have become indelible in the memory of witnesses. A half mile from Nazareth, the cortege was met by all the Sisters, students, and servants, and by "nearly all the citizens of the town and neighboring counties." Young Sister Mary Vincent Hardie reported the silent procession as a heartbreaking difference from the "gentle, welcoming smile" and "extended hand" they usually had when greeting "our dear, dear Mother."[14]

At the church, Bishop Spalding, Father Haseltine, and clergy of the Bardstown area received the body, and the coffin was opened. No mourner among the many who came was remembered more than one, Teresa Carrico, whose "bent and trembling form . . .

was to be seen kneeling in prayer beside the loved remains, her face expressive of grief and resignation." The bishop performed the funeral Mass and rituals Catherine herself had attended for so many others. Her grave, by her own wish, was made in front of Bishop David's. Bishop Spalding suggested a headstone a little taller than the others, carved with a sunburst to recognize her as foundress.

Shock and grief were not soon softened at Nazareth. On March 30, Margaret Bamber, one of Catherine's most effective and loyal associates in the Louisville cholera and the Nashville crisis, died after severe suffering. Columba Carroll wrote, "To be bereft in one brief week of two so loved and so devoted is a bitter trial. . . . I am too sad to write more."[15]

But more loss had to be borne. Mother Frances wrote that "Poor Sister Teresa was nearly killed at Mother Catherine's death. The separation will not be long—I believe." Teresa Carrico was not yet seventy but seemed aged. To the younger members, she was "dear old Sister Teresa," a wonder for her longevity, left by God among her Sisters as a "perfect exemplar of all the virtues which their state of life called for." She could never be the public person Catherine had been; humility, untiring domestic labor, prayer, and the sweetness of charity in her every contact were the virtues cited to explain the enormous respect, reverence, and love the entire community gave to Teresa. She was, moreover, noted for her devotion to Catherine; and on April 23, Teresa Carrico, first pioneer in the log house, joined Catherine in the "heavenly mansion" both had desired.[16]

Catherine Spalding's life story, in a very real sense, has no "conclusion." At her death, an obituary by Catholic historian Ben Webb lauded "this extraordinary woman—extraordinary in the influence she possessed and exerted for good, as well as for those characteristics by which she was enabled, through the blessing of God, and for so great a length of time, to increase and widen that influence."[17] Catherine herself could not have imagined the reaches of her influence, the extent to which her heritage would be discussed and cherished by her Sisters and their lay and clerical collaborators into the twenty-first century and beyond the boundaries of her nation.

If these persons are asked to describe Catherine Spalding's spirit and legacy, they are sure to cite her pioneer spirit, her perception of the needs before her and her willingness to take risks to meet them, the enormous faith in Providence that enabled her to try so much and accomplish so much, and the simplicity with which she regarded and spoke of those achievements. They will mention her love for the church as she collaborated with and sometimes challenged its leaders, and her love for community as she challenged Sisters of various ancestries to live in loving union. And they will note that at the heart of all these traits are her prayer, her personal and communal center in the Eucharist, and her solid Vincentian spirituality that knew charity as the revelation of God's love to us and through us to all others, especially the poorest among us.

SCN history attests that Catherine's legacy has lived in the lives and works of hundreds of Sisters and laity who absorbed her spirit and motivation. In the rest of the nineteenth century, the mission of education exploded. Schools were opened throughout the American South, Midwest, and Northeast. New hospitals and orphanages began service. SCNs nursed on the battlefields of the Civil War and in Louisville's Pest House, taking the risk of smallpox. Most of these ministries lasted well into the twentieth century, some beyond it, expanding to all levels of education and varied forms of health services.[18]

In 1947 Catherine's expansive spirit, her risk taking and openness to new peoples and cultural experiences, urged the SCNs to move in mission to India and, later, to welcome India's women into the community. There, too, the poor and sick in cities and villages have been educated and healed, and the economically advantaged in another Nazareth Academy challenged to turn their education to the betterment of their society. Similar needs, similarly expanded visions of mission, of geography and culture, took Sisters to Belize in Central America and welcomed into community women of that nation's several ethnic groups. When the Sisters in India considered the risk of moving into the kingdom of Nepal, the decisive word was, "If Mother Catherine were here, she would go." In all these missions, lay collaborators have served as they did with Catherine, increasingly as committed Associates. Certainly, if Catherine were here in the twenty-first century, she would write with renewed pleasure of "our very large family."

For Sisters in the United States, as for their nation, one great challenge has been dealing with the legacy of slavery, its long-lived ramifications in minds, hearts, and social structures. What Catherine would think, feel, and do, or where she would go, had she lived to see the issue more clearly and widely discussed, was and remains a persistent question of her heritage. Within five years of the Civil War, Sisters began education for black children in a Bardstown school. Such schools and a hospital multiplied in the South over the years. Social and spiritual vision had to expand as the nation outgrew legally mandated segregation. Sisters engaged in the civil rights movement, and since 1960, some African American women and women of color from the Caribbean have found their home as Sisters at Nazareth. In 2000, the Year of Jubilee and Reconciliation, the Sisters of Charity of Nazareth engaged in a formal ceremony of apology and reconciliation for their part in slavery and pledged continued and expanded cooperation in the effort to reverse its legacy of injustice. This pledge took a unique form in the decision to go where Catherine could never have dreamed of going but would certainly affirm, to Botswana in Africa, primarily to care for and educate the children orphaned by AIDS. It is yet to be seen how Catherine's family will expand there.

Catherine Spalding's ministries were education and the care of the sick, the impoverished, and the orphan. As social programs and opportunities changed, so did the forms of these ministries among her Sisters. Education may be informal, under trees on the outskirts of a village, or tutoring in a home for urban single women with children. Health care may be in a village clinic where no hospital exists or in a clinic or shelter for persons with AIDS. Religious instruction may be pastoral service in a parish. The orphans may be the adult homeless and their children in day shelters. Catherine's urge of charity toward unmet needs remains the same.

"If Mother Catherine were here . . . ," where would she go, what would she want to do on the frontiers, not of America alone but of the globe? Of the myriad possible answers, some must always be selected by those who cherish the values by which she lived and the example she left. As long as Sisters of Charity of Nazareth and their "very large family" live by Catherine Spalding's goals and parallel her actions, she lives in her legacy.

Which Spalding's Daughter?

Multiple efforts to identify Catherine Spalding's parents have led to discordant conclusions. Confusion and controversy arose from the lack of official records, a church fire, a "lost" letter, disputed dates, an undocumented footnote, and similarity of names. Remaining documents and the few solid traditions about Catherine's birth and childhood make virtually conclusive the case for Edward Spalding and so for Juliet Boarman, his wife, yet the matter still requires a fair sifting of the missing or conflicting evidence.[1]

What would be conclusive documents are among the missing—birth and baptismal records. In Maryland counties at the time of Catherine's birth, no records of vital statistics were kept. Birth dates must be traced by family Bibles, guardianships, wills, tombstones, or any documents that might mention a person's age. The most relevant remaining documents relate to Basil Spalding, known to be the father of Catherine's guardian aunt, Elizabeth Spalding Elder, and thus Catherine's grandfather. Basil's seven sons and five daughters are all known from a Bible record, and all are named in their father's 1791 will, two years before Catherine's birth. Unless there was another son, excluded from both the Bible and the will, with a wife of unknown identity, who left behind no documentation of his own existence (all very improbable), then Catherine's father must be found in the list of Basil's known sons: Henry, John, William, James, Basil, Edward, and George Hilary.

The four oldest sons were not living in Charles County at the time of Catherine's birth. According to the 1790 census, Henry was in Frederick County, John and James in Prince George's. William does not appear in the Maryland census of 1790, probably being then in Virginia; he would move to Baltimore and die there. All the sons except Edward died in Maryland, all of them too late to have left Catherine an early orphan. James died when she was only six, but his wife not before 1825. All Basil Jr.'s children are known from a Bible record, and George Hilary married six years after Catherine's birth. The numbers, names, and birth dates of all these men's children also exclude Catherine from among them.[2] Thus, existing records eliminate all the sons of Basil Spalding except Edward, who moved to Kentucky in 1797 or 1798, leaving in Maryland no records of his older children's births.

Nor can baptismal records offer proof of Catherine's origin. The traditional explanation for this lack is the destruction by fire, on December 27, 1868, of St. Ignatius Church and St. Thomas Manor at Port Tobacco, seat of Charles County, Maryland. All records of the Jesuit missions in the county—marriages, births, baptisms—were lost to history. Given the certainty that Basil Spalding was Catherine's grandfather, she must have been baptized in the area around Pomfret, site of his family home. However, it is uncertain whether baptisms at the time of Catherine's birth were performed by the Jesuits at Port Tobacco or by Father John Baptist David at Bryantown, or possibly even by Father Charles Neale, chaplain of the Carmelites who settled at Port Tobacco in 1790, closer to Pomfret than St. Thomas Manor. Father David as celebrant of Catherine's baptism has perhaps the strongest claim by virtue of his known presence, from 1792 to 1803, in "Sechia" (or Zachia), the area that included St. Mary's, Bryantown, and the Pomfret locale. However, his register of baptisms at St. Mary's, Bryantown, begins in 1793, before Catherine's December birth, yet she does not appear in it.[3]

Father David was supposed to have stated his claim to having baptized Catherine to his friend Father Simon Bruté, around 1813, in a letter copied from the Bruté collection at Notre Dame, sent to Nazareth, and translated but later lost. A fragment presumed to be from this letter reads: "She was in my parish and received the sacrament from me in 1793. After her father's death, she came to Kentucky with her mother and her aunt Elizabeth, who was married to Thomas Elder. They made their home in Fairfield." Brother Thomas Spalding examined all the original David letters to Bruté in the carefully kept Bruté papers in the Notre Dame Archives but could not find this quotation in any of them. Internal evidence, he says, also renders the quotation suspect: the word "parish" (paroisse) was never used at that time, but rather "the [place-name] congregation." Nor was the name "Fairfield" used until 1820. Before that the settlement was called "Turkey Town."[4]

This doubtful quotation, besides offering no parental names, initiated the confusion and dispute about Edward's paternal claim, since he did not die in Maryland but migrated with his family to Kentucky in late 1797 or 1798. But the assertion that Catherine's father died in Maryland and that she and her mother came to Kentucky with the Elders is undermined by other facts. Thomas and Elizabeth Elder did not sell their farm in Maryland until 1800. Elder moved his family to Kentucky sometime before September 1801, when Catherine was nearly eight years old. If she and her mother came with them, the tradition that she was a very small child at the time is wrong. So is her 1858 obituary, which says, "In 1795 her mother removed to Kentucky" and died two years later. The discrepancy of a move two years earlier than Edward's is not as difficult to explain as four years after it, and in fact, Edward Spalding's wife did die within two years of her arrival in Kentucky.[5]

Historian Ben J. Webb created yet another challenge to Edward's paternity. In 1884, twenty-six years after Catherine's death, he gave her an indelible but totally undocumented footnote: "Her father, Ralph Spalding, was a second cousin of Richard, father of the Most Rev. Martin John Spalding, Archbishop of Baltimore."[6] Because Webb was a conscientious historian and had actually known Catherine, others have tried to account for this unknown Ralph.

But the simple fact is that no Ralph Spalding has been found in any records of Charles County. None is in Basil's very specific will, yet all the sons he does name can be amply proved by land

and probate records. A Raphael Spalding is noted in the records of St. Mary's County in 1778 and 1789, but it is a stretch of belief to make him Basil Spalding's son, move him to another county, cut him out of his father's will, then bring him back to Charles County for his child's birth. As for Catherine's link to Archbishop Spalding, he claimed relationship to her and knew her well, but he said he had no information to give to a book on the family. Brother Spalding notes that neither Webb nor anyone before Boldrick and Johnson would have known the exact relationship of Catherine and the bishop, which required knowledge of four generations back to the immigrant ancestor (see genealogies). Webb, he says, was a serious and careful historian for his own day but not by modern standards.[7]

Webb's footnote, despite its lack of documentation, generated several searches for a Ralph and a nameable wife, as well as a series of correspondences and "conclusions." These letters express "certainties" without documentation acceptable to professional historians and genealogists. They identify the wrong son of Basil Spalding or create contradictions with known persons and dates.[8] In time, the efforts to maintain Ralph began to look a bit desperate. Sister Mary Ramona Mattingly, historian and archivist at Nazareth, remarked wryly that "each investigator comes up with a different solution." Brother Spalding is surely logical and factual in stating that these searches yielded only "curiosities" and that "Ralph has only Webb to sustain him."[9]

Edward Spalding, son of Basil Spalding, however, has more than a name in his father's will to sustain him. His claim, if not his honor, as Catherine Spalding's father is supported by evidences of his own life; by his migration to Kentucky in late 1797 or 1798, when Catherine was about four; and by the court records of his connection there to Thomas and Elizabeth Elder and of the disposition of his "orphans." What, then, can explain his disappearance from recorded connection to his daughter? Or the similar lack of tradition that she had siblings other than Ann? Decidedly, she had four siblings if Edward was her father. And the record of Edward's children suggests strongly that she was one of them, unless some remarkable coincidences can be otherwise explained. Four children are named in court records: Ralph, Rosella, Louisa, and Ann. The reasons those four are named help explain why Catherine is not, but they cannot explain the coincidences if she is not their sister.

Edward Spalding's migration to Kentucky, his dealings and debts there, his desertion of his family and disappearance, the ensuing guardianship of his children by Thomas and Elizabeth Elder, and Elder's need for a writ of habeas corpus to reclaim Edward's daughter Ann—these are all a matter of record. Where and exactly when Edward died cannot be ascertained, but court disposition of three of his children began in 1809. On January 9, 1809, a court bound "Ralph Spalding Orphan of Edward Spalding Dec'd of the age of Seventeen Years next month to Benedict Smith to learn the Art of a house Carpenter." There was then, for certain, one Ralph Spalding, born in February 1792, not quite two years before Catherine's birth. On January 26, 1809, Thomas Elder granted permission for his ward Louisa Spalding to marry Leonard Pierce. A few years later, in 1813, "Rosella Spalding orphan of Edward Spalding" was married to Ceda Wathen, with "the consent of Richard Clark her relation with whom she has lived for several years." Catherine Spalding is known to have also moved from the Elder home to that of his daughter Clementina Elder Clark, wife of Richard. Her obituary states that she had lived with the Elders "till she was sixteen years old"; 1809 was her sixteenth year.[10] If she was not one of Edward's children, the coincidences are remarkable. And if Edward's daughter Ann was not her sister, then the Elder household simultaneously sheltered two Ann Spaldings, nieces of the Elders and cousins to each other.

But if four of Edward Spalding's children can be verified from court orders, why not the fifth? Apprenticeship and marriage were registered, in addition to a writ of habeas corpus; but there are no guardianship records in Nelson County prior to 1823.[11] No court order was required to place the girls in the home of a relative, and Rosella, Catherine, and probably Ann were evidently so placed. From the Clark home, Catherine went to Nazareth, another action requiring no civic record.

A much trickier question is why these siblings never were part of the Nazareth tradition about Mother Catherine.[12] A few plausible conjectures can be made. Ralph Spalding, the probable brother, virtually disappears from the records after his apprenticeship. Judge Boldrick mentions a lawsuit in which "his tools were seized, he having been an apprentice carpenter," but notes he disappeared from Louisville after the suit, perhaps to enlist in the War of 1812. Hughes Spalding cites a hazy "SCN tradition" that a certain Ralph Spalding occasionally visited Catherine at Nazareth and caused her "some embarrassment."[13] If that tradition has any truth, her Sisters may have chosen to let his memory fade. Rosella Spalding Wathen and Louisa Spalding Pierce may have moved from Nelson County, perhaps beyond Kentucky; distances or simply lack of visits could account for their absence from any records or memory. Juliann Pierce, daughter of Louisa, however, will reappear in letters as "a relative," close enough in kinship to be making claims, but not necessarily the kind of relative one gladly keeps in mind. A few letters show that Mother Catherine maintained some correspondence with the Spaldings of Maryland.[14] Still, in a time when travel was difficult and letters were time-consuming, she had made a life of her own. And the life she had made and embraced was given to so many people—Sisters, students, orphans, others—that those she seldom or never saw or heard from could easily drop from her conversation and the remembered tradition of her listeners.

Finally, it must be acknowledged that at that time and long after, the gospel admonition to "leave father and mother, brothers and sisters" was practiced rather literally. In the interest of forming strong and egalitarian bonds of community, one did not often "talk about one's family." Aside from official records (minimal in Nazareth's early days), its members might be unknown, even to one's close companions.

In reflection on the evidence, then, one must say with Brother Spalding that we have "no direct or conclusive evidence that Edward Spalding was the father of Mother Catherine," but it is hard to see how it could be anyone else.[15] If she was not Edward's daughter, she would have to be the daughter of his unknown, unacknowledged brother, have lived with his children at the Elders' home, have had both a sister and a cousin Ann Spalding living there at the same time, and have moved with her cousins and probably her sister to the Clark home at the same time. That is not an impossible scenario, given the sizes and practices of extended families on the frontier. But it is far less probable than the simpler assumption that she, too, was "orphan of Edward Spalding." About him she could have had few happy memories to share or preserve.

Appendix B

Genealogies

The Spalding Family

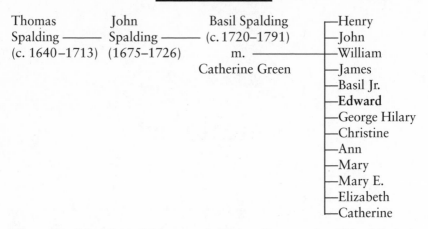

Thomas   John   Basil Spalding   ┌─Henry
Spalding ───── Spalding ───── (c. 1720–1791)   ├─John
(c. 1640–1713) (1675–1726)   m. ──────────────┼─William
                              Catherine Green   ├─James
                                                     ├─Basil Jr.
                                                     ├─**Edward**
                                                     ├─George Hilary
                                                     ├─Christine
                                                     ├─Ann
                                                     ├─Mary
                                                     ├─Mary E.
                                                     ├─Elizabeth
                                                     └─Catherine

Three of Basil Spalding's children married Elders. Henry m. Ann Elder; Elizabeth m. Thomas Elder; Catherine m. Francis Elder. These three Elders were siblings, children of William Elder (1707–1775) and Jacoba Livers (1717–1807). Thomas and Elizabeth Spalding Elder were the guardians of Edward Spalding's children.

The Boarman Family

William   John   Raphael
Boarman ──────── Baptist ──────── Boarman
(b. 1630)   Boarman   (b. 1736)   **Juliet**
                 (b. 1689)   m. ──────────── **(Julianna)**
                                 Sarah Adderton   **Boarman**
                                                         m.
                                                     Edward
                                                     Spalding
                                                     10/8/1789

The Spalding/Boarman Family

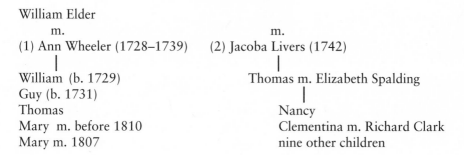

Edward
Spalding
m. ——————
Juliet
(Julianna)
Boarman

┌─Ralph (b. 2/2/1792)
├─Rosella (b. 2/2/1792) m. Ceda Wathen
├─Catherine (b. 12/23/1793)
├─Louisa (b. ?) m. Leonard Pierce — Juliann Pierce
└─Ann (b. 1798 ?)   m.
                                        Harley Skinner

The Elder Family

William Elder
m.   m.
(1) Ann Wheeler (1728–1739)   (2) Jacoba Livers (1742)
| |
William (b. 1729)   Thomas m. Elizabeth Spalding
Guy (b. 1731) |
Thomas   Nancy
Mary m. before 1810   Clementina m. Richard Clark
Mary m. 1807   nine other children

Either Mary might be the Polly of the "Tempest in Turkey Town."

Spaldings Connected to Catherine

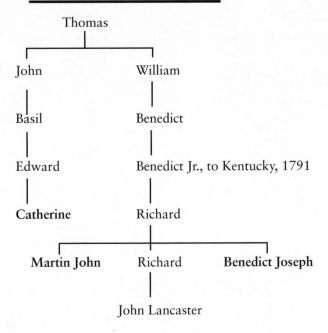

Martin John Spalding became Bishop of Louisville. His brother, Benedict Joseph, became pastor of the Cathedral in Bardstown. Both were closely associated with Catherine's ministry in her later years.

Sources

Donnelly, Mary Louise. *William Elder: Ancestors and Descendants.* Burke, VA: privately printed, 1986.

————. *Major William Boarman: His Descendants.* Ennis, TX: privately printed, 1990.

Spalding, Thomas [David], CFX. Historical Notes. Ts.

————. "The Mystery of Mother Catherine Spalding's Parents." *Records of the Historical Society of Philadelphia* 71 (1960): 118–23.

————. *Martin John Spalding: American Churchman.* Washington, DC: Catholic University of America Press, 1973.

Notes

Abbreviations

Several collections of Annals, Minutes, Letters, and Clippings located in the Nazareth Archives will be cited frequently by abbreviations. Letters will be cited by the collection, volume, and date of the letter, not by the page of the particular volume. Clippings will be cited by naming the original source, if possible, then the volume and page number.

BT	Minutes of the Board of Trustees of Nazareth Literary and Benevolent Institution
CCL	Letters of Mother Columba Carroll
Cl	Clippings, multivolume
CM	Minutes of the Council of Nazareth
CSL	Letters of Mother Catherine Spalding
DEA	Duplicate Early Annals
DLB	Duplicate Letter Books, multivolume
EAMM	Early Annals by Marie Menard, SCN
FA	First Annals
FDL	Flaget David Letters
FGL	Letters of Mother Frances Gardiner
FL	Flaget Letters in 3 volumes
SVO	Annals of St. Vincent Orphanage

Introduction

1. Catherine's English ancestry is a matter of conjecture. Probably as early as the eighth century, a town of Spalding existed in Lincolnshire, but consistent family surnames came into common usage in England only in the fourteenth to sixteenth centuries; Catherine's remotest ancestor of the Spalding name is lost in the mists of that era. In the seventeenth century, many Catholics joined the migration to Lord Calvert's colony of Maryland. Other post-Reformation migrants came as indentured servants; they or their families were converted by the Jesuits. Among these may have been Thomas, the first identifiable English Spalding in Catherine's history. Extant wills and other records of the Reformation period give no indication of any Spaldings being Catholic. Much about Catherine's ances-

try simply cannot be known with certitude (Thomas Spalding, CFX, Historical Notes from personal research, ts. For an earlier view, see Columba Fox, SCN, "Spalding, Catherine, Co-founder of the Sisters of Charity of Nazareth" ts. for *Revised Catholic Encyclopedia,* n.d.).

2. Immigrants who could not afford ocean passage often relied on such an agreement of indenture to a family member or friend who could pay their way. Brother T. Spalding has summarized Thomas's acquisitions of land between 1667 and 1688: some was awarded as his bequest from Shercliffe, and more as his freedom dues and his wife's, the final lot by actual purchase, 267 acres in all, "not an overly impressive amount of land" (T. Spalding, Historical Notes).

3. John Hope Franklin, *From Slavery to Freedom: A History of American Negroes,* 3rd ed. (New York: Knopf, 1967) 76–77.

4. Sara Ann Abell, SCN, "How We Came to the Conclusion That Pleasant Hill Is Home of Catherine Spalding," ts.; John B. Brady, "Sermon Delivered on the Occasion of a Pilgrimage to Pleasant Hill, Pomfret, Maryland, 29 March 1987," ts.

5. Basil Spalding, "Will," probated on 5 Mar. 1792, copy in Nazareth Archives.

6. David [Thomas] Spalding, CFX, "The Mystery of Mother Catherine Spalding's Parents," *Records of the American Catholic Historical Society of Philadelphia* 71 (1960): 120; Hughes Spalding, *The Spalding Family of Maryland, Kentucky, and Georgia from 1658 to 1965,* 2 vols. (Atlanta: Stein, 1965) 2: 252–53. T. Spalding says that Boldrick and Johnson, the foremost researchers of Spalding genealogy, evidently found a gravestone for Rosella Spalding Wathen. They gave her dates as b. 2 Feb. 1792, d. 10 Feb. 1869. (Notes)

7. The maiden name of Basil Spalding's wife is given as Edelen by some researchers. The evidence for Green seems stronger; probably no definite conclusion is possible (H. Spalding 2: 251). Basil's will names "Catherine, my darling beloved wife"; that name was her primary gift to her granddaughter.

8. Women of that era often returned to the parental home for an assisted and more private delivery, their husbands remaining at their home with other children and the responsibilities of their livelihood.

9. Samuel J. Boldrick and Joseph E. Johnson, "The Spalding Family of Maryland and Kentucky," ts. in Nazareth Archives, pp. 25–31; B. Spalding, "Will."

10. Clyde F. Crews, *An American Holy Land: A History of the Archdiocese of Louisville* (Wilmington, DE: Michael Glazier, 1987) 35–38 (hereafter Crews, *AHL*).

1. Kentucky Girl

1. See D. Spalding, "Mystery," for Edward's move and the family's early experiences in Kentucky; H. Spalding 2: 247.

2. D. Spalding, "Mystery" 121, 122, 124. In his Notes he offers possible explanations for Edward's debts as gambling and trickery by the Edwards brothers. He adds, "More work needs to be done on Hayden and William Edwards to see if they lured more people into debt in this way, to see in what capacity Edward came to know them." Historian Walker Gollar pointed out to me that

swindling of buyers and legal disputes were common problems in frontier land transactions.

3. Letter, Badin to Carroll, 17 Nov. 1807, quoted in D. Spalding, "Mystery" 121.

4. D. Spalding, "Mystery," 122.

5. Ben J. Webb, "Mother Catherine Spalding" (hereafter "MCS"), *Guardian* 1 May 1858: 1–2; T. Spalding, Historical Notes. Thomas Elder was born in 1748 and married in 1771. When his land was no longer productive, he first contracted for other land in Maryland but moved to Kentucky instead, probably because neighbors and relatives were already there.

6. Ben J. Webb, *The Centenary of Catholicity in Kentucky* (Louisville: Charles A. Rogers, 1884) 122–25. For many years, Ben Webb, journalist and printer in Louisville, was the chief historian of Kentucky's early Catholics. Later researchers have both cited and corrected his information.

7. T. Spalding, Historical Notes; Crews, *AHL* 27, 41–43, 51–53.

8. Dominican priests also arrived in 1805; they taught and ministered in Washington County. Catherine and the Elders would have known them chiefly as contrasts to Badin and Nerinckx. For accounts of the lives, ministries, and spirituality of Badin (1768–1853) and Nerinckx (1761–1853), see J. Herman Schauinger, *Cathedrals in the Wilderness* (Milwaukee: Bruce, 1952) and *Stephen T. Badin: Priest in the Wilderness* (Milwaukee: Bruce, 1956); Helene Magaret, *Giant in the Wilderness: A Biography of Fr. Charles Nerinckx* (Milwaukee: Bruce, 1952); and Crews, *AHL* chap 2.

9. Jansenism was a theology rooted in the writings of Bishop Cornelius Jansen (1585–1638) concerning predestination, free will, and grace. After Jansen's death, his ideas were developed and promulgated throughout France by the writings of influential religious leaders. They viewed human nature as corrupt, pulled between concupiscence and grace, in high risk of damnation, and in need of rigorous penance. God was incomprehensible and inaccessible, Jesus a severe redeemer. Their most dangerous teaching was that sacramental absolution was not valid without perfect contrition, and one should not receive communion without it. St. Vincent de Paul was a leading opponent of Jansenist theology and practice. Although condemned as theological error, Jansenism spread from France, especially into Ireland and the United States. For the complex but fascinating story and personalities involved, see *Catholic Encyclopedia* (New York: McGraw-Hill, 1967), vols. 1, 4, 7, 11.

10. Mary Ramona Mattingly, SCN, *The Catholic Church on the Kentucky Frontier, 1785–1812* (Washington, DC: Catholic University of America Press, 1936) 60–61, 90 (hereafter Mattingly, CC).

11. Mattingly, CC 105–6, 122–28; Crews, *AHL* 50–51, 60.

12. Fox, *Encyclopedia*. A large white house on a hill overlooking St. Michael's cemetery in Fairfield marks the location of that house, Gardiner's Station, where Catherine attended Mass until the church was built in 1807. From his extensive holdings, Clement Gardiner donated the land for church and cemetery.

13. DLB 1: 3 Dec. 1839.

14. Mattingly, *CC,* 140–41.

15. Mary Nona McGreal, OP, ed., *Dominicans at Home in a New Nation, 1786–1865,* Vol. 1 of *The Order of Preachers in the United States: A Family History* (Strasbourg, France: Editions du Signe, 2001) 1: 86 and n. 36. Crews, *AHL* 62–68; Schauinger, *Cathedrals* 27–30; John B. Boles, *Religion in Antebellum Kentucky* (Lexington: University Press of Kentucky, 1976), 59–64; and Mattingly, *CC* 140–41, give accounts of the practices of the two missionaries and the Dominicans' efforts to moderate them. Today, the story is a bit comical; the Elders and their neighbors were seldom amused.

16. Mattingly, *CC* 26–28. See also Martin John Spalding, *Sketches of the Early Catholic Missions in Kentucky* (Louisville: B. J. Webb, 1844) 25–31.

17. Mattingly, *CC* 28–30.

18. C. Walker Gollar, "The Role of Father Badin's Slaves in Frontier Kentucky," *American Catholic Studies* 115 (2004): 1–23, especially 6, 8, 10–14, 19; Mattingly, *CC* 105. With rare exception, the American Catholic Church failed to condemn slavery or promote abolition. The reasons for this failure and the story and issues of slavery at Nazareth will be treated in chapter 6.

19. Mattingly, *CC* 142–48; FDL, 25 Aug. 1811.

20. Mattingly, *CC* 129–31; Crews, *AHL* 40, 55.

21. Mattingly, *CC* 149–50.

22. Mattingly, *CC* 167–73, 178; Crews, *AHL* 33–35, 53–55.

23. T. Spalding, Notes on "The Tempest in Turkey Town." His account is drawn from research in the Archives of the Archdiocese of Baltimore. Other detailed accounts of this episode are Crews, *AHL* 68–71, and Schauinger, *Badin* chap. 9.

24. T. Spalding, Notes on "The Tempest in Turkey Town."

25. Ibid.

26. Benedict Joseph Flaget (1763–1850) was ordained in the Society of St. Sulpice in 1788 and taught in its seminaries in Nantes and Angers, along with his Sulpician friend John Baptist David (1761–1841), until the French Revolution forced both of them to take refuge in America in 1791. Flaget ministered in Vincennes, Indiana, then taught at Georgetown College, Havana, Cuba, and at the seminary in Baltimore until his appointment as bishop. David also taught in Baltimore until he went to Kentucky with Flaget. Flaget's life is detailed by Charles Lemarié, CSC, *A Biography of Msgr. Benedict Joseph Flaget,* trans. Mary Wedding, SCN (Bardstown, KY: 1992), ts. David's is recorded by Columba Fox, SCN, *The Life of the Right Reverend John Baptist Mary David* (New York: United States Catholic Historical Society, 1925).

27. T. Spalding, Notes on "The Tempest in Turkey Town."

28. For a full, often humorous account of Flaget's efforts, see Lemarié 1: 103–25. All accounts of Flaget indicate he was naturally sociable and humorous yet also subject to bouts of melancholy. His appointment and move to Kentucky activated both sides of his temperament.

29. Fox, *Life* 46–47. For accounts of the journey and the early days of the diocese, see Schauinger, *Cathedrals;* Crews, *AHL,* M. Cajetan Spelman, OP, "The Catholic Church of the Kentucky Frontier as Seen in the Letters of Bishop Flaget, Fa-

ther David, Father Badin, and Father Chabrat to Father Bruté (1811–1821)," (M.A. thesis, University of Notre Dame, 1945); W. J. Howlett, *Old St. Thomas' at Poplar Neck, Bardstown, Kentucky* (1906; rpt., Cleveland: Dillon/Liederbach, 1971); and especially the letters that Flaget and David wrote back to their fellow Sulpician, refugee, teacher, and close friend, Simon Bruté, at the seminary in Baltimore. David's letters especially are filled with both physical details and the feelings evoked; they contain a rich account of the seminary and the early Sisters of Charity.

30. FL 1: 7 June 1811; FDL 17 June 1811. St. Stephen's is the present site of the Loretto Motherhouse. A replica of Father Badin's own house may be seen there.

31. Thomas Howard, Last Will, 28 May 1810, Nelson County Court House Records, copy in Nazareth Archives. It should be noted that the see of Bardstown actually included the entire frontier west of the Appalachians, from Michigan to Tennessee.

32. FDL 6 July 1811, 8 Sept. 1812. It should be noted that in April 1812, Father Nerinckx organized a few women, at their request, into a new religious community for precisely the same purpose. These grew into the Sisters of Loretto, not far from St. Thomas. Flaget and David knew of this foundation, approved of it, but obviously still wanted another community under their own sponsorship.

33. FA 1; Flaget, "Report of the Establishment of the Sisters of Charity of Nazareth, in Kentucky, United States of America" in FDL (hereafter "Report"); Schauinger, *Cathedrals* 81, 102; EAMM 4.

34. The first and not entirely reliable Annals say the beginning on December 1 was in a log house a half mile away. That would be the tenant's house first intended for the convent. But see David's 1812 letters to Bruté in FDL; "Nazareth Centennial, 1912" ts. in Miscellany, vol. 10:11ff. in Nazareth Archives; "Report"; also Howlett 36–37; Columba Fox, "Mother Catherine Spalding" (hereafter Fox, "MCS"), ts. 1925, in Nazareth Archives. The Howard house, later called the Bishop Flaget house, was restored between 2002 and 2006 to its original condition, with poplar siding to preserve the logs. A family of means like the Howards could afford such a dwelling.

35. William Clark, OP, to Mary Cassilda Stey, SCN, DLB 29: 19 Sept. 1954. Father William's ancestry runs back four generations to Richard Clark. M. Rita Hayden Vaughn preserved the memorandum written by her grandmother, Betty Clark Bell, granddaughter of Richard and Clementina Elder Clark. A genealogical sheet gives their dates; both, by coincidence, were born in 1780 and deceased in 1851. Their graves are in St. Michael's cemetery, Fairfield. No search of church records or tombstones has yet located the graves of Thomas and Elizabeth Elder. Nancy Elder, surely their daughter, was buried in St. Joseph Cemetery, Bardstown, in March 1842.

2. Pioneer at St. Thomas

1. FDL 9 Jan. 1812; Howlett 36; FDL 18 Apr. 1812.

2. "Report"; EAMM 6. Unless another source is noted, the biographical

information about individual Sisters is found on their record cards, in the Annals, in the Biographical Sketches, or in Ben J. Webb, "Mother Catherine's Early Companions," *Guardian* 8 May 1858: 1–2; all are in the Nazareth Archives. Teresa Carrico's character is attested by long oral tradition in the community and occasional references to her in letters of her time.

3. They opposed "trusteeism" (the legal ownership of church property by laymen). In 1834, after a struggle with the trustees of St. Joseph College, Flaget wrote to them that they had "only to act as generous and dutiful children under the direction of a prudent and beloved father" (Fox, *Life* 149).

4. FDL 3 Nov. 1811, 16 Sept. 1811.

5. Clyde Crews, interview, 17 July 1996. Crews's works noted in the bibliography are thorough and very readable histories of the diocese and especially of the character of its first bishop. The spirituality he describes is vividly expressed in the extant publications of Bishop David found in the archives of Nazareth and of the Louisville archdiocese.

6. Quoted in Schauinger, *Cathedrals* 122.

7. Schauinger, *Cathedrals* 168–69; Benedict Joseph Flaget Diary, 21 June 1815, ts. in Nazareth Archives; Howlett 52. Lemarié's *Biography* gives a very full account of Flaget's personality and activity throughout his episcopacy. It does not deal in much detail with his relations to the Sisters of Charity.

8. Flaget to Garnier, FL 1: 8 Apr. 1816. David had already written two long protests to the Sulpician Superior General in Paris, detailing the same reasons (DLB 2: 14 Sept. 1814, 2 Mar. 1815). See also Fox, *Life* 80–83.

9. DLB 1: 41.

10. Anna Blanche McGill, *The Sisters of Charity of Nazareth Kentucky* (New York: Encyclopedia Press, 1917) 14; DLB 24: 28 May 1816; Schauinger, *Cathedrals* 179, 213.

11. The term refers to the cleric appointed by the bishop to represent him in relation to a community of religious established in his diocese. This superior's authority is considerable and so calls for tact and collaboration with the community's own elected leaders. Father David, as the founder of the Sisters of Charity of Nazareth, was ecclesiastical superior until the 1830s; a succession of priests held the role after him until 1912, when the status of a "papal congregation" (accountable to authority in Rome) was granted and the position was no longer applicable.

12. Accounts of this conflict—a history that still produces uneasy reactions to David's name among the daughters of Elizabeth Seton—are found in Joseph I. Dirvin, *Mrs. Seton: Foundress of the American Sisters of Charity* (New York: Farrar, 1962); Ellin M. Kelly, SC, comp. and ed., *The Seton Years, 1774–1821*, vol. 1 of *Numerous Choirs: A Chronicle of Elizabeth Bayley Seton and Her Spiritual Daughters* (Evansville, IN: Mater Dei Provincialate, 1981); and Regina Bechtle, SC, and Judith Metz, SC, eds., *Elizabeth Bayley Seton: Collected Writings*, 2 vols. (Hyde Park, NY: New City Press, 2002) 2: 86–87, 106–7, 120, 122. In her biography of David, Columba Fox, understandably, takes his perspective on most matters.

13. Duplicate Early Annals (DEA) 7. No copy remains of this Rule, which David based on his memory of the one in Emmitsburg. A sure clue to its contents is found in *True Piety, or The Day Well Spent*, a *Manual of Chosen Prayers, Devout Practices, and Solid Instructions Adapted to Every State of Life,* which David had compiled in his Maryland years. Its "Rule of Life" covers the day from a mode of rising piously, through prayers, meals, employments, and "amusements," to night prayer, the ensuing "greater silence," and devout thoughts in bed. The link to *True Piety* can be attested by any Sister of Charity who remembers "chosen prayers" and "devout practices" that remained in place until the 1960s. See also FDL 7 Sept. 1813; Fox, *Life* 69.

14. FDL 12 July 1813; EAMM 6–7.

15. Letter, 30 Sept. 1912, of Sister Aquin, OP, granddaughter of Richard and Clementina Elder Clark, citing his stories of Catherine's going to Nazareth, Clippings (Cl) 6: 100, in Nazareth Archives.

16. EAMM 9.

17. "Report"; DEA 10; EAMM 8; Schauinger, *Cathedrals* 104; Lemarié 2: 105. The number and names of the slaves at St. Thomas at this time are not recorded.

18. Flaget Diary 34; EAMM 8.

19. FA 2–3.

20. EAMM 6.

21. FDL 12 July 1813; EAMM 5.

22. EAMM 7.

23. FDL 7 Sept. 1813, 21 Apr. 1814; EAMM 9–10.

24. EAMM 10.

25. FDL 7 Sept. 1813; EAMM 6. "Philothea"—Gr.f. "one who loves God."

26. Register. Betsey Wells found her goal again as a Dominican Tertiary serving the priests at St. Rose Priory, where she died in 1851, almost seven years before Catherine. She was buried in the Dominican Sisters' cemetery in Springfield, Kentucky (Archives of Dominican Motherhouse).

27. David to Carroll, 7 Sept. 1814; and Carroll's reply, n.d., on the back of David's letter; Catherine Spalding to Flaget, CSL 6 July 1841. The story of the negotiations with Emmitsburg may be traced further in the following letters, all in FDL: Flaget to Bruté 13 Oct. 1811; 13 July 1813; David to Bruté, 3 Nov. 1811; 7 Sept. 1813; 21 Apr. 1814; also in Fox, *Life* 72–74; Kelly 176–77; Schauinger, *Cathedrals* 103–4.

28. FA 1; Register of the Sisters of Charity of Nazareth; "Report." Until very recent times, the distinctive dress ("habit") of a religious community was considered an almost essential sign of an individual's public religious commitment and of the communal identity. The latter purpose explains why a change in the habit became so large an issue in 1841, when the separate identity of the SCNs was under siege.

29. FDL 7 Sept. 1813, 21 Apr. 1814. The seven Sisters at that time were Teresa Carrico, Betsey Wells, Catherine Spalding, Harriet Gardiner, Polly Beaven, Ann (Nancy) Lynch, and Mary Gwynn.

30. EAMM 9.

31. FDL 28 July 1813.

32. Schauinger, *Cathedrals* 104; McGill, 23; Webb, *Centenary* 247.

33. Fox, *Encyclopedia.*

34. The early Annals and various later documents all attest to Catherine's and Ellen's lively traits. See also Biographical Sketches; Webb, "Companions"; and McGill, 85–90, 94, for descriptions of the early Sisters.

35. DLB 24: 27 Jan. 1828; EAMM 158.

36. EAMM, 10–11; DEA, 9; Agnes Geraldine McGann, SCN, *Sisters of Charity in the Apostolate* (Nazareth, KY: privately printed, [1976]) 21.

37. CSL 3 June 1852 and other letters. The delicate, browning document sent by Bruté, a guarded treasure at Nazareth, is exactly the Rule developed by Ss. Vincent de Paul and Louise de Marillac and the first Daughters of Charity and published by Vincent's successor in 1672.

38. "Common Rules of the Daughters of Charity, Servants of the Sick Poor," trans. Mary Wedding, SCN, ts. All quotations are from this translation of the Rule sent in French by Bruté; it seems needless to cite chapter and article numbers for each phrase.

39. FDL, especially 7 Jan. 1815, 17 May 1815, 19 June 1815.

40. Fox, *Life* 96; EAMM 13.

41. Register; "Report." The vow formula was found in the file of Idalie Geoffsion SCN (d. 1952). She herself probably used it yearly after her first vows in 1897. Earlier use cannot be authenticated. No formula for vows is included in either the first Rule or the 1890 Regulations, but the latter does have a form for written petition for vows that names a vow of Perseverance.

42. Throughout this book, all dates of entrance, reception of habit, profession of vows, departure, or death are drawn from the community Register in the Nazareth Archives.

43. FDL 13 Sept. 1816; EAMM 11; "Report"; FL 2: 29 Oct. 1816.

44. Lemarié 2: 370.

45. CSL 19 May 1821. Accounts of the Vincentians at St. Thomas are given in Schauinger, *Cathedrals* 146–52; and Fox, *Life* chap. 7.

46. EAMM 14; DEA 9; Fox, "MCS" 9. The exact location of the building was long conjectural. It must have been adjacent to the existing school, therefore about a half mile from the seminary. Today, at about that distance, at the approach to St. Thomas, may be seen an old stone foundation; numerous bricks have been turned up from the soil over years of gardening. Even more telling, an archaeological dig in the summer of 2001 uncovered a portion of flooring in the basket weave pattern of bricklaying. If these were not the foundation and the floor or entrance of the brick school, it is hard to guess what else they were.

47. FDL 1 Dec. 1818. The following quotations are also from this letter.

48. An obvious and probable cause has been pointed out: parental panic at two deaths, of a Sister and a student, from consumption on campus just before the date of David's letter. Or the outbreak could have been widespread in the area (Eugenie Coakley, SCNA, letter to author, 8 Dec. 2003). Consumption was the

general term of that time for tuberculosis. It had no cure.

49. Rules chap. 1, art. 8.

50. FA 3; EAMM 14–15.

51. Another cause for the rampant consumption was pointed out by a specialist in the study of infectious disease. The construction of a spring house for a dairy in 1816 implies that cows were milked on campus. Tuberculosis can spread from cows to milk to humans if the milk is not pasteurized, and pasteurization was not invented until 1860 (Eugenie Coakley, SCNA, letter to author, 8 Dec. 2003).

52. EAMM 15–16.

53. FA 3–4; DEA 8; EAMM 18–19.

54. EAMM 16; Register; Biographical Sketches. The Gardiners were granddaughters of Clement and Henrietta Gardiner, the pioneers who had supported the Catholic community and church in Fairfield. Other pioneers were Cecily O'Brien, Elizabeth Suttle, Angela Spink, Susan Hagan, Agatha Cooper, Betsy Bowling, and Mildred Stuart—all of them names to be repeated and remembered in Catherine's story. Of the seven, only Susan, Cecily, and Elizabeth outlived her; Elizabeth, in 1866, was the first Golden Jubilarian.

55. See Howlett 65–70; Fox, *Life* 86–92; and Schauinger, *Cathedrals* 175–80, for accounts of these diocesan events.

56. "Report."

57. EAMM 18; Fox, *Life* 98.

58. Register.

59. McGill 100; Webb, "MCS" 1.

60. FDL 3 May 1821; "Report."

61. "Report"; see EAMM 19–21; Webb, "Companions" 89, for the full account of this foundation.

3. Leader to New Frontiers

1. Fox, *Life* 100.

2. Howard will, in Nazareth Archives.

3. FDL 9 June 1815. The two portions were the homestead that Mrs. Howard was to have during her widowhood (which she had ceded to the bishop for the seminary), and another plot bought of a Mr. Campbell. Badin had ceded only the Campbell portion.

4. FL 2: 16 Feb. 1815; Schauinger, *Badin*, 179. Detailed and objectively fair accounts of the entire dispute are given in Schauinger, *Badin* 171–83, and Peter Guilday, *The Life and Times of John Carroll*, 2 vols. (New York: Encyclopedia Press, 1922) 2: 696–97. Schauinger gives extensive quotations of the letters written by both Flaget and Badin. Howlett, 35, refers to the dispute but says that it was "satisfactorily arranged, and the title finally vested in the Ordinary of the diocese in accordance with the idea of the testator." He gives no date for this happy ending.

5. Today, one can only suppose that both Flaget and David felt that they

had been thoroughly deceived in 1815 and might still be in any subsequent litigation, that the diocesan claim to inheritance might be disputed after Mrs. Howard's death, as well as any ensuing right to transfer the land to the Sisters. One can imagine the trouble in such a dispute had the Sisters been allowed to remain until the death of Mrs. Howard; she lived until 1836.

6. Fox, *Life* 100–101.

7. EAMM 22–23.

8. EAMM, 22–23.

9. "Report"; EAMM 22–23.

10. Father Chabrat escorted Mrs. O'Connor and others from Baltimore. To Flaget, he wrote that she was "young and very pious . . . in no way destitute of talent" and "quite well off in the world, having valuable property." She brought and donated $3,000, her silverware, dresses (which became vestments), a clock that long remained the sole timepiece at Nazareth, and a black family, who were to be freed in a year. Mrs. Tyson probably came to Nazareth with her sister-in-law; she was one of the elderly women who boarded there. In 1828, Mrs. Tyson wrote Flaget a witnessed letter stating her contentment with the disposition of her share of the O'Connor estate, saying that Sister Scholastica only regretted that the property given the community was "so small a donation." DLB 1: 22 June 1821; EAMM 34–37; DLB 15: 64, 65.

11. FDL 17 Sept. 1822; DEA 11; EAMM 22–23; "Report"; Fox, *Life* 103.

12. EAMM 23. The Register is the best source to resolve discrepancies on the numbers that first came to Nazareth; it shows who was then in the novitiate. Scholastica O'Connor's slaves seem not to have been included in the move. They must have been given the promised freedom.

13. FDL 17 Sept. 1822; DEA 11.

14. FDL 17 Sept. 1822, 4 Feb. 1823; Schauinger, *Cathedrals* 220; DLB 24: 27 Aug. 1823.

15. DLB 15: 11 Mar. 1824; DLB 2: 1 Feb. 1825.

16. EAMM 23–26.

17. EAMM 26; DLB 2: 23 Feb. 1811, 29 Dec. 1809.

18. CSL 13 Nov. 1852, 19 Oct. 1856, n.d. 1856.

19. Webb, *Centenary* 250; EAMM 27–28.

20. EAMM 36; DLB 24: 14 June 1823; FDL 1 Dec. 1818.

21. FDL 4 Feb. 1823; Ann Bolton Bevins and James R. O'Rourke, *"That Troublesome Parish": St. Francis/St. Pius Church of White Sulphur, Kentucky* (Georgetown, KY: St. Francis and St. John Parishes, 1985) 93; Register.

22. DLB 10: 30 Apr. 1823.

23. The full account of St. Pius Parish is given in Bevins and O'Rourke 62–73, 91–93; Fox, *Life* 105–7; Schauinger, *Cathedrals* 219–20; James Maria Spillane, SCN, *Kentucky Spring* (St. Meinrad, IN: Abbey Press, 1968) 103–5; Webb, *Centenary* 92–93; Paul E. Ryan, *History of the Diocese of Covington, Kentucky* (Covington: Diocese of Covington, 1954) 81–87. Ryan edited Flaget's letter to delete the entire passage on the Sisters' "Via Crucis."

24. Bevins and O'Rourke, 85, 88–9; EAMM 24–5. How long Abe was kept

at Scott County cannot be ascertained; slaves' movements must be inferred from scattered references. He may have returned to Nazareth with Catherine. At her later visit to Scott County, it is said the Sisters had only one servant, twelve-year-old Ben, who regularly ran away, was jailed, and returned (Bevins and O'Rourke 96).

25. Bevins and O'Rourke 93, 94; Lexington, *Cross Roads,* Cl 1993: 413.

26. Bevins and O'Rourke 94–95; Cl 1: 67. Letters to the editor of the *Lexington Intelligencer* praised the Sisters and students, noted the Sisters' "exemplary conduct" and respect for the religion of non-Catholics, and expressed hope that no such prejudice would be found in Lexington.

27. EAMM 108–9, 112; Bevins and O'Rourke 95–96.

28. FDL 4 Sept. 1821.

29. EAMM 41.

30. EAMM 40–41.

31. EAMM 42–44; Webb, *Centenary* 251; Webb, "Companions" 1.

32. Register; EAMM 24, 28–29; McGill 96–97, 150–51. Martha Drury was famous in community for strength, charity, and nearly seventy years in various missions as both teacher and nurse; she was also one of Sister Marie Menard's chief resources for the memories of Catherine in the early Annals.

33. EAMM 28–31. Columba Fox thought this tale "not deserving of record" because "such conduct" in a novice and senior Sisters was "incomprehensible" ("Commentary," Nazareth Archives). She acknowledges, however, Martha's reliable memory; her objection is probably less that the story is "mythical" than that it is "not edifying." Since the tale involved Martha's direct quotes, and as Ellen O'Connell's rather bold wit was well known, one may credit the account. Its value is in what it says about the Sisters' view of Catherine's exercise of authority.

4. Educator and Mother

1. DLB 24: 17 Mar. 1825; FL 3: 18 Apr. 1825.

2. EAMM 32; DLB 2: 1 Feb. 1825; DLB 22: 4 Jan. and 10 Feb. 1825.

3. EAMM 41; Fox, *Life* 107.

4. Accounts of this episode can be found in EAMM, esp. 41; Fox, *Life* 107, and "MCS" 13–14; McGill 36–37, 40, 47–48; and Schauinger, *Cathedrals* 220–21. David's letter to Rose White (DLB 1: 18 June 1825) carries a copyist's dating of June 1824; because Mother Agnes died in September 1824, the correct date must be 1825. This corresponds to a similar letter to Bruté.

5. DLB 2: 1 Feb. 1825; DLB 22: 23 Dec. 1825. Flaget here says the "Grand Almoner of France received last April a very long letter" describing the "different institutions" and "the happy outcome which will result" if "they help me" to strengthen them and begin new ones. That letter is surely the 1825 "Report," written in French, which was found in the Vatican Archives by Brother David (Thomas) Spalding, CFX, and given to Nazareth, where it was translated. The original language and the content indicate a French recipient; Flaget's letter seems to identify him.

6. DLB 1: June 1825; DLB 24: 25 June 1825. In fact, the Sisters were not conveniently lodged until 1855, after the building of the second academy.

7. FL 2: 29 June 1825; FDL 19 Nov. 1825.

8. Eliza Crozier Wilkinson, "Memoir," quoted in EAMM 47–48; DLB 1: June 1825; FDL 23 Dec. 1825, Good Friday 1826, 5 June 1826; DLB 24: 13 Nov. 1826, 17 Aug. 1827; DLB 1: 15 June 1828; Fox, "MCS" 14. These sources are not without some discrepancies. The early Annals are seldom explicit or exact about dates. Mrs. Wilkinson's memory may have been inexact; the priceless value of her narrative is its account of the various Sisters and the student life, and here, in her revelation that Catherine had sacrificed her own privacy in a separate room.

9. FDL 5 June 1826; Webb, "MCS"; McGill 48.

10. EAMM 33, 55.

11. CSL 9 May 1829.

12. Licensed graphoanalysts studied the handwriting of this letter. They said it reveals Catherine as "highly responsive—strong emotions with considerable depth of feelings—she could be hurt deeply, but she would not keep that hurt a long time." This capacity for personal hurt seems to be in conflict—or in balance?—with "a definite absence of self-consciousness and sensitivity" to criticism, based on her "self-confidence." Her control on the emotions is "pride and poise . . . a certain dignity." Peter Krusling and Peter Marie Murphy, MM, "Mother Catherine Spalding: A Personality Study Based on Analysis of Her Handwriting" (Nazareth: SCN Health Corporation, 1987) 6–7.

13. DLB 15: 22 May 1828. Bills of sale indicate the slaves were a woman, Louisa, and two boys, William and Henry; they may have been the first slaves to come to Nazareth by bargain or direct purchase. Mrs. Wescott had previously taken in a Mme. Brolius in a dying condition, along with her sister, two children, and a niece (DLB 24: 23 Dec. 1825). These are probably the niece who went to Nazareth and the dependents to be supported. The circumstances may explain Mrs. Wescott's wish to retire there as well and Catherine's charity in agreeing to it.

14. Rules, chap. 1, art. 1.

15. FDL Flaget, Memoir to Rome, 1836.

16. DLB 24: 9 Oct. 1827; EAMM, 66.

17. DLB 24, 27 Nov. 1827; Wilkinson, "Memoir."

18. DLB 1: 18 June 1825; FDL 5 May 1826; "Report."

19. DLB 24: 27 Jan. 1828.

20. DLB 24: 1 Nov. 1827; McGann, *Apostolate* 23–24; DLB 24: 27 Nov. 1827.

21. DLB 24: 27 Jan. 1828.

22. Accounts of the examinations are found in EAMM 44–47, 54–55; Schauinger, *Cathedrals* 239; and McGill 120.

23. *Bardstown Herald,* July 1830, Cl 1: 30; McGill 120.

24. EAMM 53.

25. FL 3: 1 May 1830; DLB 24: 8 Feb. 1830. As girls with a largely nominal

Protestant identity were attracted to Catholicism by positive school experiences, fears of the Catholic academies grew. By the mid-1830s, these fears were mounting to opposition that would become severe in the 1850s.

26. DLB 22: 4 Dec. 1828.

27. EAMM 50–57. The quotations from the Wilkinson memoir that follow are taken from these pages of the Annals.

28. EAMM 55; DEA 25.

29. EAMM 57.

30. EAMM 52–53.

31. Biographical Sketch of Mother Catherine Spalding, 27. The "heavily built" is made doubtful by the only certain photograph, a tintype made apparently in Catherine's later years.

32. Senator Ben Hardin, quoted in Fox, *Life* 218.

33. For the full newspaper account of the debate in the legislature and Hardin's speech, see Fox, *Life* 215–20. Other accounts of the incorporation were given by Bishop David to Sister Fanny Jordan (DLB 1: 29 Dec. 1829); Flaget to the Pope (DLB 33: 14 Apr. 1830); McGill 50–55; and Agnes Geraldine McGann, *SCNs Serving since 1812* (Nazareth, KY: privately printed, [1985]) 10–12.

34. BT 3 May 1830, 7 May 1830, 2 Dec. 1830.

35. EAMM 37–40, 66–67; McGill 51.

36. FDL 27 Aug. 1823; McGill 44.

37. DLB 24: 4 Oct. 1828.

38. FDL 27 June 1825, 23 Dec. 1825; DLB 24: 17 Aug. 1827, 22 Sept. 1831.

39. Letters of Mother Columba Carroll. This kinship of character was noted on tape by James Maria Spillane, SCN. Agnes Geraldine McGann, SCN, and Maria Vincent Brocato, SCN, have made short studies of Columba Carroll's life; these are in the Nazareth Archives.

40. Crews, *AHL* 100; EAMM 65–66.

41. See EAMM 59–64, for a full account of Harriet and for two of her letters to her sisters, the last written ten days before her death. In reporting her death to Bruté, David blamed it chiefly on the ignorance and imprudent advice of a doctor (FDL and DLB 24: 13 Nov. 1826). Flaget lamented in a letter to Rome that the school at Vincennes had "gained great fame," but the superior, "scarcely 30 years old" with "conspicuous" and "excellent gifts," had died, and that "such a loss can scarcely be replaced" (DLB 1: 9 Nov. 1826).

42. EAMM 73–75; Register.

43. The story is best found in the letters of Bishops Flaget and David, who wrote in detail to Bishop Rosati in St. Louis and to Bruté in Maryland as events were unfolding: FL 2: 21 Feb. 1827, 13 Apr. 1827, 20 Aug. 1827, 2 Nov. 1827; DLB 24: 31 Oct. 1827, 1 Nov. 1827, 27 Nov. 1827, 8 Jan. 1828, 8 Apr. 1828. Earlier references to Coomes are in FDL 9 Jan. 1812, 12 July 1813, 13 July 1813. The story is also told by Bevins and O'Rourke 95, 98–99; and Lemarié 2: 214–22. Historian Ben Webb, then twelve years old and in a front pew, recounts the climactic excommunication in his *Centenary* 94.

44. FL 2: 21 Feb. 1827; DLB 24: 31 Oct. 1827.

45. FL 2: 21 Feb. 1827.

46. Ibid.

47. FL 2: 13 Apr. 1827.

48. Coomes died in 1830, only three years after his marriage. Webb says he never justified himself by impugning the Catholic faith and practice and died "heartily repenting the scandal he had occasioned." Frances Alvey Coomes lived on as "devotedly Catholic"; she was buried in the parish cemetery. They had twins, Charles and Mary Anne; the latter is known to have married, lived as a Catholic, and raised a large family.

49. DLB 1: 3 June 1825; DLB 24: 15 Jan. 1828; DLB 1: 25 Apr. 1828. How many conferences were sent is not known. A modern printing is in four volumes: *The Conferences of St. Vincent de Paul to the Sisters of Charity,* trans. Joseph Leonard, CM (Westminster, MD: Newman Press, 1952).

50. The Loretto story is contained in Schauinger, *Cathedrals* 76–80, 184–85, 222–24. Details and dates have been verified by Sister Kate Misbauer, SL, archivist at Loretto. In 1821, the Sisters opened a mission named Bethania, near Fairfield; eleven died there in just over two years, the first five in less than six months. Chabrat, pastor in Fairfield and their confessor, intervened with Flaget to require a change in the austere rule. Flaget tried to mediate, but Nerinckx, convinced he could not prevail, asked to retire to Missouri, where he died a few months later, August 1824. Chabrat was made ecclesiastical superior of Loretto; he set about obliterating Nerinckx's influence by burning his writings. Flaget then required the Sisters to move their motherhouse to property he had given them at St. Stephen's, Badin's former home; they did so in November 1824 but burned the buildings they were forced to leave.

51. FDL 5 June 1826.

52. McGill 49–50.

53. CSL 9 May 1829.

54. Schauinger, *Cathedrals* 255–57; Cl 1: 28.

55. Cl 1: 28.

56. Register.

57. DLB 21: 22 Jan. 1832.

5. Pioneer in Louisville

1. Carl E. Kramer, "City with a Vision: Images of Louisville in the 1830s," *Filson Club History Quarterly* 60 (1986): 445.

2. Mattingly, CC 91; Kramer 427; *Louisville Directory for the Year 1836,* ed. G. Collins (Louisville: Prentice and Weissinger, 1836), 1; *Louisville Directory for the Year 1838,* ed. G. Collins (Louisville: J. E. Marshall, 1838), 9.

3. Map, *Louisville Directory for the Year 1832* (Louisville: Richard W. Otis, 1832); Mary Michael Creamer, SCN, "Mother Catherine Spalding—St. Catherine Street, Louisville, Kentucky," *Filson Club History Quarterly* 63 (1989): 207; Fox, *Life* 128–29; Kramer 431–38; Reuben T. Durrett, *The Centenary of*

Louisville, Saturday, May 1, 1880 (Louisville: Filson Club Publications, 1893) 99–100; Mattingly, *CC* 90–93. The westside boundary extended diagonally from Twelfth Street at the river outward to what became Nineteenth Street. The east side extended diagonally from the wharf at Second Street outward to Preston and the open lots beyond it; population, however, had extended as far east as Wenzel and the present Bardstown Road. In the center city, population thinned below Jefferson Street. The new St. Louis Church replaced the first and only Catholic church at Tenth and Main Streets since 1811; Catholic growth by immigration had made it too small.

4. Kramer 433–34.

5. *Louisville Directory for the Year 1832*; *Louisville Public Advertiser* 7 May 1836: 1 (hereafter *LPA*); Schauinger, *Cathedrals* 214.

6. "History of Presentation Academy," ts. 1931; Berenice Greenwell, SCN, "Nazareth's Contribution to Education 1812–1933" (Ph.D. diss., Fordham University, 1933) 83; *1832 Directory* 136–37.

7. CM 18 Sept. 1831. The community Council consisted of the Mother and elected officers. The ecclesiastical superior was also a part of it in these years. It is to be distinguished from the Board of Trustees of NLBI, the legal identity of the congregation.

8. CM 3 Oct., 5 Oct. 1831. Serena Carney is called Theresa in the minutes; her baptismal name, however, is given as Ellen. It is worthwhile to note something of the character of the priest with whom Catherine pioneered Catholic education in Louisville. Robert Abell, her senior by one year, entered the seminary at St. Thomas, where Catherine knew him and attended his ordination in 1818. Later David thought it would be good for him to join the Jesuits as only their strict obedience could subdue "that character so excessively republican." A big man, six feet, four inches, Abell was a powerful preacher, widely admired, and well loved. He was a faithful friend of Mother Catherine and a major influence on and most effective supporter of the developing mission in Louisville. (Schauinger, *Cathedrals* 162–64, 267; John A. Lyons, *Bishops and Priests of the Diocese of Bardstown* (Louisville: privately printed, 1976), 20–22; Clyde F. Crews, *Presence and Possibility: Louisville Catholicism and Its Cathedral* (Louisville: Archdiocese of Louisville, 1973) 19.

9. *1832 Directory* 139. Floyd Mansberger, *Archeological Investigations at the Cathedral of the Assumption, Louisville, Kentucky* (Springfield, IL: Fever River Research, 1990) chap. 8, analyzes all the documentary and archaeological evidence for the presence and activities of the Sisters on the site of St. Louis Church.

10. Crews, *AHL* 114–15; *LPA* 27 Feb. 1836: 1. No mention of Presentation has been found in the extant Louisville papers of the time. The name was chosen to honor an old Christian tradition that Jesus' mother, Mary, as a young girl, had been presented in the temple at Jerusalem. The ancient feast was celebrated on November 21.

11. *1832 Directory* 139; EAMM 74; Fox, *Life* 130; "Presentation Academy," ts., Presentation Archives.

12. David to Bruté, 28 Feb. 1832, quoted in John A. Lyons, "Fr. Lyons Collection: Entries in Publications, 1782–1961," 19, Cathedral Heritage Collection; CM 29 Mar. 1832.

13. *1832 Directory* 139.

14. DEA 19–20; the story is also told in EAMM 80–82; Fox, *Life* 131–32; and Louisville's diocesan paper, the *Record* 4 June 1884, Cl 3: 224. Because Eliza Jenkins, the older of the two children, remained a devoted friend of the Sisters and collaborated in work for the orphans, it is likely that Sister Marie Menard received the story directly from her. Later accounts were certainly derived from these two women. It is assumed that the boys remained with their father.

15. Fox, *Life* 132. Two stories are found in the *Record,* 4 June 1884: Cl 3: 223; McGill 52; DEA 20.

16. Fox, "MCS" 24.

17. DEA 20; EAMM 82.

18. *Record* 4 June 1884, Cl 3: 223. The twelve women as listed were Mrs. J. D. Colmesniel, Mrs. Elizabeth Baldwin, Mrs. M. D. Kennedy, Miss Catherine Cauffman, Mrs. John Carroll, Mrs. Daniel Smith, Mrs. James Rudd, Mrs. Alfred Tarleton, Mrs. (W.) Cirode, Mrs. Goring, Mrs. Breen, Mrs. Benjamin Harrison.

19. SVO.

20. Cholera is caused by a bacterium that flourishes in filth, garbage, and sewage, invades the small intestine, and releases a toxin that shreds the intestinal lining. Extreme and painful nausea and diarrhea lead to severe dehydration, cramps, shock, and death, often within a few hours. Prevention requires clean water and handling of food—also garbage and sewage disposal away from water supplies. Treatment requires abundant clean replacement fluids. Jacquelyn G. Black, *Microbiology: Principles and Applications* (Upper Saddle River, NJ: Prentice Hall, 1996) 11–12, 620–21, 639–40.

21. *LPA* 18 Feb. 1832: 2.

22. FDL 18 June 1832; *LPA* 26 June 1832: 2.

23. *LPA* 26 Sept., 1 Oct., 6 Oct., 9 Oct., 13 Oct., 15 Oct., 25 Oct. 1832.

24. CSL 10 Feb. 1834; DLB 12: 53.

25. CM 17 Oct. 1832.

26. The following account is drawn from accounts in EAMM 77–78; DLB 12: 53; DLB 4: 71; *LPA* 1 and 8 Feb. 1832, 15 Nov. 1832, 1 Dec. 1832; Kramer 450–51; Cl 1: 39–40, 44; McGill 53.

27. An anonymous paper found in the Archives.

28. BT 5 Nov. 1832.

29. EAMM 82–83; SVO; Webb, *Centenary* 541–42.

30. Stories of the Bardstown/Nazareth cholera, its victims, and the courageous charity of the various religious orders are detailed in Schauinger *Cathedrals* 274; EAMM 90–102; Fox, *Life* 138–39; and in letters by David: DLB 24: 8 July 1833; FDL 2 Dec. 1833, 13 Feb. 1834; and by Flaget: FL 2: 5 July 1833; DLB 22: n.d. or recipient, but clearly written by Flaget.

31. CSL 10 Feb. 1834.

32. EAMM 85; SVO, "Notes and Lists of Orphans"; Webb, *Centenary* 542–43. Differing numbers reflect variations in the sources.

33. DEA 20.

34. EAMM 85.

35. CSL 31 Aug. 1839.

36. CM 10 Dec. 1834.

37. The story is documented chiefly in Council Minutes, in Marie Menard's Annals drawn from the living memory of senior Sisters, and in numerous letters of Bishop David, especially those he wrote to Sister Elizabeth Suttle at St. Vincent's in Union County (DLB 2). In these letters, he vents his extreme pain over "ungrateful daughters" and his "exile"; he also mentions talking with Mother Catherine at a Board meeting (DLB 2: 6 May 1836). Elizabeth Suttle was one of Marie Menard's sources.

38. Register; CM 19 Feb. 1833; Mary Buckner, SCL, *History of the Sisters of Charity of Leavenworth, Kansas* (Kansas City, MO: Hudson-Kimberly, 1898; rpt., 1985) 34–38; Julia Gilmore, SCL, *Come North! The Life Story of Mother Xavier Ross* (New York: McMullen, 1951) 23–28.

39. The rage of Ann's father especially was probably exacerbated by the anti-Catholic tracts of the time that told horror stories of Protestant girls being lured or stolen away by Catholic nuns and of the repressive life in convents.

40. *LPA* 9 Apr. 1836.

41. McGloin to Catherine Spalding, 18 Dec. 1836, quoted in EAMM 120; *LPA* 21 May 1836: 3.

42. SVO, "Notes and Lists of Orphans."

43. BT 2 May 1836; CM n.d. 1836, 24 Aug. 1836; EAMM 121–22.

44. CM 5 Oct. 1836; BT 7 Sept. 1836, 9 May 1837.

45. Historical Maps, 1858, in Louisville Free Public Library; *Directory 1838–39;* SVO, "Notes and Lists of Orphans."

46. CM 24 Aug. 1836; BT 7 Sept. 1836; Mansberger chap. 8; Ignatia Murphy, SCN, "Recollections of Presentation Academy," ts., 1919; Frederick Doyle, "The Old Presentation Academy of Louisville," ts., 1948. "Old Presentation," however "hodge-podge," lasted well beyond Catherine's lifetime. It was replaced in 1893 by a new construction at Fourth and Breckinridge Streets.

47. CM 24 Aug. 1836.

48. DEA 21–22.

49. *1832 Directory* 130–31, 140; Crews, *AHL* 115–16; SVO; *Record* 4 June 1884, Cl 2: 223–24; J. Stoddard Johnston, ed., *Memorial History of Louisville from Its First Settlement to the Year 1896*, 2 vols. (Chicago: American Biographical, 1896) 1: 364–65; Creamer 203–4; M. Joblin and Co., *Louisville Past and Present: Its Industrial History as Exhibited in the Life-Labors of Its Leading Men* (Louisville: John P. Morton, 1875) 220–21. Variation of name spellings is common in nineteenth-century records; usually context will tell when the same person is meant.

50. DEA 21–22; EAMM 83–84, 118, 122–23; Rosati to Catherine Spalding, 17 June 1833, quoted in SVO.

51. BT 7 May 1838.
52. DEA 22; EAMM 122–23.
53. DLB 1: 17 Jan. 1837.
54. DLB 1: 18 Jan. 1833. George Hilary Spalding was a younger brother of Edward, Catherine's father. His older brother, Basil Jr., inherited Pleasant Hill; B. R. Spalding, author of the letter, was almost certainly Basil's son and heir.
55. DLB 1: 22 Apr. 1838, 31 May 1838; DLB 2: 23 Aug. 1838.

6. Mother and Administrator

1. The three journal entries are in DEA 1–2; all citations are from these pages. Before the election on August 14, 1838, 137 women had entered; 19 had died; 56 had left. Catherine had said farewell to more women than remained with her (Register). Election was for three years, with one possible reelection; Catherine's "third" term was technically her fifth and sixth.
2. DLB 2 and CM, both 23 Aug. 1838.
3. DLB 2: 23 Aug. 1838; DEA 2; EAMM 132–34. The two deaths were of Sisters Rose Greenwell and Bridget Madden. Both were severe losses to Catherine of effective ministers and good companions.
4. Edwin Weber, chemist, provided information on the disease and the danger in nineteenth-century treatments. Quotations are from Rabley Dunglison, MD, "Fever, Congestive," "Mercurial," "Salivation," *A Dictionary of Medical Science* (Philadelphia: Blanchard and Lea, 1857), and Samuel Henry Dickson, MD, *Elements of Medicine: A Compendious View of Pathology and Therapeutics; or the History and Treatment of Diseases* (Philadelphia: Blanchard and Lea, 1855) 245–50. In case the "iodide of mercury and quinia" is not effective, Dickson suggests other treatments, such as both heat and ice, mustard, hot baths, friction with acids, leeches, and "brandy and ether in no timid quantities." It is perhaps just as well that we cannot know whether any of these remedies were applied to Catherine.
5. DLB 2: 17 Sept. 1838, 2nd Sunday of Advent 1838, 21 Apr. 1839.
6. DLB 2: 2nd Sunday of Advent 1838, 21 Apr. 1839, 10 Nov. 1839; EAMM 135–38, 174.
7. DEA 6; for other descriptions of Father Haseltine's character and work, see McGill 59, 114, 122–23, 130–31, 365–67; Fox, *Life* 153–54; and Schauinger, *Cathedrals* 224, 239. His role at Nazareth lasted until his sudden death in 1862. His name is alternately spelled "Hazeltine"; he himself mostly used the "s" as easier to write.
8. *Cincinnati Catholic Telegraph; Louisville Catholic Advocate* Cl 1: 49–52; 63–64; DLB 11: 20 Dec. 1836, 16 Sept. 1836, 11 Sept. 1837. Numerous letters concerning the school at this period can be found in DLB 11.
9. BT 7 May 1838.
10. BT 13 Nov. 1838; EAMM 133.
11. CM 15 Nov. 1838.
12. EAMM 148–49.

13. EAMM 148.

14. EAMM 149. Most if not all early slaves came as part of the postulants' dowry or were born on the property; later Sisters long supposed that such was always the norm and practice. In 1836, however, the Council purchased two women and two children, the first recorded purchases (CM 5 Oct. 1836, n.d. 1836). Catherine was in Louisville that year.

15. CSL 15 Aug. 1840.

16. See 1 Aug. 184?, 23 Feb. 1844, 20 May 1844, 12 Dec. 1847, 12 May 1849, 18 Nov. 1850, 8 Mar. 1851, 17 June 1851, 22 May 1852, 11 Nov. 1854, 5 Jan. 1856.

17. Most of these names match those in the list of "Nazareth Servants and Their Children" (n.d.) in the Archives. It names fourteen men, twelve women, and thirty-eight children of five mothers. In the 1840 Census, servants at Nazareth are enumerated: six adults over age twenty-four, fourteen ages ten to twenty-four, and seven children under ten. It seems the slave population grew chiefly by births into family units.

18. CM 22 Jan. 1844; C. Walker Gollar, letter to the author, 26 July 2004, offered insights on this episode.

19. DLB 1, n.d.; CSL 22 May 1852. Kentucky law forbade education of slaves, but enforcement was not strict.

20. CM 21 Aug. 1844.

21. DLB 11: 3 Jan. 1855; CM 20 and 27 Aug. 1845; DLB 3: 7 Jan. 1843; CM 19 Apr. 1836, 15 Jan. 1841; "Servants" list. The 1854 sale involved Mary Ann, who had five children, most born in Catherine's third term; three died early. The fifth, Sylvester, was "sold with his mother"; he would have been about nine.

22. *Catholic Advocate* 23 Mar. 1836, quoted in C. Walker Gollar, "Catholic Slaves and Slaveholders in Kentucky," *Catholic Historical Review* 84 (1998): 51; Gollar, "Catholic Slaves" 51–52. For detailed information and discussion of slavery in the various religions, see Gollar, "Catholic Slaves"; Boles; Eugene D. Genovese, *The Slaveholder's Dilemma: Freedom and Progress in Southern Conservative Thought, 1820–1860* (Columbia: University of South Carolina Press, 1992); Albert J. Raboteau, *Slave Religion: The "Invisible Institution" in the Antebellum South* (New York: Oxford University Press, 1978); and Kenneth J. Zanca, comp. and ed., *American Catholics and Slavery: 1789–1866: An Anthology of Primary Documents* (Lanham, MD: University Press of America, 1994).

23. Zanca 42–44. By 1837 there were fourteen dioceses: Baltimore, New Orleans, Boston, Philadelphia, New York, Bardstown, Richmond, Charleston, Cincinnati, St. Louis, Detroit, Dubuque, Natchez, and Nashville—an even split between the North and the South.

24. The Catholic position is delineated in Gollar, "Catholic Slaves"; Cyprian Davis, OSB, *The History of Black Catholics in the United States* (New York: Crossroad, 1990); Richard R. Duncan, "Catholics and the Church in the Antebellum Upper South" in *Catholics in the Old South*, ed. Randal M. Miller and Jon L. Wakelyn (Macon, GA: Mercer University Press, 1983) 77–98; other essays in Miller and Wakelyn; Nathaniel E. Green, *The Silent Believers* (Louisville: West

End Catholic Council, 1972); and the numerous primary documents reprinted in Zanca. In summary, the American bishops differentiated the international slave trade, condemned by Gregory XVI, from domestic slavery of those born in the United States. They believed slavery was not contrary to natural law or biblical norms, and immediate abolition would create social anarchy and worse suffering for the unprepared slaves. They advocated social order and respect for law, and so upheld the Fugitive Slave Law and defended Catholic Justice Taney in the *Dred Scott* decision—both in Catherine's lifetime. Even if most bishops hoped for gradual emancipation, they saw it as a political matter, not a call on their spiritual ministry. This depressing picture must be fairly balanced with the fact that some abolitionist groups did advocate and practice violence and were also rabidly nativist and anti-Catholic. The bishops were anxious to present the Catholic Church as unified and the Irish and German Catholic immigrants as loyal, law-abiding, and peaceable Americans. They devoted themselves to developing the immigrant church and deplored the abuse of slaves but not the system. They thus avoided a sectional split of the American Catholic Church but forfeited moral leadership for emancipation and racial equality.

25. On Sunday, December 3, 2000, a reconciliation service was held in the Bardstown Cathedral, sponsored by the Sisters of Charity and of Loretto and of St. Catharine (Dominicans), and attended by many Sisters and African American Catholics. The leaders of all three congregations asked forgiveness for their communities' participation in slavery and committed themselves to the contemporary work of racial justice. Representatives of the local African American community accepted this apology and pledge of collaboration.

26. Cl 1: 64.

27. FL 3:12 Oct. 1839. These "distinguished families" included that of Jefferson Davis, three of whose nieces from Davis Bend, Mississippi, made the annual trip by steamboat to attend school at Nazareth (McGill 130).

28. Letters written to Mother Catherine are chiefly in DLB 11. Some parents or agents refer to letters received from her; these are regrettably lost. Many replies from Father Haseltine are extant; these are chiefly in DLB 3: 1841–51.

29. Nazareth had severe problems obtaining payments across state lines. The United States did not then have a common currency. Specie was almost out of circulation, and paper money flooded the country in all kinds and denominations, in private bills and bank notes called "shin plasters." Ben Casseday, *The History of Louisville from Its Earliest Settlement till the Year 1852* (Louisville: Hull and Brother, 1852) 142.

30. DLB 11: 11 Jan. 1842.

31. DLB 11: 13 and 14 Aug. 1839, 11 Jan. 1842, 7 Apr. 1843.

32. DLB 11: 5 May 1843; DLB 3: 21 Aug. 1843, 17 Nov. 1841; DLB 11: 19 July 1842–18 Jan. 1843, 6 June 1845.

33. DLB 13: 8 Oct. 1842; DLB 3: 21 Dec. 1841, 8 Jan. 1842, 30 Dec. 1842; CM 30 Dec. 1842; BT 7 June 1843. St. Louis Church became the cathedral when the see of the diocese was moved in 1841 from Bardstown to Louisville.

34. DLB 3: 16 Sept. 1842, 12 Oct. 1842.

35. DLB 11: 11 Nov. 1846, 18 July 1844, 22 June 1843, 22 Nov. 1847, and any of the more than thirty letters in DLB 11 from McKay to Mothers Catherine or Frances, from early 1842 through 1848.

36. DLB 15: 66–69; DLB 3: 27 June 1842, 20 Sept. 1842, 3 Jan. 1841.

37. DLB 11: 16 Apr. 1841, n.d., 17 Jan. 1842.

38. DLB 11: 14 Aug. 1841, 30 Aug. 1838, 6 Mar. 1843, 3 Sept. 1843, 11 Mar. 1843, 3 May 1845.

39. DLB 11: 24 May 1844, 15 Aug. 1838, 12 Oct. 1838.

40. DLB 1: 17 June 1841.

41. CM: 5 Dec. 1838; 16 Oct. 1839; 15 Jan. 1841; 8 July 1842.

42. CSL 31 Aug. 1839.

43. DLB 4:2; CM 3 Dec. 1838; DLB 2: Dec. 1838; EAMM 140.

44. DLB 2: Jan. 1839. Guy Ignatius Chabrat was Flaget's "first son" in ordination and ever a special object of his affection. In 1816, the bishop noted his "piety and talents, especially for controversy"; he would not be surprised if he were his successor one day (FL 2: 29 Oct. 1816). Flaget almost made that happen by insisting on Chabrat for coadjutor, over the protests of both priests and laity, notably the ladies of Louisville, who objected to another French bishop. The priests simply disliked Chabrat's talent for humorless controversy, quick and arbitrary judgments, and general dominance. Loss of eyesight prevented his succession to Flaget, but in 1838, Chabrat may have enjoyed taking on a just fight with the ladies of Louisville, one manager against others. For accounts of Chabrat, see FL 2; Boles 74–76; Crews, *AHL* 101–3; Jay P. Dolan, *The American Catholic Experience: A History from Colonial Times to the Present* (Garden City, NY: Doubleday, 1985) 120; Schauinger, *Cathedrals* passim.

45. CM 13 Feb. 1841; Register; Card file in Archives; DLB 3: 28 Apr. 1845. These Sisters, who joined the Religious of the Sacred Heart, must be the referents in Catherine's letter to Flaget, saying that "they returned not to the world" (CSL 6 July 1841).

46. The five span the period from 9 Apr. 1840 to 26 June 1842. Four of the deaths are described in EAMM 147, 158, 181–82, 187.

47. EAMM 158.

48. DLB 2: 7 Aug. 1839, 17 Feb. 1840. David's final days are recounted in EAMM 170–78; Fox, *Life* 179–87; Lemarié 3: 231–32. In October 1839, Sister Elizabeth Suttle was transferred from St. Vincent's to Presentation. One hopes David did have the "great satisfaction" to see her again; she may have attended his deathbed or funeral. She lived not "a few years" but until 1873, a principal carrier of his memory and story.

49. CSL July 1844. Her request was honored. The picture hangs in the office of the current president of the SCN Congregation.

7. Community Life-Giver

1. After much painful and practical consideration and public relations efforts with those who favored or opposed the move, the authorization from Rome

had arrived in the spring of 1841. See Schauinger, *Cathedrals* 303–4; Crews, *AHL* 106–7; FL 2: 18 Mar. 1841, Aug. 1841.

2. Lemarié 2: 254, 350–52; DLB 24: 8 Aug. 1834. The story of the 1841 independence crisis is told in nearly all sources of SCN history. See especially Fox, *Life* 180–85; McGann, *Apostolate* 5–9; McGill 57–69.

3. Lemarié 3: 89, 218–21; DLB 24: 8 Aug. 1834; DLB 2: 10 Sept. 1834.

4. Register; CM 23 Oct. 1836. The story of Eulalia's departure, the bishop's role in it, and her later life can be followed in FL 3: 5 Sept.1834; DLB 21: 24 Aug. 1835; DEA 71; CM 23 Oct. 1836, 5 Oct. 1839; EAMM 173–74; and Dropfile of Nazareth Archives. Lemarié intersperses his biography of Flaget with a full and often amusing account entitled "The Ballad of Sister Eulalia": 2: 239–44, 389–93; 3: 202–4, 221–22, 303–9. Eulalia's volatile personality had to be some challenge to Mother Catherine. Even young Eliza Crozier saw that Eulalia's primary devotions were France and "mon oncle." Yet when she accompanied the bishop in 1835, she sent silver medals to Mothers Catherine and Frances and agreed to Flaget's four proposals by which he hoped she might be received again in the community. Despite the refusal, she seems to have retained good feelings for Nazareth and in her later years asked one correspondent to "say a thousand amiable things to Mother Catherine Spalding."

5. CM 5 Oct. 1839.

6. Lemarié 3: 218; Fox, *Life* 180.

7. CSL 17 Apr. 1841. Flaget's letter is unfortunately lost.

8. McGann, *Apostolate* 7–8; quoted in full in McGill 61–63. Marie Menard (EAMM 160) says that Haseltine and other clerical friends of Nazareth did not want the change but that Chabrat believed Nazareth needed reform and was acting for Flaget.

9. FL 2: 6 June 1841.

10. Fox, *Life* 185; Schauinger, *Cathedrals* 302; EAMM 160.

11. CSL 6 July 1841, quoted in full in McGill 63–69.

12. FL 2: 20 July 1841.

13. Lemarié 3: 220.

14. DLB 1: 2 Feb. 1854. For detailed accounts of the union from differing viewpoints, see Daughter of Charity, *1809–1959* (Emmitsburg, MD: St. Joseph's Central House, 1959) 45–73; and Judith Metz, SC, and Virginia Wiltse, *Sister Margaret Cecilia George: A Biography* (Mt. St. Joseph, OH: Sisters of Charity, 1989). From first to last, the union of Emmitsburg with France was clerically motivated and directed and conducted in secrecy. In 1845, the Sulpicians were ordered to give up governance of religious communities. Deluol redoubled his efforts to transfer his authority to a Vincentian priest and effect the union. He was abetted by the American Vincentian superior, the archbishop of Baltimore, and his friend the bishop of Natchez. Of the Sisters, only Mother Etienne Hall was involved. Either she genuinely desired the union and so "ardently" petitioned Paris for it, or she believed it inevitable and so cooperated as expected. She seems never to have informed or consulted the Sisters. Most did not know of the plans until they were told to don the French habit and renew vows on March 25, 1850,

to the Superior General in Paris, by the formula of the Daughters of Charity. Far from effecting a real union, the process created two new divisions, the Sisters of Charity of New York and of Cincinnati. However, a century later one sees enrichment from the connection of American and French Vincentian traditions and from the voluntary association of all the communities in the Charity Federation.

15. Lemarié 3: 206–7, 237; DLB 1: 25 Jan. 1842.

16. A copy of this meditation is preserved in the Nazareth Archives, with the notation of Catherine's ownership. The original booklet is not there.

17. See, for instance, CSL 1 Aug. 1844, 12 Dec. 1844, 20 Sept. 1848, 29 Aug. 1850, 3 June 1852, 13 Nov. 1852.

18. DLB 12: 23 Jan. 1843.

19. These notes were found in an old book. They are filed in DLB 25: 29. A portion of the text is repeated in Biographical Sketch of Mother Catherine Spalding 27–28.

20. DEA 122.

21. CM 30 June 1839, 8 and 9 Aug. 1840, 2 and 24 Mar. 1843, 7 Aug. 1843, 12 May 1844, 20 Mar. 1842.

22. DEA 122.

23. CSL 20 May 1844, 23 Feb. 1844, 12 May 1849, 29 Aug. 1850, 22 May 1852, 5 Jan. 1856.

24. *Catholic Advocate* 29 Apr. 1843, 27 May 1843, in Lyons, "Collection" 29.

25. V. F. O'Daniel, *The Father of the Church in Tennessee* (Washington, DC: Dominicana, 1926) passim, especially 201, 207–9, 341; Thomas Stritch, *The Catholic Church in Tennessee: The Sesquicentennial Story* (Nashville: Catholic Center, 1987) 50–51.

26. O'Daniel 260, 377–78.

27. DLB 1: 2 Nov. 1841, 15 Dec. 1841.

28. CM 17 Aug. 1842.

29. A Nashville "Methodist Paper," as quoted in *Catholic Telegraph*, 17 Sept. 1842; O'Daniel 379, 400, 414–15; Stritch 106. McGill 114, dates the opening of both a school and a hospital in 1841 and is cited by Gilmore 302, n.10. The Council Minutes, however, show the school, St. Mary's, opening in 1842 and the first assignments to the hospital, St. John's, in October 1848, after Catherine's term had expired.

30. DLB 1: 16 Oct. 1843; Gilmore 34. Detailed accounts of the establishment in Nashville are found in Gilmore and Buckner. O'Daniel's biography of Bishop Miles is a revealing source, basically favorable to Miles's views and actions in the ensuing history.

31. CSL 15 Nov. 1843?, 3 Feb. 1844; 20 May 1844. A dating puzzle exists here: Claudia's assignment is given as 15 Aug. 1843 in DEA 146 but as 16 Jan. 1844 in the more reliable Council Minutes and her official card in the Archives. If the later date is correct, the first cited letter cannot be 1843. But by November 1844, Catherine was back in Louisville, and the letter is clearly from Nazareth.

32. CSL 10 Aug. 1844.

33. DLB 1: Sept. 1844; CSL 31 Aug. 1839.

8. Louisville's "Mother Catherine"

1. Crews, *AHL* 108–9.

2. In 1927, the "Civic Opinion" cited the 1840 census report ("only 3616 Germans . . . nearly 1000 Irish") as pleasing evidence that Louisville had always been a "purely American city" with "practically all-American labor" (Clipping Files of Kentucky Division of Louisville Free Public Library). By 1850, however, the census recorded 12,500 Germans in Louisville, part of the wave that created the "German Triangle" of Milwaukee, St. Louis, and Cincinnati and caused the Ohio River to be dubbed the "Rhine of America"; with them were 3,100 Irish (Crews, *AHL* 139). Anti-immigrant feeling grew in proportion and endured.

3. Crews, *AHL* 117–18, 123.

4. Crews, *AHL* 104–5. The heated, even dangerous, atmosphere was not without its humor. A lecture titled "All the Abominations of Rome Exposed at Once (Ladies Excluded)" was countered by "Exposition of Catholic Thought (Ladies Invited)" (Crews, *AHL* 130). For accounts of the general attitudes and the League, see Agnes Geraldine McGann, *Nativism in Kentucky in 1860* (Washington, DC: Catholic University of America Press, 1944) 1–12; Stritch 71–74; Crews, *AHL* 128–33, 138–39.

5. Crews, *AHL* 128–29. The Millerites were a fairly large millennial Christian group with literal interpretations of Scripture, apocalyptic expectations, and highly emotional meetings. They were notably anti-Catholic.

6. McGann, *Nativism* 12–21, 27–28. No evidence suggests Clay was personally anti-Catholic. He was a friend of Flaget and had used his influence in Congress to counter anti-Catholic legislators and uphold the rights of Catholics as citizens (Schauinger, *Cathedrals* 231–33, 243, 267). Prentice's Whig *Louisville Journal* was rivaled by the Democratic *Louisville Courier*.

7. Peabody Poor, *Directory and Business Advertiser for 1844–45* (Louisville: W. N. Haldeman, 1844) 37; CSL 25 Feb. 1845.

8. SVO, 1868 "Charter and By-laws" 1–3. The later admission policies must have stemmed from Catherine's practice.

9. DLB 1: 26 Mar. 1845; DLB 14: 31 Mar. and 14 Apr. 1849, 20 Jan. 1846; DLB 1: 11 June 1847, 25 June 1846; SVO.

10. DLB 14: 20 Jan. 1846; CSL 21 Nov. 1844; DLB 1: 9 and 10 Apr., 11 June 1849.

11. *Catholic Advocate* 4 Oct. 1849, Cl 2: 3–4.

12. Catherine's letter is lost. Sister Margaret's reply is in DLB 1: 26 Aug. 1849. All quotations are from this letter. For "Martha," cf. Luke 10: 38–42.

13. Gilmore 32. This account tells that the cold so settled in Sister Xavier Ross's ears as to start her gradual deafness.

14. EAMM 120–21. The account says this episode occurred at a time of "forty or fifty girls, the oldest of whom was now twelve years old" and that Eliza Jenkins, the Penn Baby of the 1830s, was Catherine's companion on this and other begging tours.

15. SVO, "By-laws" and "List of Orphans Received."

16. Letter to Father Aud at St. Thomas, almost certainly from Mother Catherine (DLB 1: n.d. but after 1835); SVO, "By-laws." Barbara Dosh became Sister Mary Lucy Dosh of Civil War fame. She died as a volunteer nurse of soldiers from both sides, who then escorted her remains from Paducah back to St. Vincent's, Union County, under a flag of truce ("The True Story of Sister Mary Lucy Dosh," in booklet prepared for the Market House Museum of Paducah, Kentucky).

17. DEA 25.

18. DLB 1: n.d. but before 1847; CSL n.d., probably 1847 by internal evidence.

19. CSL 20 Sept. 1848.

20. DLB 1: 6, 17, 30 Mar. 1845

21. DLB 1: 27 Apr., 5 May 1845. Gray refers to letters by Catherine written on 12 and 23 Mar., 21 Apr. 1845. His letters have survived and indicate the content in hers.

22. DEA 24.

23. FGL; DLB 1: n.d.

24. DEA 24.

25. Johnston 1: 82–83.

26. DEA 24. The prominent men included James Guthrie and James Speed, both members of presidential cabinets, and James Stephens Speed, who would become mayor of Louisville. Notable visitors included Lincoln, Webster, Dickens, Whitman, Emerson, and Clay. Catherine knew their hosts (Crews, *AHL* 120–21; John Kleber, "Speed," *The Encyclopedia of Louisville* [Lexington: University Press of Kentucky, 2001]; Lyons, "Collection" 19).

27. Creamer 200–201; Lyons, "Collection" 28, 29, 31, 35, 38; *Catholic Advocate* 29 Nov. 1849, Cl 2: 6, 72; DLB 1: 16 Nov. 1849.

28. DLB 1: 25 Dec. 1844, 31 Dec. 1844.

29. St. Joseph Infirmary, "Leaves of Old Records" 7, and "Annals" 3.

30. DLB 1: 22 Mar. 1849, 18 Sept. 1845.

31. "The Orphan's Casket," Oct. 1845; Nov. 1848. This paper is eight large pages of "original tales, poems, essays, &c." published and sold each day of the fair by B. J. Webb and Brother. "Casket" evidently denoted a jewel box. Announcements and advertisements at the end best describe the fair. Many issues are in a bound volume in the Archive of Spalding University, Louisville. Quotations are taken at random from the issues cited.

32. The *Catholic Advocate* reported that people had purchased expensive articles, then donated them to other tables, some three or four times (9 Nov. 1851, Cl 2: 26).

33. DLB 14: 14 Feb. 1846, 17 June 1849.

34. Polly's father, Alexander Scott Bullitt, was delegate to the state constitutional conventions of 1792 and 1799 and the state's first lieutenant governor. His son William C. was heir to the large family estate, Oxmoor, and delegate to the convention of 1849. James Guthrie was a hugely successful businessman and Democratic politician, who had already served in the state house and senate and helped Louisville get city status. The Whig *Journal* said sourly, "The city is but

another name for Mr. Guthrie." With large interests and knowledge in the arts and sciences, Guthrie highly valued Mother Catherine and the education given his daughters and voted for the NLBI charter. Objectivity cannot have been easy for her in this case (Kleber 362–63; Creamer 219).

35. The Bullitt family history, some depositions for the 1845 trial, summaries of proceedings, and the judge's charge to the jury are in the Bullitt Family Papers in the Special Collections of the Filson Historical Society, Louisville. Depositions by people supporting the Guthries are in the State Archives in Frankfort, Kentucky; they have been copied and added to the Bullitt collection.

Some Sisters' depositions are preserved in the Bullitt papers; they are cautious in describing Polly's limitations. Many listed depositions are missing, including Mother Catherine's and the first depositions of Father Haseltine and Sister Emily Elder, who was in charge of Polly. The 1845 charge to the jury and the 1849 Bullitt letters indicate Mother Catherine's testimony favored the Guthries' position; this was probably true of other Sisters' testimonies as well.

36. Bullitt Family Papers, charge to the jury, 2 May 1846.

37. *Louisville Daily Journal*, 30 Apr., 7, 8, and 9 May 1849; these newspapers and the two letters of William Bullitt's daughters, in the Bullitt Family Papers, provide the sequence and lively drama of the 1849 trial.

38. Letter in Bullitt Family Papers; Lyons, *Bishops* 44. The priest was the Reverend Walter S. Coomes, assistant at St. Louis Church, whose name as witness is on the will. Clay had tried to make him unsure of his own handwriting.

39. Lyons, "Collection" 33; Register.

40. Vallée: Permanent record in card file; DEA 125, 146.

41. DLB 1: 8 Feb. 1846. Neither the arsonist nor the motive is known today.

42. FGL 3 Mar. 1846.

43. An 1872 record states unequivocally: "When Sister Ann Spalding died from the poison administered by a black servant girl, [1848] Sister Ambrosia had received a dose that came very near putting an end to her life" ("Record of Daily Facts" handwritten by Sister Marie Menard, Cl B: 157). A coroner's inquest was done on the death, implying special circumstances. Receipt for the coroner's expenses is in Original Letter Book (hereafter OLB) 42: 25.

44. Annals of St. Catherine Academy 29, quoted by McGill 92–93.

45. DLB 1: n.d. but 1839, 26 Jan. 1840; EAMM 11–12.

46. Annals of St. Catherine Academy; McGill 92–93.

47. *Catholic Advocate* 8 July 1848, Cl 1: 148.

48. CM 18 and 19 May 1848, 15 June 1848, 24 and 26 Aug. 1848.

49. CSL 20 Sept. 1848.

50. DLB 14: 14 Jan. 1847; Webb, "MCS."

51. Father Clark taught at St. Joseph's and St. Mary's colleges and was pastor at St. Charles. Lyons, *Bishops* 39 gives an account of his life.

52. CSL 21 Nov. 1844; 8 Jan. 1849. See Lyons, *Bishops* 95–99, for accounts of the brothers Spalding. Martin John became bishop of Louisville and archbishop of Baltimore; Benedict Joseph largely directed construction of the Louisville Cathedral and served as vicar general and administrator of the diocese.

53. CSL 24 July 1846, 22 Sept. 1848.

54. DLB 1: 26 Mar. 1845, 27 Oct. 1845.

55. BT 6 May 1850. Only five meetings of the Board are recorded in this period, none between July 1845 and September 1847. Mrs. J. D. Colmesnil was the president chosen at the first meeting in August 1832 of the ladies organizing a fair for the orphans (*Record*, 2 July 1849, Cl 45: 33).

56. CSL 25 Feb. 1845.

57. Quotations throughout this section from the letters to Sister Claudia Elliott are taken at random from CSL 1 Aug. 184?, 2 Nov. 1846, 12 Dec. 1847, n.d., possibly 1847, 20 Sept. 1848, 30 Apr.–12 May 1849.

58. Nazareth Academy Records; Register; CSL 24 May 1848.

59. DLB 1: 17 Jan. 1846. John sent Catherine's letter with one of his own to Father Ben Spalding in Bardstown. He refers to her as "the late Catherine Spalding." The "late" may refer to her former lay status; he had no reason to think her dead. Why he did not answer her directly is puzzling. Father Ben forwarded John's letter to Catherine.

60. CSL 24 May 1848. All quotations of Catherine to Juliann are from this letter.

61. CSL 30 Apr.–12 May 1849.

62. DLB 1: 18 Sept. 1845; DLB 14: 20 Jan. 1846.

63. *Catholic Advocate* 22 Apr. 1848; 8 July 1848, Cl 1: 148; Stritch 107; CM 29 Aug. 1849. Ivo Schacht came from Belgium at an appeal from Bishop Miles, who ordained him in 1843 and shortly made him pastor of the cathedral, director of the Academy, and spiritual director of the Sisters of Charity (O'Daniel 390, 447–49).

64. *Louisville Journal*, 6 May 1849; Crews, *AHL* 121.

65. Crews, *AHL* 131–32.

66. Lemarié 3: 258–60, 267; FL 2: 15 Jan. 1843, 16 Apr. 1847?, 21 Sept. 1847; Schauinger, *Cathedrals* 306–7. Thomas W. Spalding, *Martin John Spalding: American Churchman* (Washington, DC: Catholic University of America Press, 1973), is the fullest account of Bishop Spalding's life.

67. Schauinger, *Cathedrals* 309–10; Lemarié 3: 284–87. The *Journal* 13 Feb. 1850, took brief notice of the death, citing the bishop's holiness and the public's esteem. Cl 2: 8–9, gives a full description of the elaborate obsequies and temporary burial at the Good Shepherd house until the new cathedral would be built.

68. Population from 1850 Census, cited in SVO.

9. Builder for a Future

1. CSL 29 Aug. 1850.

2. Register; DLB 1: 4 June 1846, 8 Feb. 1846; DLB 21: 25 Aug. 1855; CSL 5 Jan. 1856.

3. CM 13 Jan. 1846, 23 Mar. 1846; DLB 1: 4 June 1846. Advance specifications in the Council Minutes do not fully agree with the enthusiastic description of Sister Clementia Paine to Claudia, but the general picture is clear enough.

4. DLB 13 contains numerous letters to or from Father Haseltine, many combining business with small talk and best wishes to Mothers Catherine and Frances and Sister Columba. All the schoolgirls knew him; some are as chatty with him as if to a Sister or another woman.

5. FGL n.d. 1848 or 1849.

6. *Catholic Advocate* 2 Nov. 1850, Cl 2: 23; CM 4 Dec. 1850; Howlett 115; McGann, *Apostolate* 73–74. The *Advocate* urged that since the female orphans were well cared for at St. Vincent Asylum, it was now "incumbent on all, to think of the future destiny of the Youthful *Lord* of *Creation*" and to rescue as many as possible "from the devouring jaw of the monster of infidelity and immorality."

7. EAMM 24; Fox, "MCS" 19–20. Marie Menard's account, closer to the time and the sources of the story, supersedes McGill's statement (71–72) that Catherine never returned after the first trip. For an account of Father Chambige and his connections with Nazareth, see Lyons, *Bishops* 34–35.

8. CM 30 Aug. 1851, 16 Jan. 1852.

9. CM 20 Apr. 1852, 5 Nov. 1852, 1 Jan. 1855; DLB 22: 20 May 1856.

10. DLB 3: 9 May 1848, 26 Sept. 1848. The letters do not state the fifty dollars was annual payment, but this may be logically inferred.

11. CM 29 Aug. 1849; DLB 3: n.d.

12. DLB 1: 1 Aug. 1850. Bishop Miles was traveling the diocese on horseback throughout 1850 and was seriously ill at the end of the year. Schacht also made begging tours to other areas.

13. CM 22 Aug. 1850, 27 Aug. 1850, 1 Nov. 1850, 15 Nov. 1850, 1 Dec 1850.

14. Buckner 19–23, especially 22; Stritch 107–8. For the New York and Cincinnati separations, see chap. 7, n. 14; Metz and Wiltse 55–57, 66–74.

15. O'Daniel (448–49) insists that the plan was Schacht's, that the bishop, a Dominican, would never have wished to divide a religious community and did not know Schacht's intent until some Sisters were too engaged in it to be happy again at Nazareth. It is not easy to accept this fully; Miles might be expected to know something was afoot and to stop what he really opposed.

16. Quoted in O'Daniel 449–50 and Gilmore 43.

17. DLB 1: n.d., but her wish for the New Year dates the letter in the winter after her assignment to Louisville and before her return to Nashville in summer 1851.

18. Gilmore 17–18, 27; Xavier Ross, permanent record card; CM 17 Aug. 1842, 29 May 1843, 22 Aug. 1847. See also chapter 5.

19. DLB 1: 4 Jan. 1847, 9 Aug. 1846.

20. James Maria Spillane, SCN, on a tape about Mother Catherine made for the author.

21. George Morris, SJ, "Graphoanalysis of Mother Xavier Ross," ts. in Archive of Sisters of Charity of Leavenworth, Kansas, n.d.; Krusling and Murphy 19. While the scientific nature of graphoanalysis is not universally accepted, the qualities of the two women noted by these analysts are amply verified in other records of their personalities.

22. Register.

23. DLB 1: n.d. except "Wednesday night."

24. CM 2 July 1851.

25. Buckner 23; Haseltine to Frances Gardiner, DLB 1: 2 Feb. and 22 May 1852; CM 14 Jan. 1853, re Baptista Carney. The Sisters who remained in Nashville were Johanna Bruner, Mary Vincent Kearney, Baptista Carney, Ellen Davis, and Jane Frances Jones. Their dates of departure in Nazareth's Register are 2, 3, and 5 July 1851, probably the dates they declared a decision.

26. The others were Sisters Christine Coomes, Agnes Smith, Gabriella Todd, Dorothy Villeneuve, and Cornelia Paine.

27. Mother Catherine might have known through Bishop Spalding the subsequent history of the Sisters at Nashville until 1857. They expanded their ministry and membership from 1851 through 1856. With borrowed funds Father Schacht began construction of an academy and motherhouse. In 1857, however, he began to have conflict with the bishop, leading to Schacht's suspension and departure from the diocese. When the creditors heard it and demanded their money, the bishop refused to assume responsibility for the debts, which O'Daniel says had been incurred without his authorization. He stresses that Miles was aging and ill, severely exhausted in mind and body by his labors (O'Daniel 538–42; Stritch 107–8). Other traditions support this, including one that Mother Xavier never blamed him for the way all the trouble fell on the Sisters. They had to sell everything to pay the debts and find another bishop to receive them. Xavier went to a council of bishops in St. Louis, where Bishop Miege of the Northwest Territory welcomed her to transplant her community to Leavenworth, Kansas (Buckner, chaps. 4, 6; Gilmore, chaps. 7–10 give the entire story). Mother Catherine was out of office before this trouble developed, and she died before the resettlement in Leavenworth at the end of 1858. For some years the two communities had little or no contact, but in 1933, for the Diamond Jubilee of the Sisters of Charity of Leavenworth, Sister Mary de Lourdes Macklin wrote a tribute:

> Nazareth your Mother rejoices
> . . . .
> There was work for the Master awaiting
> Hearts and hands in the land of the West.
> God's Providence guided your footsteps
> As you heeded His loving behest. (Gilmore 279)

In the years since, the friendship of the two communities has continually deepened by visits to the motherhouses and other forms of association.

28. Stritch 107; CM 14 July 1851, 7 Aug. 1851, 11 Sept. 1851; DLB 3: 21 July 1851; BT 25 Oct. 1851; DLB 11: 12 Jan. 1856.

29. DLB 1: 2 Feb. 1852; see 22 May 1852 for Haseltine's comment.

30. Sisters Pauline Gibson and Dorothy Villeneuve returned to Nashville in 1852 and 1853 (Register). Neither went to Kansas. For Baptista Carney, see CM 14 Jan. 1853, 11 May 1853.

31. DLB 1: 28 Nov. 1851.

32. Numerous letters and Board and Council Minutes refer to these problems: DLB 10: 8 July 1830, 19 Apr. 1834; DLB 1: 28 Nov. 1851, 29 Dec. 1851, 2 Feb. 1852, 2 Mar. 1852, 22 May 1852, 3 Aug. 1852; BT 7 May 1849, 6 May 1850; CM 6 May 1836, 13 Nov. 1842, 16 Dec. 1842, 3 May 1843, 5 Aug. 1843, 2 May 1848, 28 Aug. 1849, 1 Dec. 1850, 7 Aug. 1851, 5 Mar. 1852, 26 Dec. 1852 (when Mother Frances was relieved of office there), 10 Mar. 1854. Sacred Heart Church was the parish for St. Vincent Academy and located on the same land.

33. CM 18 Nov. 1852, 18 Jan. 1853, 2 Feb. 1853, 24 Oct. 1853; BT 18 Nov. 1853.

34. CSL 9 Jan. 1855. A reference to Father Durbin locates the recipient at St. Vincent's.

35. DLB 2: Aug. 1835. Angela is not listed among the Sisters at St. Vincent's renewing vows in 1840. In 1842, she is listed at the motherhouse. CM 2 Mar. 1840, 28 Feb. 1842, 6 Mar. 1843, 27 Aug. 1845, 9 Nov. 1848, 7 Aug. 1851, 5 Mar. 1852, 10 Mar. 1854.

36. Register; CSL 22 May 1852; 5 Jan. 1856.

37. CSL, 12 May 1849, 17 June 1851, 11 Nov. 1854, 9 Jan. 1855; DLB 1: 4 May 1854, 15 July 1854.

38. CSL 5 Jan. 1856; Register.

39. CSL 13 Nov. 1852, 3 June 1852; CM 7 Aug. 1853; CSL 1 Apr. 1853, 15 Jan. 1855.

40. CM 30 Mar. 1852, 20 Apr. 1852, 27 Apr. 1852, 8 Sept. 1852; Creamer 208–9. Seven acres were purchased from Guthrie.

41. Flaget had bought the lot in 1841 as the site for a new cathedral. The Jesuits had St. Aloysius College there until they left for New York (1849–52). When the cathedral was built on the site of St. Louis Church, the disappointed and irrepressible Badin performed a ritual of mourning and departed for Cincinnati, where he died in April 1853. Catherine led a ritual of mourning for him at Nazareth. Lyons, *Bishops* 24, 26; Schauinger, *Cathedrals* 309–10; Crews, *AHL* 124; Cl 2: 30; "Leaves" and "Brief History" in archival box of St. Joseph Infirmary; Webb, *Centenary* 543; Johnston 2: 47.

42. Creamer (209–19) argues this naming with ample documentation. She describes, in detail and with a map, the land transactions of 1852 and 1854. The city put the name on its official 1856 map, thus ratifying the honor in Catherine's lifetime.

43. CM 2 Feb. 1853, 24 Oct. 1854; Cl 2: 29; DEA 72. St. Mary's on Jefferson Street served eight years until a parochial school was opened in the area.

44. Crews, *AHL* 127; CM 22 July 1855, 10 Oct. 1855.

45. DLB 14: Mar. 1856; DLB 10: 27 Mar. 1856; DLB 26: 26 Mar. 1856. Spalding, however, was impressed at that time by the success of the Nashville Sisters and thought the idea of a motherhouse in each diocese might have its value.

46. DLB 1: 28 Jan. 1853, Feb. or Mar. 1854, Feb. 1854, n.d. but in 1854.

47. CM: 6 Mar. 1849; DLB 1: 29 Dec. 1851.

48. CSL 18 Nov. 1850, 8 Mar. 1851.

49. CSL 8 Mar. 1851.

50. DLB 1: 29 and 31 Dec. 1851; CM 14 Feb. 1852; CSL 9 Jan. 1855.

51. CSL 22 May 1852, 3 June 1852.

52. CM 29 Aug. 1853, 5 Dec. 1853; BT 6 May 1854; CSL 12 Sept. 1854; CSL 4 Nov. n.d., after 1854. Kate has been tentatively identified from a list of boarders for 1853–54 as Mary Catherine Smith; her education at Nazareth terminated in June 1854.

53. CCL 15 July 1854, 22 Jan. 1855; CSL 8 Feb. 1854, 6 Mar. 1854; DLB 1: 13 Mar. 1854.

54. CSL 30 Apr. 1854; DLB 1: 4 May 1854, 15 July 1854.

55. CSL 30 Apr. 1854, 9 Jan. 1855.

56. CSL 9 Jan. 1855.

57. DLB 11: 2 Mar. 1855, 28 Apr. 1855, 9 July 1855, 7 Sept. 1855, 19 Dec. 1855; Cl 2: 18, 58; CSL 29 June 1852; DLB 23: Notice to Parents, 1856.

58. OLB 5: 123–23a; CM 5 Nov. 1854; DLB 1: 6 Mar. 1855, 21 Sept. 1856; DLB 21: 29 Apr. 1856.

59. DLB 11: 5 Dec. 1851, 22 Feb. 1855, 21 Apr. 1855, 9 June 1855, 2 Mar. 1855. More than twenty such letters sent to Catherine in this term of office are extant, most collected in DLB 11.

60. CM 11 Apr. 1851; BT 16 Nov. 1855.

61. CSL 25 May 1857.

62. T. Spalding, *Martin John Spalding* 19–22, 79–85; CM 29 Aug. 1849, 28 Oct. 1849; DLB 1: 11 Jan. 1853.

63. CSL 20 May 1852.

64. CM 17 Mar. 1853, 27 May 1853, 31 July 1853. Gabriella Todd was one of those who returned from Nashville; she died an SCN in 1899.

65. CCL 2 Feb. 1854; DLB 1: 13 Mar. 1854.

66. CSL 20 Oct. 1854. All subsequent quotations of Catherine to Bishop Spalding are from this letter.

67. CM 4 Dec. 1854.

68. Boles 76; T. Spalding, *Martin John Spalding* 68–70. An excellent short account of the day and its antecedents is Crews, *AHL* 140–47. A full history is McGann, *Nativism* especially chap. 4. Local reminiscences are in the Filson Historical Society of Louisville and issues of the local newspapers in the Louisville Free Public Library.

69. DEA 23; CSL 22 Sept. 1856.

70. DLB 11: 3 Dec. 1855; DLB 1: 9 May 1850, 7 Nov. 1852, 9 Oct. 1850; "Reminiscences," DLB 22: 48.

71. CSL 18 Aug. 1856; Luke 10:42.

10. Final Harvest, Global Legacy

1. CSL 22 Sept. 1856; DEA 28.

2. CSL 18 March, 13 June 1857. The tradition of Catherine as a figure of

charity on the streets of Louisville is long-standing in both city and SCN community. It passed to the author from Sister Patricia Kelly from Sister Mary Rita Knight from Sister Emerentia Wales (1850–1937), who said that in her childhood, her mother pointed out Mother Catherine in the street, always with a child, and told her, "That is a very holy woman!" Sister Emerentia was many years a teacher and superior in Yazoo City, Mississippi; at her death, the local paper cited her acquaintance with all Nazareth's Mothers, including the foundress (Annals of St. Clare Academy 1: 12).

3. The SVO Annals, SCN Register and permanent record cards, and the 1860 official census of the Louisville First Ward 12–15 offer data for a composite picture, but not a perfectly certain list for 1856–58.

4. CSL n.d. but mid-1857, 23 Jan. 1858.

5. CSL 30 Oct. 1857.

6. *Louisville Journal* 12, 17 Mar. 1857; *Louisville Courier* 13, 19, 28 Mar. 1857; *Bardstown Gazette* 25 Mar. 1857; copies in Cl 2: 64, 67, 68; FGL 13 Mar. 1857. The story went as far as the *New York Herald;* Simon Fouché considered it would make "only a squall . . . the reputation of Nazareth is solidly established" (DLB 21: 27 Apr. 1857).

7. CSL 19 Oct. 1856, n.d. probably 1856, n.d. but Dec. 1856 or Jan. 1857, 14 Jan. 1857.

8. The following discussion draws at random from six letters for brief quotations and frequently similar examples: CSL 18 Aug. 1856, 22 Sept. 1856, 25 May 1857, 11 Jan. 1858, 13 June 1857, n.d. but after May 1857. Sister Cleophas Mills later succeeded Catherine in the line of Mothers (1885–91, 1897–1903).

9. CSL 22 Sept. 1856; 19 Oct. n.d. probably 1856, to Claudia; 25 May 1857.

10. CSL 25 May 1857.

11. CSL 23 Jan. 1858.

12. The account that follows is drawn from several sources: DEA 26–28, written by a Sister who received her account from the attending physician and Sisters; CCL: "Thursday night" [17 Mar.], 30 Mar. 1858, and DLB 1: 19 Apr. 1858; Webb's obituary in the *Louisville Guardian* and tributes in the *Bardstown Gazette* and *Louisville Courier* Cl II: 76–84; Fox, "MCS" 22; and McGill 76–78. McGill says Catherine went on her errand of mercy to a poor workman; the earlier sources cite a family.

13. The meaning of this request has been much discussed. It has been taken, perhaps accurately, as a traditional sign of poverty or surrender to mortality. Contemporary nurses have also noted that persons dying of lung disease are often restless and beg to be moved to alleviate pain and inability to breathe. The early annalist's account seems to corroborate this interpretation (DEA 27).

14. The transfer was on Monday, March 22, arriving at Nazareth about 4:00. The records are not fully clear whether the funeral was that same day or the next morning.

15. CCL 30 Mar. 1858.

16. FGL Apr. 1858; DEA 18; Register.

17. Webb, "MCS" Cl 2: 76. Similar tributes appeared in papers of Louisville and Bardstown (Cl 2: 84).

18. McGann, *Apostolate* 15–18.

Appendix A

1. A detailed sifting of all the evidence—lost, found, reconstructed, interrelated—is found in D. Spalding, "Mystery." Brother Spalding searched all existing and relevant records in churches and courthouses in Maryland and Kentucky, as well as the research compiled by Judge Samuel Boldrick and Dr. Joseph E. Johnson, who researched all records in the two states, and the genealogies compiled in the same way by Mary Louise Donnelly. Hughes Spalding, in his chapter on Mother Catherine, summarizes what these predecessors learned. All came to the same conclusion. What follows relies heavily on Brother Spalding's clear summary of all this evidence; he cites all relevant specific court documents. It also relies on his written notations and oral comments, drawn from his extensive files of research (T. Spalding, Historical Notes).

2. Boldrick and Johnson 25–31; T. Spalding, Historical Notes, and "The Parentage of James Spalding of Cox's Creek" 1, 3–4. Boldrick and Johnson did the first solid genealogical research of the Spaldings. Brother Spalding has demonstrated, however, that they erred in identifying James, son of Basil Sr., as the James Spalding who lived in Cox's Creek.

3. Sulpician records, cited in T. Spalding, Historical Notes.

4. T. Spalding, Historical Notes.

5. Webb, "MCS"; T. Spalding, Historical Notes.

6. Webb, *Centenary* 254 n.

7. T. Spalding, "Mystery" 120–21; H. Spalding 2: 242–43; T. Spalding, Historical Notes.

8. Edward E. Kirwan, Correspondence with Mother Bertrand Crimmins, 5 and 8 July 1952; Mattingly, Mary Ramona, SCN, Correspondence with Crolian Edelen, 5 Jan. 1957–27 Feb. 1958; with Hughes Spalding and others, 27 June 1960–1 Dec. 1974; "Charles," letter, n.d.; T. Spalding, Historical Notes, "Mystery" 122. All the letters are in the Nazareth Archives.

Kirwan asserted that Catherine was "certainly the daughter of Ralph Spalding"; it is "less certain . . . quite probable, her mother was a . . . Edelen." He cites a 1928 book by J. W. S. Clements on the Clements and Spalding families that says Priscilla Clements Edelen's granddaughter married Ralph Spalding; that work is no longer cited by reputable genealogists.

Crolian Edelen, probably from family interest, named as Catherine's father Basil Spalding's son James, adding "probably James Raphael—married 'Mollie' (Mary) Edelen. . . . d. c. 1800 in Prince George's County, Md, left two sons and two daughters." Edelen is correct on this James's data, but there is no evidence for tacking Raphael to his name—nor to Edward's, even though he gave it to his son. Second names, despite George Hilary, were rare at the time. Edelen's solution also makes the death of Catherine's father much later than believed and leaves two sons to be accounted for. Kirwan and Edelen simply accepted the father's name given by Webb; they were in search of the mother's maiden name.

Most "curious" of all is a letter from "Charles" to "Norbert" on the letterhead of the St. Mary's Historical Society, dated without a year; it states, "Everyone knows that Mother Mary Catherine Spalding's father was Ralph Spalding. [She] herself wrote this. [What] cannot be proved is whose son was Ralph." "Charles" thinks Ralph was the son of John Spalding, who moved from St. Mary's County to Charles County. That solution would make Catherine's father a brother, not a son, to Basil Spalding, and Catherine a cousin, not a young niece, to Elizabeth Spalding Elder. If Mother Catherine herself ever wrote that her father was Ralph, that document is lost.

9. D. Spalding, "Mystery" 122, and conversations with the author.

10. D. Spalding, "Mystery" 121–22; Webb, "MCS."

11. D. Spalding, "Mystery" 123 n. 7.

12. The lack of that tradition, rather than the dubious character of Edward, caused Sister Mary Ramona Mattingly's reluctance to accept the paternity of Edward as proved. It ran, she wrote to Hughes Spalding, "contrary to all information we have and to every tradition concerning Mother's close relatives" (14 Oct. 1965). She noted that there were so many Spaldings in Maryland and Kentucky that not all of them could be traced, and she was more inclined to think Basil Spalding had a son omitted from his will because he was already the ne'er-do-well Edward became. Hughes Spalding, however, relying on the research of Boldrick and Johnson and Brother David (Thomas) Spalding, held to his conviction (Mattingly correspondence with H. Spalding).

13. Boldrick writes Johnson, "You know Sr. Columba [Fox] told us that it was a tradition in the order that Ralph was not much force." He also cites Sister Columba for the tradition that Ralph was Catherine's father but discounts it as error (DLB 31: 14 Dec. 1942). Hughes Spalding cites the embarrassing visits (244). Brother Thomas Spalding says he was told directly by Sister Augustine Porter that she had heard directly from Sister Marie Menard about Ralph, Mother Catherine's brother, who occasionally came to Nazareth begging. Marie Menard's sources for her Annals were yet older Sisters who knew Catherine directly. The tradition thus has some weight. Hughes Spalding thinks it accounts for the later citation of Ralph as the father's name.

14. H. Spalding 2: 249; CSL 24 May 1848; DLB 1: 18 Jan. 1833, 11 Jan. 1846.

15. D. Spalding, "Mystery" 122.

Bibliography

Primary Sources

Note: Most of these materials are in the Archives of the Sisters of Charity of Nazareth at Nazareth, Kentucky. Others are in the Kentucky Room of the Louisville Free Public Library, the Cathedral Heritage Collection, and the Filson Historical Society. Items with contents not readily identified have been annotated.

Administrative Documents

Book of Elections. Handwritten official accounts of elections of Mothers and Council members from 1813 to 1882.

Card and Drop Files of Nazareth Archives. Summary record of individual Sisters' data.

Charter, Constitution, and By-laws of the St. Vincent's Orphan Asylum. Louisville: J. C. Webb & Co., 1869.

Members of the Board of Trustees for NLBI. Dates of meetings and members present of the Nazareth Literary and Benevolent Institution from May 1830 to May 1932.

Minutes of the Board of Trustees, 1829–1932. Original handwritten Minutes of the Board of Trustees of Nazareth Literary and Benevolent Institution (NLBI).

Minutes of the Council of Nazareth, 1831–1911. Handwritten "true copy from the original manuscript" of minutes of the Nazareth Council.

Nazareth Academy Records.

Register of the Sisters of Charity of Nazareth. Ts. Contains dates of entry, reception of habit, vows, death or departure of the Sisters.

Annals

Annals of St. Catherine Academy, Lexington, KY.
Annals of St. Clara Academy, Yazoo City, MS.
Annals of St. Joseph Infirmary, Louisville, KY.
Annals of St. Vincent Orphanage, Louisville, KY. Vol. 1.
Duplicate Early Annals. A gathering in Duplicate Letter Book 4 of various collections and notes. "Annals of Mother Catherine and Others" are especially important.
Early Annals by Marie Menard, SCN. A narrative composed by Sister Marie from her 1870 interviews with earliest Sisters. A key historical source. One copy, in a ring binder, is cited by page number in the notes of this book.
First Annals. Five pages of notes by early Sisters, copied in 1967. In a binder with the Duplicate Early Annals.

Correspondence

Clark, William, OP. Letter to S. Mary Cassilda Stey, SCN.
Duplicate Letter Books. 42 vols.
Flaget David Letters. 1 vol. Trans. S. Edward Barnes, SCN. Includes most letters of David to Bruté.
Flaget Letters. 3 vols. Trans. S. Edward Barnes, SCN.
Kirwan, Edward E. Correspondence with Mother Bertrand Crimmins, 5 and 8 July 1952, 23 Aug. 1957.
Letters of Mother Catherine Spalding.
Letters of Mother Columba Carroll. Vol. 1.
Letters of Mother Frances Gardiner.
Mattingly, Mary Ramona, SCN. Correspondence with Crolian Edelen, 5 Jan. 1957–27 Feb. 1958; with Hughes Spalding and Others, 27 June 1960–1 Dec. 1974. Discussions of evidences of the paternity of Mother Catherine.
Original Letter Books. Vol. 5

Newspapers

Bardstown Herald
Catholic Advocate, Louisville, KY
Catholic Telegraph, Cincinnati, OH
Daily Public Advertiser
Louisville Courier
Louisville Daily Journal

Louisville Guardian. Early Catholic paper in Louisville
Louisville Public Advertiser
Record. Later Catholic diocesan paper of Louisville

Other Sources

Biographical Sketch of Mother Catherine Spalding by a Member of the Community. Nazareth: Mother House, 1912. Centennial booklet.
Biographical Sketches of 5 Ecclesiastical Superiors and Some Chaplains of the SCN Community. SCN Administration Book.
Biographical Sketches of SCNs. 4 vols. Ts.
Boldrick, Samuel J., and Joseph E. Johnson. "The Spalding Family of Maryland and Kentucky." Ts. Earliest research of Catherine Spalding's family origins.
Bullitt Family Papers. Special Collections, Filson Historical Society, Louisville.
Clipping Files of Kentucky Division of Louisville Free Public Library.
Clippings, multivolume. Paginated folders containing clippings from journals and newspapers, 1826–60.
"Common Rules of the Daughters of Charity, Servants of the Sick Poor." Trans. Mary Wedding, SCN, from Rule in French copied by Simon Bruté, SS. Ts.
The Conferences of St. Vincent de Paul to the Daughters of Charity. 4 vols. Trans. Joseph Leonard, CM. Westminster, MD: Newman Press, 1952.
David, John Baptist Mary. *A Catechism of the Catholic Religion.* New revised edition. Louisville: J. C. Webb & Co., n.d. Described in the preface as "chiefly a reprint" of an 1825 edition. Archives of Archdiocese of Louisville.
———. "A Manual for the Sisters of Nazareth." Handwritten book of advice on religious duties.
———. *A Spiritual Retreat of Eight Days.* Ed. M. J. Spalding. Louisville: Webb and Levering, 1864. Contains introduction, biographical sketch of Bishop David, his "Method of Mental Prayer," and his "Manual for the Sisters of Charity" as an appendix. Archives of Archdiocese of Louisville.
———. *True Piety, or, the Day Well Spent, being a Catholic Manual of Chosen Prayers, Devout Practices, and Solid Instructions. Adapted to Every State of Life.* Taken Partly from the French. From the Second American Edition. By the authority of the Right Rev. Bishop David. Lexington: Kentucky Gazette Office, 1824.

Donnelly, Mary Louise. *Major William Boarman: His Descendants*. Ennis, TX: privately printed, 1990.

———. *William Elder: Ancestors and Descendants*. Burke, VA: privately printed, 1986.

Doyle, Frederick. "The Old Presentation Academy of Louisville." Ts. 1948. Personal recollections of Presentation in 1888.

Flaget, Benedict Joseph. *Diary*. Copy in ts.

Historical Maps, 1858. Louisville Free Public Library.

Howard, Thomas. Last Will, 28 May 1810; probated 16 July 1810. Nelson County Court House Records.

"Leaves from the Old Records of St. Joseph's Infirmary." Booklet for the Seventy-third Anniversary of Infirmary on Fourth Street, Louisville.

Louisville Census, 1860.

Louisville Directory for the Year 1832. Louisville: Richard W. Otis, 1832.

Louisville Directory for the Year 1836. Ed. G. Collins. Louisville: Prentice and Weissinger, 1836.

Louisville Directory for the Year 1838. Ed. G. Collins. Louisville: J. E. Marshall, 1838.

Lyons, John A. "Fr. Lyons Collection: Entries in Publications, 1782–1961." Copies in binder of cards made from primary sources on the history around the Louisville Cathedral. Cathedral Heritage Collection.

Murphy, Ignatia, SCN. "Recollections of Presentation Academy." Ts. 1919.

"Nazareth Centennial, 1912." Miscellany. Vol. 10. Ts.

"Nazareth Servants and Their Children." List.

Orphan's Casket, The: A Journal Published during the Fair for the Benefit of St. Vincent's Orphan Asylum. Louisville: B. J. Webb & Brother. Spalding University Archives, Louisville, KY.

Poor, Peabody. *Directory and Business Advertiser for 1844–45*. Louisville: W. N. Haldeman, 1844.

"Report of the Establishment of the Sisters of Charity of Nazareth, in Kentucky, United States of America." C. 1825. In Flaget David Letters. An account of the foundation, signed by Bishops David and Flaget, discovered by David (Thomas) Spalding, CFX, in the Vatican Archives, and translated by Sr. Edward Barnes, SCN.

Spalding, Basil. Will, 5 Mar. 1792. Copy.

Spalding, Julia Sloan. "Reminiscences of My School Days at Nazareth Academy 1853–1858." Ts. Duplicate Letter Book 22: 48–54.

Webb, Ben J. "Mother Catherine Spalding." *Guardian* 1 May 1858: 1–2,

in Clippings 2: 76–77. Mother Catherine's obituary in Louisville
Catholic paper.
———. "Mother Catherine's Early Companions." *Guardian* 8 May
1858: 1–2, in Clippings 2: 88–89.
Wilkinson, Eliza Crozier. "Reminiscences of Nazareth in 1825–26." Ts.
in Duplicate Letter Book 4 and Early Annals of Marie Menard.

Secondary Sources

Note: Some of the following sources are of long-standing and particu-
lar usefulness for background history of the city, state, diocese, and
SCN community: Casseday, Fox, Johnston, Crews, McGann, Mattingly,
Schauinger, Yater, and Webb.

Abell, Sara Ann, SCN. "How We Came to the Conclusion That Pleasant
Hill Is Home of Catherine Spalding." Ts.
Bechtle, Regina, SC, and Judith Metz, SC, eds. *Elizabeth Bayley Seton: Col-
lected Writings.* 2 vols. to date. Hyde Park, NY: New City Press, 2002–.
Bevins, Ann Bolton, and James R. O'Rourke. *"That Troublesome Par-
ish": St. Francis/St. Pius Church of White Sulphur, Kentucky.* George-
town, KY: St. Francis and St. John Parishes, 1985.
Black, Jacquelyn G. *Microbiology: Principles and Applications.* Upper
Saddle River, NJ: Prentice Hall, 1996.
Boles, John B. *Religion in Antebellum Kentucky.* Lexington: University
Press of Kentucky, 1976.
Brady, John B. "Sermon Delivered on the Occasion of a Pilgrimage to
Pleasant Hill, Pomfret, Maryland, 29 March 1987." Ts.
Buckner, Mary, SCL. *History of the Sisters of Charity of Leavenworth,
Kansas.* Kansas City, MO: Hudson-Kimberly, 1898. Rpt., 1985.
Casseday, Ben. *The History of Louisville from Its Earliest Settlement till
the Year 1852.* Louisville: Hull and Brother, 1852.
Creamer, Mary Michael, SCN. "Mother Catherine Spalding—St. Cath-
erine Street, Louisville, Kentucky." *Filson Club History Quarterly* 63
(1989): 191–223.
Crews, Clyde F. *An American Holy Land: A History of the Archdiocese
of Louisville.* Wilmington, DE: Michael Glazier, 1987.
———. "Benedict Joseph Flaget: First Bishop of the West." In *Patterns of
Episcopal Leadership.* Ed. Gerald P. Fogarty, SJ. New York: Macmil-
lan, 1989.
———. *Presence and Possibility: Louisville Catholicism and Its Cathedral.* Louisville: Archdiocese of Louisville, 1973.

Daughter of Charity. *1809–1959*. Emmitsburg, MD: St. Joseph's Central House, 1959.

Davis, Cyprian, OSB. *The History of Black Catholics in the United States*. New York: Crossroad, 1990.

Dickson, Samuel Henry, MD. *Elements of Medicine: A Compendious View of Pathology and Therapeutics; or the History and Treatment of Diseases*. Philadelphia: Blanchard and Lea, 1855.

Dirvin, Joseph I. *Mrs. Seton: Foundress of the American Sisters of Charity*. New York: Farrar, 1962.

Dolan, Jay P. *The American Catholic Experience: A History from Colonial Times to the Present*. Garden City, NY: Doubleday, 1985.

Duncan, Richard R. "Catholics and the Church in the Antebellum Upper South." In *Catholics in the Old South*. Ed. Randall M. Miller and Jon L. Wakelyn, 77–98. Macon, GA: Mercer University Press, 1983.

Dunglison, Rabley, MD. *A Dictionary of Medical Science*. Philadelphia: Blanchard and Lea, 1857.

Durrett, Reuben T. *The Centenary of Louisville, Saturday, May 1, 1880*. Louisville: Filson Club Publications, 1893.

Fox, Columba, SCN. *The Life of the Right Reverend John Baptist Mary David*. New York: United States Catholic Historical Society, 1925.

———. "Mother Catherine Spalding of the Sisters of Charity of Nazareth." Ts. 1925.

———. "Spalding, Catherine, Co-founder of the Sisters of Charity of Nazareth." Ts. of article for *Revised Catholic Encyclopedia*, n.d.

Franklin, John Hope. *From Slavery to Freedom: A History of American Negroes*. 3rd ed. New York: Knopf, 1967.

Genovese, Eugene D. *The Slaveholder's Dilemma: Freedom and Progress in Southern Conservative Thought, 1820–1860*. Columbia: University of South Carolina Press, 1992.

Gilmore, Julia, SCL. *Come North! The Life Story of Mother Xavier Ross*. New York: McMullen, 1951.

Gollar, C. Walker. "Catholic Slaves and Slaveholders in Kentucky." *Catholic Historical Review* 84 (1998): 42–62.

———. "The Role of Father Badin's Slaves in Frontier Kentucky." *American Catholic Studies* 115 (2004): 1–24.

Green, Nathaniel E. *The Silent Believers*. Louisville: West End Catholic Council, 1972.

Greenwell, Berenice, SCN. "Nazareth's Contribution to Education 1812–1933." Ph.D. diss., Fordham University, 1933.

Guilday, Peter. *The Life and Times of John Carroll*. 2 vols. New York: Encyclopedia Press, 1922.

"History of Presentation Academy." Ts., 1931.

Howlett, W. J. *Old St. Thomas' at Poplar Neck, Bardstown, Kentucky.* St. Louis, MO: B. Herder, 1906. Rpt., Cleveland: Dillon/Liederbach, 1971.

Joblin, M., and Co. *Louisville Past and Present: Its Industrial History as Exhibited in the Life-Labors of Its Leading Men.* Louisville: John P. Morton, 1875.

Johnston, J. Stoddard, ed. *Memorial History of Louisville from Its First Settlement to the Year 1896.* 2 vols. Chicago: American Biographical, 1896.

Kelly, Ellin M., SC, comp. and ed. *The Seton Years, 1774–1821.* Vol. 1 of *Numerous Choirs: A Chronicle of Elizabeth Bayley Seton and Her Spiritual Daughters.* Evansville, IN: Mater Dei Provincialate, 1981.

Kleber, John, ed. *The Encyclopedia of Louisville.* Lexington: University Press of Kentucky, 2001.

Kramer, Carl E. "City with a Vision: Images of Louisville in the 1830s." *Filson Club History Quarterly* 60 (1986): 427–52.

Krumpelman, Frances, SCN. *A History of the Prayer and Prayer Books of the Sisters of Charity of Nazareth, 1812–1995.* Nazareth, KY: privately printed.

Krusling, Peter, and Peter Marie Murphy, MM. "Mother Catherine Spalding: A Personality Study Based on Analysis of Her Handwriting." Nazareth, KY: SCN Health Corporation, 1987.

Lemarié, Charles, CSC. *A Biography of Msgr. Benedict Joseph Flaget.* 3 vols. Trans. Mary Wedding, SCN. Bardstown, KY: Sponsored by the Flaget-Lemarié Group and St. Joseph Proto-Cathedral Archives, 1992. Ts.

Lyons, John A. *Bishops and Priests of the Diocese of Bardstown.* Louisville: privately printed, 1976.

Magaret, Helene. *Giant in the Wilderness: A Biography of Fr. Charles Nerinckx.* Milwaukee: Bruce, 1952.

Mansberger, Floyd. *Archeological Investigations at the Cathedral of the Assumption, Louisville, Kentucky.* Springfield, IL: Fever River Research, 1990. Cathedral Heritage Collection.

Mattingly, Mary Ramona, SCN. *The Catholic Church on the Kentucky Frontier, 1785–1812.* Washington, DC: Catholic University of America Press, 1936.

McGann, Agnes Geraldine, SCN. "Historical Sketch of Nazareth Academy and Nazareth College 1814–1971." Nazareth, KY: privately printed [1979].

———. *Nativism in Kentucky in 1860*. Washington, DC: Catholic University of America Press, 1944.

———. *SCNs Serving since 1812*. Nazareth, KY: privately printed, [1985].

———. *Sisters of Charity of Nazareth in the Apostolate*. Nazareth, KY: privately printed, [1976].

McGill, Anna Blanche. *The Sisters of Charity of Nazareth Kentucky*. New York: Encyclopedia Press, 1917.

McGreal, Mary Nona, OP, ed. *Dominicans at Home in a New Nation, 1786–1805*. Vol. 1 of *The Order of Preachers in the United States: A Family History*. Strasbourg, France: Editions du Signe, 2001.

Metz, Judith, SC, and Virginia Wiltse. *Sister Margaret Cecilia George: A Biography*. Mt. St. Joseph, OH: Sisters of Charity, 1989.

Miller, Randall M., and Jon L. Wakelyn, eds. *Catholics in the Old South*. Macon, GA: Mercer University Press, 1983.

Morris, George, SJ. Graphoanalysis of Mother Xavier Ross. Ts. Archives of Sisters of Charity of Leavenworth, Kansas.

O'Daniel, V. F. *The Father of the Church in Tennessee*. Washington, DC: Dominicana, 1926.

"Pleasant Hill: Birthplace of Catherine Spalding." Ts. Author unknown; some errors cited by Thomas Spalding, CFX.

Raboteau, Albert J. *Slave Religion: The "Invisible Institution" in the Antebellum South*. New York: Oxford University Press, 1978.

Reibel, R. C. *Louisville Panorama*. Louisville: Liberty National Bank and Trust, 1956.

"Rules of the Daughters of Charity, Servants of the Sick Poor." With introduction. *Vincent de Paul and Louise de Marillac: Rules, Conferences, and Writings*. Ed. Frances Ryan, DC, and John E. Rybolt, CM, 167–99. The Classics of Western Spirituality. NY: Paulist Press, 1995.

Ryan, Paul E. *History of the Diocese of Covington, Kentucky*. Covington: Diocese of Covington, 1954.

Schauinger, J. Herman. *Cathedrals in the Wilderness*. Milwaukee: Bruce, 1952.

———. *Stephen T. Badin: Priest in the Wilderness*. Milwaukee: Bruce, 1956.

Spalding, David [Thomas], CFX. "The Mystery of Mother Catherine Spalding's Parents." *Records of the American Catholic Historical Society of Philadelphia* 71 (1960): 118–24.

Spalding, Hughes. *The Spalding Family of Maryland, Kentucky, and Georgia from 1658 to 1965*. 2 vols. Atlanta: Stein, 1965.

Spalding, Martin John. *Sketches of the Early Catholic Missions in Kentucky.* Louisville: B. J. Webb, 1844.

Spalding, Thomas W. [David], CFX. Historical Notes from personal research. Ts. Notes gleaned by Spalding for the author, now placed in Nazareth Archives.

———. *Martin John Spalding: American Churchman.* Washington, DC: Catholic University of America Press, 1973.

———. "The Parentage of James Spalding of Cox's Creek." Ts.

Spelman, M. Cajetan, OP. "The Catholic Church of the Kentucky Frontier as Seen in the Letters of Bishop Flaget, Father David, Father Badin, and Father Chabrat to Father Bruté (1811–1821)." M.A. thesis, University of Notre Dame, 1945.

Spillane, James Maria, SCN. *Kentucky Spring.* St. Meinrad, IN: Abbey Press, 1968. A historically based account in popular style of the life of Mother Catherine after 1812.

Stritch, Thomas. *The Catholic Church in Tennessee: The Sesquicentennial Story.* Nashville: Catholic Center, 1987.

Wade, Richard C. *Slavery in the Cities: The South 1820–1860.* New York: Oxford University Press, 1964.

Wakelyn, Jon L. "Catholic Elites in the Slaveholding South." In *Catholics in the Old South.* Ed. Randall M. Miller and Jon Wakelyn, 211–39. Macon, GA: Mercer University Press, 1983.

Webb, Ben J. *The Centenary of Catholicity in Kentucky.* Louisville: Charles A. Rogers, 1884.

Yater, George. *Notes to Two Hundred Years at the Falls of the Ohio: A History of Louisville and Jefferson County.* Louisville: Heritage Corporation of Louisville and Jefferson County, 1979.

Zanca, Kenneth J., comp. and ed. *American Catholics and Slavery: 1789–1866: An Anthology of Primary Documents.* Lanham, MD: University Press of America, 1994.

Index